# PAUL NIZAN

# PAUL NIZAN

## Committed Literature in a Conspiratorial World

### W. D. REDFERN

PRINCETON UNIVERSITY PRESS
PRINCETON, NEW JERSEY
1972

Publication of this book has been aided by
grants from the Research Board of the
University of Reading and the Graduate
School of Contemporary European Studies,
Reading, England, and the Whitney Darrow
Publication Reserve Fund of Princeton
University Press

This book has been composed in Linotype Granjon
Printed in the United States of America
by Princeton University Press

*To Angela*

# CONTENTS

# ACKNOWLEDGMENTS

I would like to express my gratitude for helpful advice and opinion from the following: Jean-Albert Bédé, Mme. H. Besse, Simone de Beauvoir, Jean-Jacques Brochier, André Chamson, F. W. Deakin, Ariel Ginsbourg, Jean Guéhenno, Pierre Naville, Henri Peyre, Rima Drell Reck, Gilbert Sigaux, Pierre-Henri Simon, Geoffrey Strickland, Alexander Werth.

I am especially grateful to Mme. Henriette Nizan for informative and delightful conversations, and for allowing me to see Nizan's letters to her.

In a category apart, I thank my wife for help with typing, for criticism, for encouragement, and for all the priceless rest.

Chapter 5, which appeared in a different form in *Romanic Review*, is included here by permission of the journal. Translations of quotations, unless indicated otherwise, are my own.

# PAUL NIZAN

# INTRODUCTION

"THAT VIGOROUS CORPSE, NIZAN. . . . During his hibernation, he grew younger every year."[1] In the last decade, there has been a rebirth of interest in the person and the work of Paul Nizan. Three of his essays have been reprinted by that excellent progressive, François Maspero (who publishes Debray, Fanon, Che Guevara). They have sold well, especially among the young. Nizan, in addition, pricks the consciences of the dissatisfied older generation. Maurice Nadeau confesses: "Nizan speaks to the youth of today over the top of our heads which we bow in submission."[2] Nizan induces such mea culpa. He is, as Sartre says, "a spoilsport. He issued a call to arms, a call for hatred between the classes."[3] Nizan's appeal to contemporary youth probably stems from his tone of tonic disgust; he urges a new mental and social hygiene, a purgation of what no longer serves or of what serves only a privileged minority. In the fullest sense, he has *got a nerve*. He never apologizes for his violent prejudices. He is not crippled by self-conscious embarrassment.

He did not suffer from that widespread twentieth-century intellectuals' malady: creeping agnosticism, which invades every fibre. "As we move out of our hardened positions of belief and disbelief, it is felt that we may be meeting on common ground somewhere in the centre. Perhaps it's felt that both sides might get together and form a new, united church, with a *dubito* instead of a credo."[4] The joke strikes home. Whereas Nizan, as a Marxist, wed himself to the belief that opposites necessarily coexist and form a single whole, he never melted the differences between those opposites he saw in mod-

---

[1] Jean-Paul Sartre, "Paul Nizan," *Situations* IV, pp. 137-39.
[2] Maurice Nadeau, "Paul Nizan: deux fois mort et ressuscité," p. 16.
[3] Sartre, "Paul Nizan," p. 134.
[4] Michael Frayn, "Leaning Towers," *The Observer*, 17 December 1967, p. 20.

3

ern society: privilege and deprivation, complacency and anger, status quo and revolution. In England even more than in France, there has been a strong tradition of writers hostile to politics and practicing an apartheid in which they are the Whites and all political agents of whatever kind are the Blacks. Many writers have felt unique, superior to their fellow beings, and, because the process of writing involves inward-looking concentration, have often in their practical attitudes been anarchistic, if not downright reactionary. Writing, for such men, is a secretive trade in which the mass of men intervene only at the point of sale of the finished product. It is because of such commonly held assumptions that writers and intellectuals have often been considered suspect by militant political organizations, except when their support was useful for some public image. Artists tend to take the long view, whereas politicians have to wrestle with the immediate circumstance. But some artists are instinctively drawn to where the drama, the struggle for supremacy, is occurring at a particular historical moment. Like Malraux, like Silone, Nizan is such an artist.

During the Algerian crises, some rebels picked Nizan's name for their clandestine group. In his prison cell in Bolivia, Régis Debray was observed reading Nizan's essays. Debray in several ways resembles Nizan. Like the young man who in 1925 fled from a hated France to an even more hateful Aden, only to return with his hatred shaped into a political determination, Debray left behind the continent where he felt impotent to act, in order to immerse himself in another where his rebelliousness could find sustenance. Both were bourgeois committing class suicide. Debray talks of his move as "this moulting and this rebirth."[5] His criticism is directed not only at his class but at the deformed minds which its educational system produces. Intellectuals, he says, are not empirical. Where it should be a case of hand-to-mouth, for them it is

[5] Régis Debray, *Révolution dans la révolution?*, p. 121.

4

usually a matter of book-to-situation. He attacks "the demon of analogy" in all its forms, for it is an automatic intellectual tic which hinders straightforward and concentrated observation of the problem at hand. Like Nizan, Debray holds a Manichaean view of "total class-war," of the need to avoid any strategy that leads to compromise with the dominant authority, and is keenly aware of the possible links between education and spying. He echoes Nizan's opinion that, in reactionary eyes, rebels are a cancer in the body politic. Like Nizan, he distinguishes between Trotskyism (a nonempirical, protean, imported mystique) and the efficient man Trotsky himself.

With his belief that "revolution is not the exclusive property of anybody," that Marxism can be mingled with the working ideologies of Castro, Guevara, Lenin, Mao Tse Tung and others, Debray represents, it is true, a more eclectic revolutionary outlook than was available to Nizan in the thirties. Both men are highly conscious of their own perhaps marginal utility. Debray admits: "Overuse of strategy and shortage of tactics are delectable vices peculiar to contemplative people, and I'm giving in to them myself in writing this."[6] Yet, like Nizan, he willfully conserves hope. Of a guerrilla group he comments: "Like young children in poor countries, its chances of dying in the first few months are high but get smaller every month it survives."[7] He retains sufficient intellectual reserve to have a real sense of the strongly entrenched enemy, and of the possible and actual absurdity of any revolutionary cause. Beneath the guerrillero's jacket, the philosophy student still functions, as when he writes caustically of the theory that town parties should control the military arm: "Heaven gives orders to Earth, the soul to the body, the brain to the arms. Just as the Word took precedence over action, so the lay stand-ins for the Word—speech, palaver, nattering—take precedence over and give orders to the military branch, from some Olym-

[6] *Ibid.*, p. 60.   [7] *Ibid.*, p. 63.

pian height."[8] Despite his scorn for the verbal games of "politicos," his intelligence stands or falls by his own sensitivity towards words and to what assumptions lie behind them: "There is a saying that we steep ourselves in society; but long baths soften us up. . . . Towns, those warm incubators, turn us into infants and bourgeois."[9] Though it is difficult to visualize Nizan laboring like Debray through the Bolivian jungle in the wake of a Guevarist guerrilla, the differences of attitude and spirit between these two intellectual rebels at a distance of thirty years are not great, and, such as they are, can be explained mainly by the changes in political situations. As Debray puts it, "Parties belong to this world and have to face the harsh challenge of earthly dialectics. If they can be born, then they can also die and be reborn in another form."[10] Similarly, the revolutionary drive of a Nizan has been reborn, in a different form, in Debray.

Within the Communist Party, Nizan was not (and could hardly have survived for so long if he had been) the odd man out. Rather, he was the odd man in. Those fond of "Freudian slips" might enjoy the following erratum insertion in *L'Humanité*: "As a result of an error in the last literary column by P. Nizan, the heading 'In the Light of Marxism' was printed as 'Beyond Marxism.' "[11] Lovers of puns might think that Nizan, with his unorthodox interest in psychology, gave the Party the (Freudian) slip. His membership was serious, but never humorless. What was his "image"? By most accounts, one of taciturnity, of reserve. His arrogant silences must have seemed to many what sergeants and headmasters call "dumb insolence." By reason of his profound conviction that he was permanently on enemy territory and that life consisted of conspiracies and counterplots, his tight lips should cause little surprise. On a less tense level, anyway, few people

[8] *Ibid.*, p. 92.   [9] *Ibid.*, p. 71.   [10] *Ibid.*, p. 103.
[11] *L'Humanité*, 23 February 1936, p. 6.

reveal themselves completely to strangers or even to friends. (Nizan wrote to his wife: "Even though I don't tell you everything, you're still the only person I tell my life to.") His wife says that his secretiveness was a deliberate protection for a very thinly-covered sensibility. Others hold that, like many Bretons, he was averse to social exhibitionism. He himself cultivated the image of a man hostile to the facile obsession with "inner life." To his enemies, his silences were suspect, and, when he left the Party, were made out to be, retrospectively, the proof of his treacherous soul.

There are a good number of fictional versions of Nizan, of half-truths, quarter-truths, and lies. I try to sort out the apocryphal from the indulgent and spiteful and to find the plausible. Attempting to make sense of Nizan is rather like the difficulty of reading his correspondence. The reader has to be constantly on the alert for the allusions, the ellipses of familiarity. His handwriting is not always legible, rather crammed, but conveys an air of urgency. What he says is usually to the point, functional in the best sense. One of my duties in this book is to decide to what extent there is any visible conflict between his own writing and the "rewriting" expected of members of the Party. My own stance is partisan: "Why be coy? Why shouldn't we sing?"[12] Modesty has always struck me as a suspect quality.

I will discuss a good many other writers, some wtih enthusiasm, some with denigration, because there is a need to present for inspection and for comparison the men Nizan knew or talked about, the ideas he met, adopted, or cast aside. It is not a question of "background," but of the cultural and ideological air Nizan breathed in and out. You can tell a man partly by the company he keeps and the company he discards.

I will try to circumscribe Nizan. Not that such a plain-speaking man is really elusive. Rather it is a question of seeing him

[12] Paul Nizan, *Le Cheval de Troie*, p. 220.

7

in a context, dialectically—how the context affected him and how he responded. Hence the negative definition (negative controls), the affinities, the corroborations, the analogies across time, space, and other barriers, the delineation of differences. Nizan himself always took great care to *situate* any phenomenon—a quality which stood him in good stead both for his political observation and his fictional creation.

Nizan is not a glamorous figure like Malraux, whose characters are curiously restricted to the *heights* of experience. He is disconcerting, as are all frank people. His kind of integrity is often undervalued or overlooked. I wish to set this imbalance right, to pay respects where they are due, and to carp on those occasions when they are not. I will try to judge whether Nizan deserves the testimonial written by his son-in-law, Olivier Todd, who never met him: "Why should Nizan appeal to readers today? Because no one in France has recently managed to blend victoriously politics and literature. Because he was a radical and an artist who could tell a good story. Because *his* revolt was sensitive and intelligent."[13]

[13] Olivier Todd, "Paul Nizan: An Appraisal," p. 524.

# CHAPTER ONE

# EVOLUTION OF A YOUNG THINKER

Paul Nizan was born at Tours in 1905, the son of a railway engineer. He attended the lycée at Périgueux before going in 1916 to the Lycée Henri IV in Paris as a day pupil. There, in the "cinquième A 1," he and Sartre met and made friends. Their education was to run parallel until they finished at the École Normale Supérieure in the late 1920s. They moved together in 1922 to Louis-le-Grand in order to prepare for entry to the E. N. S. The first entrance of Nizan into Sartre's field of perception was an eerie hallucination: Nizan was the mirror image of another boy who had died a few weeks before. In some ways, Sartre seems never to have recovered from this initial jolt (and it would be wrong to underestimate the importance of superstition in Sartre's mental constitution). The new boy, because of his squint, struck the young Sartre as the "diabolical double" of the dead boy. The portrait he gives of Nizan at that age is highly colored: "Overwhelmed by violent, static emotions, he never shouted out loud but we have seen him go white with anger and stammer. What we took to be gentleness was merely a momentary paralysis. It wasn't so much truth that came from his lips as a sort of cynical objectivity which made us feel uncomfortable, because we weren't used to it. Although he naturally loved his parents, he was the only one amongst us who spoke ironically about them."[1]

Sartre is rather shaky on his dates, and it is unlikely that he is here describing the eleven-year-old boy he first met, but rather the older one, who, at sixteen, proposed that he and Sartre transform themselves into supermen and adopt Gaelic names. However supercharged Sartre's Nizan appears, the emotion that emerges most strongly from his version is that

[1] Jean-Paul Sartre, Les Mots, p. 190.

of awe and a certain degree of envy, an emotion Sartre would never grow out of with respect to his friend. Nizan had already read widely and wanted to write. "In other words he was a whole man," Sartre comments, with some self-irony. There was some cause for the envy. Nizan won the history prize in the "philo" class, and he impressed his fellow pupils as being much more gifted than Sartre, who had to sweat over his essays. Nizan, in himself, was probably at that age much more self-doubting than he appeared to Sartre. In a poem he wrote at eighteen, he wondered: "I'm not sure / whether some new thing will arise / from an ordinary act." Reality needs to be improved upon, but by everyday effort, and not by some magical intervention. He was beyond the superman mirage.

He started at the E. N. S. in 1924, the same year as Sartre, Raymond Aron, and Georges Lefranc. He read voraciously: Spinoza, Lenin, Sorel, Croce, Amiel, Stendhal, Zola, Gide. Of average height, he had dark hair and, like Sartre, a strabismus, "but one that turned inward, which was more pleasant to look at."[2] With his cane, monocle, and natty clothes, he was insolently fashion-conscious, a dandy. On the walls of the room he shared with Sartre were two crossed foils under a fencing mask. The same combination of aggressiveness and defensive dissimulation could be seen in his character. One of his more disconcerting tics was his habit, in conversation, of staring at his fingernails for long periods. He and Sartre would tramp around Paris indefatigably. Nizan often vanished for days, according to Sartre, and would be found drunk with strangers. He was unremittingly an extremist; and because he felt the physical weight of his bondage, he was a materialist. Nizan was culturally ahead of Sartre, and introduced him to Irish writers like Shaw and O'Casey and to new American novelists. Simone de Beauvoir says of the two: "They deflated every

[2] Sartre, "Paul Nizan," p. 142.

kind of idealism without pity, they mocked at good souls, noble souls, every kind of soul, and soul states, and inner life."[3] She had caught from Sartre the set way of seeing Nizan exclusively as a *negator*. According to Daniel Lagache, Nizan, Sartre, Aron, and Lagache himself once projected a scenario based on Jules Renard's *Poil de Carotte*. Sartre says of this project: "What we must emphasize is the need for tenderness."[4] These young men were not unrelenting iconoclasts all the time.

So far, we have seen Nizan mainly through the eyes of witnesses. His letters to his future wife, Henriette, enable him to speak for himself. In many of them, he apologizes for fits of rude or eccentric moodiness, which possibly stemmed from fighting a campaign against the invasion of love into his life. It is clear that he worked hard at his studies, and also that he relaxed hard. He underwent recurrent depressive states, and was often ill with facial neuralgia, which might have been the cause or the offshoot of his depressions. In one of these states of psychic lowness, he warned Henriette that he might one day enter regular orders. But, to an onlooker, his salvation certainly lay more in Henriette than in any such otherworldly vocation: "You are the best tonic I know" (8 April 1926). He learns to speak of love happily and gratefully: "It's a new and marvelous experience" (April 1927). Most of his letters were written when on holiday. After returning from Aden, his opinion of travel is blasé: "All landscapes are interchangeable. . . . I can well understand those who seek in travel some form of escape, of purification or intoxication. . . ."; but otherwise he takes the Pascalian view that men move around only because they fear sitting still with themselves (9 July 1927). Earlier, he had oscillated, in the face of new scenery, between aristocratic dismissal and enthusiasm. He said that the South of France is "the one place it is impossible to think of a new

[3] Simone de Beauvoir, *Mémoires d'une jeune fille rangée*, pp. 476-78.
[4] *Les Écrits de Sartre*, p. 24.

epithet for. It's the home of commonplaces" (July 1925). On the other hand, the "intelligent" Italian landscapes delighted him: "They're just right for people who cultivate simultaneously an elegant melancholy and rational pursuits. . . . They're too complete, too definitive, and they stop you from looking for secret worlds." The influence of Stendhal is palpable in such pithy judgments: "You know you are mortal, and you have two options: be like Cellini or St. Francis" (Genoa, 1925).

In 1927, he told Henriette that the era of groups was finished. It is time to examine the group to which he occasionally lent himself at the university. Even if the conclusion should be that he never truly belonged to it, an examination of its constituents, its personalities and ambitions, should help to illuminate Nizan himself, if only, in the main, by contrast.

This group was principally composed of Henri Lefebvre, Georges Friedmann, Georges Politzer, Norbert Guterman, and Pierre Morhange, all of whom were later to achieve varying degrees of distinction in diverse fields of intellectual enquiry. They engaged in four publishing ventures: the periodicals *Philosophies* (March 1924–March 1925), *L'Esprit* (May 1926–January 1927), *La Revue marxiste* (February 1929–September 1929), and *La Revue de psychologie concrète* (two issues in 1929). They were in their early twenties and students of philosophy. A similar age group in England at the same time was also busy erecting verbal barricades for the conflict of the older and the younger generations. But, in Orwell's account, the voice that spoke best to and for them was Housman, who "stood for a bitter, defiant paganism, a conviction that life is short and the gods are against you, which exactly fitted the prevailing mood of the young."[5] In France at that time there was a similar fashionable fixation on death, and the cultivation of the self-consoling myth of a "sacrificed gen-

[5] George Orwell, *Collected Essays*, pp. 132-33.

12

eration." In truth, of course, the sacrificed ones were their fathers and elder brothers who died in the trenches. But it is the luxury grievance, and not the common grief, that gets into the cultural headlines.

By all literary accounts, in the France of the 1920s, the thoughtful young were busy discarding their superannuated "maîtres à penser" and scouting for replacements. This was the case with both young right-wing traditionalists and would-be radicals. Here is a (praising) right-wing view of the group under consideration by J.-P. Maxence (a contributor to *Gringoire*), who is speaking of the new tendency to *extremist* thinking by the *L'Esprit* group: "They are, in the words of Albert Thibaudet, 'scornful and sensual young men.' ... When they see the disintegration of fictional characters, they attack the cult of introspection. ... They condemn en bloc and rather frantically all subjectivists (Barrès, Gide, Rivière, Valéry). ... They want a return to the object. But that involves concentrating on France, and abandoning interior bankruptcy for an external, public bankruptcy. And there again they feel the need to put themselves in the opposition."[6] Like most intellectual groups, this one was far more in agreement on its aversions than on its aspirations.

*Philosophies*, directed by Morhange, often talked of the need for a new mysticism, of meditations on God, and it published a homage to Unamuno in 1924. The periodical contained no discussion of politics, but favored instead articles on Bergson, Brunschvicg, Lavelle, or fragments from Proust, Max Jacob, Supervielle, or Cocteau. Henri Lefebvre contributed some now unreadable philosophical theory. Some space was taken up with haughty dismissal of other movements of the day, much of it incredibly woolly (e.g., "We believe in the life we have and in the one that will carry us forward"). The group went

6 Jean-Pierre Maxence, *Histoire de dix ans*, pp. 80-81.

13

in for second-degree "gratuitous acts," such as petty thefts, followed by the return or the destruction of the stolen goods so as not to benefit from their possession.[7] Acts like these, indulged in long enough, became addictive, became "necessary acts," like the absurd heroics of Malraux' early heroes. "The mania for testing ourselves had a name amongst us philosophy students. We called it testism."[8] They cultivated violence (mainly verbal or gesticulatory) as a criterion of authenticity. They were, in short, antimilitaristic diehards. It was a very programmatic era, avid for manifestoes. It was almost inevitable that the Surrealists and the *Philosophies* group would serenade each other.

There were parleys. Much of the time they proceeded like the cultural equivalent of a 1920s demarcation dispute, each side striving to preserve its "originality," its own area and methods of inquiry. Around 1925, the Surrealists so fancied themselves that they could dare to exert "political pressure" on their contemporaries in the name of a more advanced stage of revolution. A farcical meeting took place at the Centrale Surréaliste at which Lefebvre appeared as spokesman for the "philosophes." He was instructed by them to plug the highly improbable line of his group's belief in God. The natural and desired result was a breakdown in communication between the two sides.[9] Another attempt to pool their energies, and to include those of the Trotskyst *Clarté* group, in a periodical to be called *La Guerre civile* also failed, though Lefebvre, Guterman, Morhange, and Politzer signed a manifesto, "La Révolution d'abord et toujours," in *La Révolution Surréaliste*. Breton's apartheid tendencies, of course, helped to ruin any projects of mergers. Nizan appears to have taken no part in any of these approaches. Some time later, in fact, he was to reproach the Surrealists for being excessively preoccupied with

[7] Henri Lefebvre, *La Somme et le reste*, p. 386.
[8] *Ibid.*
[9] See Lefebvre, *La Somme et le reste*, pp. 396-97.

purely individual matters and for trying to live in a "timeless world," in short, for being luxury merchants.[10]

*L'Esprit* replaced *Philosophies* after the failure of the projected *Guerre civile*. In *L'Esprit*, Politzer, later to be a leading Party economic theorist, spoke curiously of "a detour through political economy," and, in general, Marxists were indignant at the call issued by *L'Esprit* for a new spiritual wisdom. Pierre Naville wrote of "the confusionist tendencies of the *L'Esprit* group," and of "the incompatibility between Judeo-philosophical jargon and historical materialism."[11] The general tone of the writing in this periodical was abstract, snobbish, and iconoclastic. It published a translation of T. S. Eliot's *Wasteland*, bits of Hegel and Engels. There was a good deal of unclarified guff about a dynamic new "wisdom," and a stated attempt to "put Christendom on trial." The whole group seemed to be in search of a spiritual or philosophical father figure.

*La Revue marxiste*, in its short life, was altogether more serious. It was financed by Georges Friedmann (the son of a banker), who joined the party in 1929. The French Communist Party agreed to its publication, and Charles Rappoport was on its editing committee. The cover bore Lenin's phrase: "No revolutionary movement without a revolutionary theory." It was in fact the first truly Marxist review in France. Marx's writings were still largely unknown (or ignored) even, or especially, at the Sorbonne. Some of Marx's 1844 texts, as well as his unpublished preface to Engels's *Anti-Dühring*, appeared in French for the first time in *La Revue marxiste*. Politzer wrote on Lenin's *Materialism and Empiriocriticism*, Nizan on state economic planning. The periodical died, or was killed off, after less than a year. Henri Lefebvre's very incomplete account of this period is ambiguous about whether the review ran into financial trouble after getting mixed up with a stranger claiming to be "a watchdog from Moscow" and to have

---

[10] Nizan, *Commune*, July 1933, pp. 85-86.
[11] Pierre Naville, *Clarté*, August-September 1926, p. 85.

a foolproof gambling system, or whether Moscow sank the review in order to drown independent Marxist thought in France.

In Lefebvre's prejudiced account the members of the group are characterized in the following terms: Guterman was "perhaps the most subtly intelligent one," nonchalant, skeptical, respected by the others for his crushing irony. Friedmann, a levelheaded scientific mind, also had his mystical side; not content with mocking the contemporary cults of "anxiety" and "availability," he wanted to make people accept "their eternal constituent." Morhange was verbally gifted, rhetorical, Messianic, tending to "talk about his work instead of writing it." Politzer was the most bizarre, outrageous, hectoring. Of Nizan, Lefebvre writes: "Beneath an apparently more abstract intellectuality, and with a darker and more secret inner self which he kept to himself, he became the most politicized member of the group; he never involved himself with it completely."[12]

When Lefebvre describes some of the group's projects and behavior, it is not difficult to see why Nizan kept his distance. Morhange, for instance, caressed the ideal of a "consortium of faith," and envisaged "the advent of a new aristocracy of ardent men, who overcame their disagreements by sharing an extremist outlook." He had another name for these new men: the "subtle brutes."[13] In his prophetic role, he craved the coming of a new syncretism, Judaism purged of some of its traditional elements and amplified by contact with other beliefs. Morhange's scheme attracted at various times young Catholics, Protestants, and scientists. His frenzied, almost inquisitorial belief in God granted him a certain awesome standing with his coevals. Other projects of the group included a manifesto against the Army, and a plan to "return to the soil" by buying a fertile plot of land and a big house to house the "philosophes." Lefebvre began arrangements to buy an island

[12] Lefebvre, *La Somme et le reste*, p. 390.
[13] *Ibid.*, p. 391.

16

("The Isle of Wisdom") in the Gulf of Morbihan. But nothing came of this variant on the theme of "the men of good will."

"There was a rather comical contrast between the lack of seriousness and the excessive seriousness with which these young intellectuals planned their activities."[14] It is sometimes difficult to keep in mind that the group was composed not of teenagers but of men well into the age of reason. A study of them reveals what young men of an age and intellectual background similar to Nizan's chose to do with their time and energy. So far we have seen mainly the more laughable aspects of their hopes and exploits. But the group represented also something more serious: a challenge to the prevailing orthodoxy of thought in the 1920s. All of them were suffering to some degree from what might be called intellectuals' schizophrenia. They were heavily influenced by and violently hostile to their philosophical masters: Blondel, Brunschvicg, and Bergson. The tension generated reveals an attempt to institute a movement of secession, in philosophy, away from the Sorbonne, to create an at first *marginal* movement of new thought. Lefebvre describes the process in these terms: "Philosophy had just been rebuilt as something violent and vehement, but it was now the product of a collective body and no longer a strictly individual meditation. We were spontaneously trying to disentangle ourselves from a dichotomy or to resolve a contradiction, that between the public and the private thinker."[15] Bergson especially, with his "shapeless philosophy, his ill-defined pseudoconcepts," was the pet aversion of the whole group. Lefebvre and Politzer delighted in playing heavy japes on the "great man" in the Victor Cousin library: Politzer, sitting just opposite him, noisily munching huge ham sandwiches, or letting loose a tortoise christened "Creative Evolution," or reading aloud extracts from his coming anti-Bergson pamphlet, *Fin d'une parade philosophique.*

[14] *Ibid.*, p. 398.      [15] *Ibid.*, p. 393.

Politzer was the member of the group closest in outlook to Nizan, and they remained good friends until 1939, not without a great deal of mutual harsh criticism on the way. Simone de Beauvoir says of Politzer: "There was a striking contrast between his dogmatism and the charming changeability of his face; though I relished his conversation, I liked even more his gestures, his voice, his freckles, and that flaming red hair, which Sartre borrowed for his Antoine Roquentin."[16] Politzer rejoiced in imagined visions of tough Russian sailors stubbing out cigarettes on the French tapestries of the Kremlin (cf. Breton's hoped-for spectacle of Cossacks watering their horses in the Place de la Concorde). But there were limits to the anti-Frenchness of this Hungarian expatriate: he aimed at marrying a Parisian beauty; and he did. He was the first of the group to publish (in 1928) a major work: *Critique des fondements de la psychologie*, which is worth examining in some detail, for its own sake and for the purpose of comparison with Nizan's work. Just as Nizan's later *Chiens de garde* seeks to inter the orthodox philosophy of the day, so Politzer's book announces "the demise of official psychology." He had already dismissed Bergson's work in a pamphlet as a "parade," a futile ritual of degenerate pomp, and he carries the onslaught into the field of psychology. He calls for a "radical reform of understanding," and aims to demythologize worn-out concepts. "The *ideology* of the bourgeoisie would not have been complete without a mystique . . . which it found in that 'inner life' dear to psychologists." By "inner life," Politzer means luxury, abstract problems, and for him such a cult is the bourgeois defense system against the threat of a genuine social revolution. In his view, psychologists only make sense to each other; their work talks only shop. Politzer (like R. D. Laing and other psychologists today) is hostile to biochemical psychology: "an abstract and impersonal script whose performers are physio-

---

[16] Beauvoir, *La Force de l'âge*, p. 220.

logical impulses and whose plot is made up of their movements through the brain cells." Traditional psychology tries to discount *dreams*, as it cannot fit them easily into its general theory. Freud, of course, altered this situation drastically. Politzer's attitude toward Freud, however, contains nuances. On the one hand, he acknowledges Freud's genuine innovations, but on the whole, he sees him more as the end of an old line than the start of a new one. Freud started off with admirable concreteness in his case studies, but ended up with abstraction in his theories. Altogether, Freud is caught in a midway state.

Politzer's own suggestions for a reform are vague. He talks a good deal about "the *dramatic* life of the individual," in a nonromantic sense, though he admits that this area is dealt with more often by novelists and playwrights than by psychologists. What he seems to mean by "drama" is something akin to the Sartrian notion of choice of a mode of life by an individual consciousness ("the actor of the dramatic life and not the passive subject of introspection"). Sartre once declared that he disliked the word "psychological" and doubted that it referred to any reality: "Let us say that we can improve the biography of the person." In all, Politzer was trying to blend a description of consciousness with some features of behaviorism. The offspring was a mongrel, more powerful in its denunciations than its proposals. The proposals are not startling, even if they are worthy. The new "concrete psychology" must be a posteriori, original (i.e., studying "facts not capable of being studied by other sciences"), and objective in method. In many ways, his views seem to foreshadow those of Sartre. He talks of "intentional" accounts by patients; he dislikes what he calls "a psychologically *blind* region," as if he wanted to believe that man is always conscious. And he declares that "the unconscious represents only that measure of abstraction which survives within concrete psychology." Within a couple of years of publishing this book, Politzer became convinced that psychology as a study and a weapon had been annexed by the bourgeois, and he renounced it, switching to Marxist economics and sociology. He could never have accepted, anyway, the later Soviet stress on impersonal Pavlovian psychology. Marx and Engels neglected psychology as a separate discipline. Politzer's doubts about its validity culminated in his abandoning the subject. This decision was reached *logically*, and not, as Lefebvre implies, as the result of pressure from the Communist Party. Whatever the technical value his book may still have (and it was just reprinted in 1967), the tone, haughty, scathing, still breathes today: "We have abandoned that conception which is at the root of most French philosophical works: it consists in positing an absolutely passive, not to say stupid, reader; so as to save him the effort of any personal reflection, everything must be presented to him on a plate." Politzer must qualify as one of Morhange's "subtle brutes."

Finally, before looking at Nizan's first published book *Aden-Arabie*, we should examine the target practice of another young critic of the time, although he had little connection with the *Philosophies* group: Emmanuel Berl, author of the modishly destructive pamphlet of 1929, *Mort de la morale bourgeoise*. Berl was principally appalled by a society composed of various types of bourgeois *clubs*, each with its own system of passwords. This chain of clubs in turn rests on a basis of closed family units, which practice another kind of exclusivity ("family chauvinism"). Berl, like Politzer, mocks the bourgeois taste for psychology, for the inner life of "the hidden man," the dichotomy of the envelope and the enveloped. He attacks Brunschvicg and "pure philosophy" in these terms: 'This philosophy cut off from its social foundations can always be used to justify any condition of society."[17] His tone in general is that of a bourgeois profaning his erstwhile gods (individualism, the religion of money). I called his pamphlet "target prac-

[17] Emmanuel Berl, *Mort de la morale bourgeoise*, p. 74.

tice," for it exhibits a sense of too much enjoyment and insufficient pain, and recalls Sade's injunction not to destroy idols in anger but to break them up in play. Berl's conclusion takes the form of a vague reference to "materialism," defined as "a certain way of belittling. It holds that the truest things are the least noble ones." For all its frequent wit, this book is essentially frivolous. Nizan, who befriended Berl for a time, came to see him as a "nonconformist Norpois," too exclusively Parisian in sensibility to be a genuine rebel. For Nizan, Berl drifted over to Drieu la Rochelle's position of ambivalence: he was unsure whether he was a dupe or an accomplice of fascism. Even a right-winger like Maxence describes Berl's materialism as inescapably bourgeois. Maxence calls Berl's pamphlets an attempt to outdo Aragon's *Traité du style* and Benda's *Trahison des clercs*. Nizan, as we will now see, was not guilty of this cultural one-upmanship, for he was not playing a fashionable game, but engaging in a desperate conflict.

Lefebvre states that those who become Marxists between 1925 and 1930 did not get over their spontaneous romanticism in a natural fashion. "They came to Marxism over the ruins of their youth . . . their absurd and boundless expectations."[18] In 1928, in reply to a survey conducted by the *Nouvelles littéraires* among students, Nizan stated, with pompous sincerity, the outlines of his belief: "I believe in a truly human order of things where men can live like human beings and not like insignificant shadows. It's an order of things that has to be built from scratch." Preceding Sartre ("man has not yet been invented"), as he so often did, he added: "Man is a creature that does not yet exist." And he quoted Marx to the effect that "mankind cannot be saved by making speeches. We must go to the roots of society and turn over the soil from which men grow."[19] Balancing his conclusion by bringing in the private

[18] Lefebvre, *La Somme et le reste*, p. 404.
[19] Nizan, *Les Nouvelles littéraires*, 7 December 1928, p. 4.

sphere, he mentioned the great importance dreams held for him. This was, then, in vague outline, Nizan's radical position the year before he finished his studies, and after he had returned from his traumatic stay in Aden. His first book, *Aden-Arabie*, was to be an onslaught on two fronts: his academic context and colonialism—the parochial and the universal intertwined. "I feel brutal and much readier to deal out punishment than to take it lying down" (letter to his fiancée, Strasburg, September 1926).

*Aden-Arabie* must have been written largely during Nizan's stay in Aden (October 1926–May 1927), when he acted as tutor to the son of Antonin Besse, the leading commercial figure in the colony. It is a bitter, violent, often witty, occasionally highly irritating book, which bears all the marks of Nizan's intellectual breeding (the recondite epigraphs from obscure travelers of previous centuries, the general literary allusiveness), and all the signs of a strong desire to break out of such a cocoon and to live responsibly and critically in the wider world. Nizan sailed from Greenock. During his journey through England, Scotland, and Wales, he kept a beady eye on the "different faces of England": the great poverty in the mining and port areas, and the toffs in London. "I'm fed up with Europe and fed up with solitude. . . . I am eager to live with my tribesmen in a moral universe" (letter to Henriette, Swansea, October 1926). All he found on board amongst the passengers was "the freemasonry of humanists," which made him take refuge in voracious reading. He was clearly running away. From what menace? Despite his harsh disdain for "the allegedly Normal and supposedly Superior School," Nizan often in fact felt nostalgic for the japes, the trips to flea pits, the long sessions in a room discussing aesthetics and women, the intellectual dogfights. But he quotes Pierre MacOrlan: "The honey of my memories makes me puke." The simple truth is that his motives were extremely confused, as revealed in the unclear opening pages of *Aden-Arabie*.

The first gambit is challenging. "I was twenty. And don't tell me it's the best time of life."[20] The French world of his experience is in a process of decomposition, and like the Malraux of *La Tentation de l'Occident* inspired by Spengler, Nizan aims at "the comparative study of decadence" (p. 66). The first grievance he levels against his academic home: the École Normale Supérieure. There he made, in that inbred elite world of "intelligence," no contact with less privileged sectors of society. He castigates himself for tolerating an intolerable situation. He has suffered from a lack of guidance from his elders: his teachers, his family, and the state. One senior man he exempts from his general charge: Lucien Herr, who introduced students to Hegel and Marx and whose words alone Nizan trusted. When he died, he left the E.N.S. "presided over by a patriotic, hypocritical, powerful little old man who respected the military" (p. 68): Gustave Lanson. Nizan attacks a world of outdated clichés about the progress of the human mind, a verbal universe based on the premise that problems will cease to exist once they are properly formulated. In a phrase anticipating the title of his second pamphlet, Nizan mentions "the wise owls of the sixteenth arrondissement, the watchdogs of vocabulary" (p. 69). Of these watchdogs, he singles out Brunschvicg for special odium, attacking not only his philosophy but the man himself, consumed by a greed for honors and an easy conscience. A whole wide world of suffering men lies, largely unseen, beyond this intellectual hothouse. The students produced there are unequipped for real understanding of their society, and its collective problems are reduced by them to the level of personal woes. These young men are self-divided: "We were alienated by inner wars and endless debates" (p. 71). In

[20] Nizan, *Aden-Arabie*, Maspero, 1960, p. 65.

23

a phrase which looks forward to *Antoine Bloyé*, Nizan speaks of "the mutilations which awaited us. After all, we know what kinds of lives our parents lived" (p. 71). He and his co-students have inklings of reality, but their ideas are mainly negative. Alain has taught them that to think is to say no: a satanic activity. Nizan keeps admitting how vague his protest was; he was unable to point to anything precise. (But, as Baudelaire said, "Infinity is the sharpest point of all.") Nizan can only call it "the underemployment of our human needs" (p. 73). He and his companions tried to take flight into drinking, the dreamworld of the cinema, or women. They were consumed with this urge to flee. The myth of travel figured widely in their imaginings.

As Nizan fled to Arabia, so Malraux went off to Indochina. In his *La Tentation de l'Occident*, Malraux described Europe as a cemetery of defunct conquerors, and the home of "an essential absurdity." His complaint was clearly more metaphysical than Nizan's, and closer to that of Drieu la Rochelle. Excited by Lindbergh's exploits, Drieu once exclaimed: "Whether we're chasing after God or Satan, we must get away from all this." In *Aden-Arabie*, Nizan works through the various forms of escapism proposed by and for the privileged youth of the 1920s. The religious "solution," particularly the fusing of prayer and poetry, blurred all the issues and so was unacceptable. Surrealism was "the last refuge where people could die in peace amidst the musty smells of castles left them by their grandfathers" (p. 78). That traditional French tactic, the cultivation of irony, could lead nowhere. There remained cosmopolitan travel, loudly championed as a panacea by Valéry Larbaud, Cendrars, and numerous other writers. The young men afflicted by a new "mal de siècle" were a light, airy generation (like Sartre's Orestes before he committed himself). They were ignorant of the new civilizations painfully constructing themselves in the East. Bookish, they were taken in by the literary promises, the talk of heavens below to be found away from Europe, or in the imagination: "the timeless utopias of inner life" (p. 85). They were living, in fact, in the Age of Ignorance: "those years when we're programmed by obscure forces, when we can't begin to understand our desires, actions, words, work, or love" (p. 85). This kind of youth is an illness which topples over into a rabbit run, "a low panic revealing all the falsity and mistaken ideas secreted in me" (p. 93). Nizan identifies with the soldier who cannot help continually taking French leave. "Freedom is the real power of wanting to be yourself" (p. 100). Nizan believes we have a core of self which is constantly threatened by various forms of mutilation. His own psychic disarray was not cured by locomotion and change of location; in fact, his dissatisfaction was made worse by the acquisition of new causes for anguish.

"Men need anchorages" (p. 111). What did he find when his ship moored in Aden? A town which has always been "emporium et oppidum": a market and a military stronghold, the scene of the centuries-old colonialism of the whites. These whites busied themselves with lining up and subtracting signs on paper: abstract records of concrete exploitation. Their world was one of hierarchies, passwords, and rites, in which Nizan felt like "a fish out of water" (p. 114). His job left him a lot of free time, yet he needed a framework he could work within, not a vacuum.

His employer, M. Besse, figures in *Aden-Arabie* under the flimsy disguise of "Mr. C." Antonin Besse had in fact begun by trading in local wares like hides and incense. His business grew rapidly into a major trading empire covering Ethiopia and other neighboring countries. M. Besse was later able to donate one million pounds to Oxford University in order to found a new college (St. Anthony's). This powerful man is transformed, in Nizan's account, to an unhappy capitalist in bondage to powers greater than himself. In a letter (Strasburg, September 1926), Nizan said that M. Besse's life could be summed up in the formula "negotium in tenebris." For him,

Besse was a "false man of action" who boasted, like Malraux's Perken, that "this country bears the scars of my doings here" (p. 119). He is trapped in the vicious circle of capitalism: "Caught up on the roundabout of capital and exchange controls which nobody could stop revolving, he gave orders to slaves lashed to the same wheel as himself" (p. 120). Yet even this fulfilled capitalist was conscious of a gap, of "the suction pump draining his life of its substance" (p. 121). When such men dream, cracks open up in the smooth superstructure of their lives. But they cannot transfer the findings of sleep to their active lives. Parts of their being remain fallow.

The caustic account of M. Besse and his like by Nizan might be explained by the fact that Nizan (as he admits, too briefly, in the book) almost yielded to the temptation of working permanently in his organization and thus becoming a full-blown exploiter himself. For a time, Nizan was carried away with excitement at the prospect (letter to his fiancée, Aden, 20 February 1927): "And we'll flood the East with synthetic oil. . . . Shell and Standard Oil will be driven to distraction." (It might be noticed that there is an aura of privateering, of the up-and-coming firm smacking down the big ones, in this capitalistic vision.) Nizan's cold, unnerving manner might well have betokened his ability to become a good decision maker and sales executive; and, odd jobs that he performed for M. Besse (for example, reporting on a Djibouti branch which had collapsed into chaos) suggest that he had a head for business. *Aden-Arabie* as a whole is a story of a near miss, and this projected venture is one aspect of it.

Nizan, in the book, confesses to starting his rebellion by criticizing the men at the top. For him, Aden represented a microcosm of Europe: "Only the essence is left after decanting . . . a dry, inhuman residue that can be analyzed" (p. 128). The smaller scale and the skeletal diagram available made Europe's mysteries easier to decipher. He could watch English regiments being sent from Aden "to civilize the Chinese. I hope the Chinese kill as many of them as possible" ( letter to his fiancée, Aden, 21 February 1927). He could study the shadow-play behavior of the two-dimensional, interchangeable puppets of the capitalist machine, their rigid timetables, their philistine rejection of any intelligent topics of conversation. Nizan is aware all the time that he is concentrating on the bourgeois end of the scale. The reason is that, at that time, the Arab and Somali laborers in the colony were still too docile for the Europeans even to feel the need of justifying their methodical exploitation of the natives. Nizan visited a Sultan who had been rewarded with a decoration and whose annual revenue of 3 million pounds was provided by the slave labor of 40,000 natives. The lower European ranks are petty-bourgeois, waiting only for a comfortable retirement back home. At times, Nizan relents. For instance, he truly admires the ability of the English to *relax* their bodies in rest, sports, or hobbies, unlike the French or Italians there. He even goes so far as to suggest that if the English concept and practice of leisure were given a theoretical extension by a Frenchman, it might approximate the Greek ideal of voluptuousness! But such moments of diversion on Nizan's part occur rarely. Most of the time, his phrases are loaded guns: "Their nervous tics kept them going. . . . They boasted of the women they'd had, the wounds they'd suffered in war, yet it was impossible to imagine living liquids like sperm or blood coming out of them" (p. 135). He refuses all charity. The whites, when crowded together, are opaque to the outsider's eye, like sheets of mica. The solution is to separate the sheets, and thus to see through the individuals.

"Thought needs an object and a goal" (p. 148). Nizan's "intentionality" at this stage is a tension, a hungering, or a disgust. A badly counseled youth confesses that he all but fell for the lie of capitalism, for what J.–P. Faye calls "the rigged ac-

27

countancy of colonial society, of university culture, of 'inner life.' "[21] "I was nearly finished off" (p. 155). In fact, Nizan almost died in an accident, when sunstroke overcame him at the wheel and his car crashed into a ditch. (Sartre, romanticizing, presents this incident as an attempted suicide, a flouting of reason, a death wish.)[22] Nizan needed the estrangement of his stay in Aden to discover for himself what he acknowledges to be elementary truths which other people realize without traveling. Though he points to his peasant ancestry and his own love of the countryside, he refuses all romantic, anthropomorphic uses of nature as a source of lessons: "Don't make me laugh with your revelations from nature and your storehouses of symbols" (p. 161). He makes it quite clear that his interest lies in *human* space: "Melancholy landscapes are ones in which children starve to death; tragic landscapes are ones covered with lines of helmeted police and convoys of guns; exalting landscapes are ones where anybody can kiss a woman without feeling afraid" (p. 161).

Europe is the trunk of the world's troubles. These must be attacked at their root. But it is the sons of Europe who must carry out this revolution, for the natives of the Middle East are too fatalistic to revolt. In Malraux' terms, Western man, in his temperate zones, can mold nature and feel that he is escaping fatality and building his own fate, whereas in the East "human desires make no impact on the eternal desert" (p. 167). But Nizan's resolve was heartened by the odious twin spectacle which greeted him on his return at Marseilles: a prison and a church. Ironically quoting Du Bellay's line "France who suckled me at your breast," Nizan sets about biting the desiccated breast that had fed him. It fed him sour milk, so his bite is neither loving nor playful. At the end of his private odyssey, he envies Ulysses' swift and vigorous settling of accounts on *his* return. France, to Nizan, conjures up

[21] Jean-Pierre Faye, *Aden-Arabie*, p. 552.
[22] Sartre, "Paul Nizan," p. 171.

the smell of embalming; it is trying to preserve itself by dreams of xenophobic impenetrability (cf. the Maginot Line), and by myths such as France "the capital of intelligence, the oldest daughter of the Church, the patron of democracy" (p. 171). By "France" he means the proprietor-class: a mean, calculating people, incapable of love or of giving, obsessed only with possessing. Like Du Bellay's complaint on returning from "exile" in Italy, Nizan's is willfully bilious: "The French hide in their burrows, defending their property at all times against neighboring property holders and the idea of property against those who possess nothing. France is a land of lawsuits over party walls. Everywhere you find steel traps, vicious dogs, barbed wire, broken glass along the tops of walls, and the Civil Code. If there's one thing they really like it's the sign: 'No Trespassing'" (p. 175). Here, as elsewhere, Nizan conducts a campaign against French agoraphobic protectionism in all its multiple forms. In a sense, France was always a foreign country to Nizan, and the passage just quoted reads very much like a foreigner's reaction to France's chauvinism and unwelcoming ways.

His enemies worship capital, and their sole ambition is to become or remain *rentiers*. In Nizan's eyes, such men have only a ghostly existence in themselves, though they exercise real and crushing powers: "Flesh-and-blood workers labor to keep these phantoms alive a bit longer" (p. 177). Though Nizan as yet had little direct knowledge of these workers, he felt equipped to attack their oppressors, with help from the Marx and Engels analyses. Homo economicus, Nizan states, is now more varied than in their day: "Banker, industrialist, valuer, broker. Some are *rentiers*, small landowners, others play the stock exchange. You may meet a homo economicus who is a civil servant, or even a worker. He's an animal happy to save his surplus profit" (p. 179). He describes the postures of this genus: its cult of the dead, its love of military processions with their "cannons more lyrical than breasts" (p. 182),

its literary idols (Anatole France and Valéry). Without noticing that he thereby condemns his own book, he exclaims: "Let
no one who is really alive waste his time telling them how
wretched and sterile they are" (p. 184). Pompously, but in
evident good faith, Nizan declares: "I am willing to spend the
rest of my life wearing a number. . . . It's time to make war
on the causes of fear, and time to get my hands dirty" (p.
185). The urge to exorcise the shadows that once terrified him
is patent. He is willing to accept the Soviet simplification of
the class war: "Let's have the guts to be crude" (p. 186). The
penultimate statements verge on hysteria, or at least melo-
drama. But the final words are too clearly charged with
Nizan's own real passion to be other than genuine: "I will no
longer shrink from hatred or be ashamed to be a fanatic. I
have to take revenge: they nearly finished me off" (p. 187).
As was said earlier, *Aden-Arabie* results from a near miss. It
has all the instinctive anger and the gratefulness for still being
alive of somebody who has survived a threatening dilemma.

The book has a tripartite structure: an initial spate of the
young man's prefabricated images, followed by his journey out
which ends in bitter disillusion, and finally his return home
filled with new and radical resolve. As his motives are confused until the gradual and painful clarification towards the
end, the commonest motif in the book is that of *vertigo*: the
squirrel's cage of capitalism, the blinding sun in a metallic
landscape, the dizzy succession of temptations whirling past a
young man's attention. The tone is violent and lordly throughout, often annoying in its would-be knowingness: "my enemies
must not count on any naïveté on my part"; but just as often
self-deflating: "what a lot of fuss about something so very
simple" (p. 158). Youths are presbyopic. Most English readers would be enviously appalled by such intellectual cocksure-
ness, such superb disdain and elegant rudeness. One reason
why some readers find Nizan's sarcastic arrogance so offensive
is that he is using a traditionally "aristocratic" register to

voice his defense of the underprivileged. It is the tone often employed by the nobs to talk of the plebs, but he turns it against the top dogs. *Aden-Arabie* can be compared, for this tone, with Aragon's onslaught in his *Traité du style*. Aragon dismisses all current varieties of escapism, and is particularly severe on religion, which he describes solely in terms of various sexual perversions. But the words are self-igniting and logor- rheic. The impression left with the reader is one of essential frivolity. This prose shimmers like diamante, rather than cuts like diamonds. In Nizan's book, the verb "saisir" recurs time and again: the clenching of an impatient fist, the effort of a hungry mind to grab hold of something valuable to believe in and fight for. This book, however, is not self-entranced. In addition to the harsh description of the Aden colonialists, there is a sensitive and nuanced portrait of a ship's captain, Blair, who is seen at his best when seeking to outwit natural obsta- cles or to solve technical crises, but who suffers boredom (like Pascal's "unattended king") when all is running smoothly.

To borrow Memmi's terms, this book is much more a "por- trait of a colonizer" than a "portrait of the colonized," but not for the same reasons that made Malraux far more entranced with the decadent capitalist Ferral than with the Chinese prole- tariat. I think Nizan in this book, as elsewhere, tries only to write of what he knows firsthand. He explains, besides, that he is starting his attack at the top. He has everything to learn about the other end of the social scale. Neither at the E. N. S., nor in Aden, nor in his private life, had Nizan yet found what he needed: an unmistakable sign. But despair does not set in. His return is energetic and determined: "For instance, we'll have to use our hands, get involved with living people, forget about the dead, explore our bodies at long last, kill our ene- mies, invent things, teach children to walk, laugh, discover the world" (p. 155). The program is vague, but it is joyous. It is the relief that comes of knowing the exact face of the embodied enemy. He had lived in a *dispersed* state in Paris before. He now refinds the violence that was his true self as a child and that he had masked for years. He discovers that life need not be an endless circling, but that it can be a positive movement forward. "I will come back stripped for action," he promised in a letter to his fiancée (Aden, January 1927). He kept that promise. *Aden-Arabie* is not, like some essays, a digestive, but a tonic emetic.

Nizan obtained his "agrégation de philosophie" in 1929. In that year he became editorial secretary on the avant-garde periodical *Bifur*, which published Sartre's *Légende de la vérité*, Chirico, Giono, Buster Keaton, James Joyce, Eisenstein, Heidegger, and extracts from Nizan's second pamphlet, *Les Chiens de garde*. He worked hard to push this luxury publication over to the extreme left. When he failed, he wrote for the communist-inclined review *Europe*, in which he arrogantly dismissed Chirico's writings as too great a luxury in an urgent age. This old argument was resurrected recently by Sartre, when he dismissed his own *La Nausée* as irrelevant at a time of starvation in India and war in Vietnam. This argument does not improve with repetition. It must occur to all writers with a social conscience at some stage of their careers. The better ones usually get over such self-defeating naïveté. Possibly Nizan was being "over-zealous" in his early years as a Party member.

Nizan married Henriette Alphen in 1927, with Sartre and Raymond Aron as witnesses. His two children were born in 1928 and 1930. He and his wife lived in an ultramodern house, provided by her parents, which induced outsiders to think them well-off, whereas Nizan had only his unimpressive journalist's salary. They were avid cinemagoers. Simone de Beauvoir tells a splendid anecdote of the making of a film on the Nizans' terrace. In the script, Nizan played the part of a priest, and Sartre, that of a prim young man educated by monks. Both were debauched by whores, and when they tore off

Sartre's shirt, a huge scapular medal blazed on his chest and Christ appeared. Christ asked Sartre whether he smoked and offered him his Sacred Heart as a lighter. The whores (played by Henriette, Simone de Beauvoir, and Berl's glamorous wife in her black lace underwear) fell on their knees and blessed God. The cassock apparently suited Nizan, who startled passersby by parading in the street wearing it, with his arm around his wife.[23] Nizan's humor was as basic as his angst. His letters reveal him as much more whimsical, poetic, and "Celtic" than many of those who met him ever suspected. There was a great deal more to him than the categorical and disconcerting militant, which was one of his necessary strategic roles but only one part of the whole man. It is essential to visualize him on his various levels, otherwise he might appear to be, misleadingly, a destructive young monster. *Les Chiens de garde* is a product of his destructiveness, and of his sense of humor. His ability to see disparities and to pierce masks reveals a comic sense, as well as a critical gift.

The traditional chauvinism of official bodies in France, especially the "Université," right up to 1939 (and often beyond), is a notorious phenomenon. Before looking at Nizan's account of it, we can first examine Sartre's.[24] Around 1925, Sartre alleges, Marx and Hegel were hardly taught at the Sorbonne, although students *were* advised to read Marx "in order to refute him." Sartre's generation lacked therefore the intellectual tools to understand historical materialism. Sartre read *Capital* and *The German Ideology*: "I felt I had a luminous understanding, but really I didn't understand a word. . . . Reading [them] didn't produce any change in me." The only available master with whom to counter the official idealist philosophy

[23] Beauvoir, *La Force de l'âge*, p. 37. A different version of this sketch and details of another, entitled *Le Vautour de la Sierra*, are given in Michel Rybalka, "Sartre et le cinéma," *L'Esprit Créateur* 8, no. 4 (Winter 1968), p. 286.

[24] Sartre, *Critique de la raison dialectique*, pp. 22-24.

was Unamuno and his theory of "the tragic sense of life," taken in a nonsocial sense. "We had been brought up surrounded by bourgeois humanism and this optimism was disintegrating because we had a vague sense that all around our town there was the huge multitude of 'sub-men conscious of their subhumanity,' but we still experienced this disintegration in an idealist and individualist fashion." On the one hand, then, there was a retarded and misguided intellectual development among the young. On the other, as a Marxist critic expresses it: "Any ruling class which feels threatened tries to hide the content of its class domination and to present its struggle to save an outdated form of society as a struggle for something 'eternal,' unassailable, and common to all human values."[25] It is this conflict between perplexed youth desperately wanting clarification and the maneuvers of the establishment to prevent or divert this challenge which occupies Nizan in *Les Chiens de garde*.

From the outset, he brutally juxtaposes philosophical quibbles exchanged between Julien Benda and the aptly named Parodi with newspaper reports of colonial repression and ill-treatment of prisoners in French jails. The philosophers are pictured as obsessed with the eternal and the absolute to the detriment of the temporal and the specific. Like J.-F. Revel, in another pamphlet, *Pourquoi des philosophes*, written thirty years later, Nizan stresses the urgency of redefining the terms and the purposes of philosophy, and of doing so in simple and lucid language. He reiterates his most compulsive themes: those of emotional poverty and psychic underemployment. Young minds hunger for substantial food for thought, but are dealt ersatz stuff. The chief ersatz offering is the belief that "the Mind" is the highest value and that the mind "controls the world since the disappearance of God" (p. 12). This cult is perhaps the real channel separating France and England.

[25] Ernst Fischer, *The Necessity of Art*, London: Penguin, 1963, p. 129.

To see what Nizan is getting at, we need to understand the fact that not only the guillotine, but traditional French philosophy since Descartes, severs the head from the body. Valéry's Monsieur Teste, that mutilated intellect who must once have been a man, is the perfect image of this tendency. Even French literary eroticism (Sade, Laclos, Malraux) is mental. The French vice is not, like its English counterpart, flagellation, a down-to-earth thing, but rather the exaltation of the mind at the expense of all the other actual possibilities of the person. With the cruel eyes of the resident alien, Nizan sees this phenomenon for what it is worth. Nizan admits, however, that, when he was sixteen and in the lycée, he swallowed this cult of the mind, that he was an intellectual snob who felt superior to manual workers because he had access to the ideas of the spiritual guides of the elite class: the "philosophes." It is this unquestioned status that he now intends to downgrade, with a vengeance. His friend Sartre took many years longer to outgrow the myth of thinker-saviors, which Nizan is here discarding: "People are not naïve enough to believe that a philosophy *agrégé* is by reason of his function a St. Bernard dog or even a person worthy of respect" (p. 13).

While some philosophers are good or bad, Nizan says, philosophy-in-itself does not even exist. It is in every sense equivocal, not univocal. There are only particular philosophies of an age or a social class. What is called philosophy is an empty quintessence that survives only by consenting convention, a convenient umbrella concealing a multitude of sins and ambivalences. Despite family likenesses, different philosophies are as hostile to one another as are jacqueries to pogroms. All the time, Nizan is thinking consequentially ("what is the logical outcome of such-and-such an assumption?"). He recognizes that intelligence is promiscuous and infidel; being only a tool, it will serve any master. For him, the proper use of intelligence is for the study of concrete individuals and statistics and not of abstract hypotheses. Life, in its deviousness, is closer to a second-class road than to a national highway; and it is the second-class citizens Nizan is interested in defending against the administrators of the highways. Philosophy must be down-to-earth and must base itself on questions of choice and judgment. He explains that "the revolting meaning of M. Tardieu's existence and, at the other extreme, the revolting meaning of the statistics of forced labor provide me with truly philosophical questions" (p. 18). He opposes the common man's demands to the lofty abstractions of official philosophy. There are sins of omission as well as of commission. The tone is one of: Stand up and be counted. Whose side are you on? He pushes away, in Engels' words, "the eclectic stews" served up to students of thought. He points out that most contemporary French academic philosophers are in fact historians of philosophy. Yet they adopt an ahistorical stance and claim philosophy to be a "pure" activity removed from the temporal realm, a kind of chessmatch *sub specie aeternatatis* in a lifeless landscape. Such ivory towers must be demolished. Nizan quotes some telling passages from the works of Boutroux and Brunschvicg which merrily list thinkers one after the other, as if they were all engaged in some relay race, passing on to each other the self-same baton of thought. This would-be, self-contained, incestuous world demonstrates the principal tactic of idealism: the melting of differences. Nizan proceeds to play the idealists at their own games by melting the differences between various thinkers he loathes, by lumping them together on the opposite side of the fence. For example, he condemns Bergson as an idealist. Bergson merely represents one of the dual tendencies of bourgeois thought: "the mystique of timeless reason and the inner mystique of the person" (p. 26). Above all, Nizan wishes to emphasize that thinkers, having no mandate, must face the music, must be answerable. No etiquette is needed: "We demand real democracy for philosophy" (p. 28).

The advice he offers: look outside philosophy for the causes which condition it. Kant, for instance, would exclude most of a nation's population from full rights of citizenship; the only complete human beings, in his eyes, were economically self-supporting. Like Kant, the leaders of the French Revolution, despite their bourgeois theories of egalitarianism, treated workers as wards. In his own age, Nizan, arguing from a position antithetical to that of Benda in his *Traison des clercs*, castigates philosophers for abstentionism, for abdicating their true function, and he sees this betrayal as reflecting a political choice, like that of Kant. Nizan's control of his material oscillates wildly at times. He is often carried away by the voluptuousness of his own scornful rhythms and sounds. For, on the one hand, he blames academic philosophers for supporting the establishment (and thereby exerting some kind of influence, of lending weight); and, on the other, he describes them as futile: "Is philosophy going to go on being women's work, the embroidery of a sterile old spinster? Will the *Revue de métaphysique et de morale* compete with *La Femme chez elle*, and the publisher Alcan with the Tedesco firm?" (p. 35). This willful juxtaposition of academic strongholds and commercial products aimed at bourgeois woman, while deliciously rude, weakens Nizan's argument elsewhere. If the enemy is nugatory, why waste time destroying him? Nizan is often on better group when he lets the bourgeois idols damn themselves out of their own mouths (e.g., when he quotes virtually identical passages from the works of Doumer and Brunschvicg, and concludes that there is little to choose between the "extreme stupidity" of the former and the "extreme subtlety" of the latter). Men like these, in the First World War, exhorted their pupils to die for their country. "The Marne appeared to M. Brunschvicg as a dazzling proof of his philosophy" (p. 42). Boutroux preached a "philosophical crusade" against Germany. The quotations on this topic from Parodi, Bergson, and Desjardins would be funny if they were not hair-raising. Men like these, Nizan adds, all claim to be humanists. None of them has the courage (like Fouché or Bismarck) to admit his disdain for his fellowmen. They live, like cuttlefish, surrounded by a cloud of ink. Nizan quotes Proust on the strange contradiction in those who claim to disbelieve in the external world yet work to carve themselves a niche in it: "Philosophers always end up by letting loose the real men hidden in them" (p. 45). It is this dropping of masks that Nizan hopes to accelerate by his criticism. His effort is sustained both by the urge to defend those beneath the elite and by the need to assert himself after having nearly fallen into the baited earlier trap: "I loathe the philosophy of the oppressors because I once felt oppressed myself" (p. 50). These *rentiers* think they have bought up a permanent place in society; it is time to evict them. Nizan is conscious of his own iconoclasm, but says that this is unimportant when compared with the urgency of refuting "this complicated Talmud of false history" (p. 52). He cannot in fact dismiss these great pretenders as inoffensively risible or he would have no argument, and so he declares: "This philosophy is not dead but it must be killed off" (p. 53).

He switches next to the class such thinkers represent, claiming that the bourgeois always seeks to justify "his temporal operations by reminding us of his spiritual mission" (p. 55). Their favored myth is that of the enlightened despot: "Directors of businesses. Directors of conscience" (p. 55). They enjoy the fruits of a readymade world: family connections, family traditions. Nizan pulls his two threads together: "The pride of the scholar confirms and reinforces the common pride of the bourgeois" (p. 57). They share the same premises: that they exercise a tutelary function, that they have the right to a mission (cf. Sartre's *L'Enfance d'un chef*). Imagining they bear a mission to lead and yet shying away from involvement, the bourgeois opt to intervene from a distance, to operate via third parties (and *Antoine Bloyé* will be just such a study of an interposed agent of the bourgeoisie). The chief bogey in Nizan's indictment is Léon Brunschvicg, who never confessed "that he loathed the workers who endangered the social order

he lives in, but only said that Marx was an enemy of that reason which we must worship" (p. 62). This attempt to keep all
discussion on some abstract level is typical of a "mathemati-
cian's religion wtih its nonhistoricity and nontemporality."[26]
In such a philosophy, the mind is conceived as enjoying pure
intellectual freedom and as obeying no dialectical laws. Nizan
objects to it on the same grounds as he rejects Leibniz: he
has no time for a vision of a world of windowless monadic
beings. He is impatient with such "pure" philosophy, for, as
Marx said, the time has come to change the world, and no
longer to interpret it. (Nizan might have quoted another in-
jurious axiom of Marx: "Philosophy stands in the same relation to the study of the actual world as onanism to sexual
love.") Brunschvicg once lectured in Rouen at the Université
Populaire. He declared: "If all our philosophers are attracted
to the Université Populaire it is because they find there the
realization of their ideal of spiritual life" (p. 64). As Nizan
comments, what must the Rouen stevedores have made of such
a spiel? Nizan keeps blatantly feigning to conduct his prose-
cution in a spirit of fair play, for the more justifications, pre-
ferably hypocritical, he can find for abstentionism by these
intellectual "skunks," the more clearly they stand condemned.
Despite the jibes and the insults, basically he is taking even
enemy philosophers seriously. He believes that "every human
thought questions the entire order of things weighing down
on our lives" (p. 66). What he attacks in bourgeois philosophy
is the *misuse* of thought, the attempt to deodorize and disperse
unpleasant questions. He denies that there are "fit" subjects
for philosophy to dwell on, such a concept being an overhang
from the seventeenth-century convention of decorum (which,
as Goethe pointed out, is a behavioral and not an aesthetic
criterion).

Because "every philosophy is a form of action," Nizan prom-

[26] Colin Smith, *Contemporary French Philosophy*, p. 107.

ises "We will involve ourselves in this world up to our necks"
(p. 77). He stresses that, as Marx and Engels themselves explained to their misinterpreters, economic reality is not the
whole picture of a class; there is also the superstructure: "a
collection of precepts, judgments, moral and juridical concepts" (pp. 78-79). And within the social class there are the
various professional groups which further diversify the whole
problem. In some respects, Nizan seems to have a Platonic
idea of "the Bourgeois": an abstract man who needs to protect
his abstract existence with a series of buffers and screens. He
quotes from Marx's *The Jewish Question* on bourgeois man as
"an imaginary member of an imaginary sovereignty, stripped
of his real individual life and filled with an unreal generality"
(p. 85). Yet these phantoms exercise real power. Their Janus
philosophy has both an esoteric side ("the self's effect on itself"), and an exoteric side (a few formulae for public usage).
It is this second, vulgarized version which is indoctrinated
from the primary school onwards. All bourgeois philosophers
talk of man as if he were a middle-class thinker. But such
assumptions are irrelevant to the workers, who need their own
philosophy ("a homogeneous vision of their world"), as a defense against the "mystification" practiced by their bosses. By
"mystification," Nizan means a campaign to invalidate the
perceptions or beliefs of others, and, by extension, to instil in
them alien doctrines. In answer to the ancient rejoinder that
men are never equal, Nizan would point to the felt need for
justice, which may not be based on any everlasting principles
but which is an unquestionable and palpable fact of existence.

Street fighting is not the whole of revolution. Lenin, Marx,
or Plekhanov did not sniff at attacking counterrevolution in
its *theorists*. "We will carry out tasks less glorious than insurrection" (p. 106). The main one of these tasks is the com-
batting of official propaganda, particularly in the field Nizan
knows well, education. Pupils, students, and young teachers
are vulnerable to the authoritative dictates of men like Parodi

(an inspector of education), Brunschvicg, and Alain. The latter is an interesting case. A liberal, he reflected the Radical belief that the individual's participation in politics should be largely negative: a compound of assent to the laws of the country and resistance to any abuse of them. As such, his thought split the temporal and the spiritual orders, and contained implicitly the notion of "mental reservation." This attitude was apparently widespread among many *députés* of the Third Republic, especially in the provinces, school teachers, farmers, and small businessmen.[27] Such theories can back up entrenchment but not the effort to change the existing situation in any radical way. Nizan cannot be as harsh on the obviously decent Alain as on Brunschvicg. But he can still stick to his conviction that such men, ultimately, are inadequate formers of opinion if France's structure is ever to be renovated. The social conjuncture is too critical to allow any compromises. Overproduction and underdistribution reveal the age as the crisis of capitalism, which Nizan presents, from the enemy's standpoint, in bitter puns. "It's just another of these growing pains that societies have been through in the past: all we need is a proper regime" (p. 119). The French try to convince themselves "that this malady is not within themselves, is not a sickness caused by their internal contradictions. . . . They try to make out that the causes of the illness are entirely external, a kind of invasion from abroad" (p. 119). All foreigners and foreign philosophies, to the French, are dangerous microbes. Communism, Nizan insists, is not the cause of France's malady, but its antidote.

As towards the close of *Aden-Arabie*, at the end of *Les Chiens de garde* Nizan swings into prophecy. Bourgeois philosophy will become more openly fascist. He welcomes the prospect of a more patent fight. He admits the merely verbal nature of his own rebellion, which is but a small corner of a

[27] Roy Pierce, *Contemporary French Political Thought*, pp. 6, 17.

large-scale, long-term program of radical renovation. Action, he hopes, will cleanse him of his rhetoric. Hackwork in the Party will be accepted without qualms. To bolster his own morale, he quotes Marx: "It is obvious that the weapon of criticism cannot replace the criticism of weapons. Material powers cannot be defeated except by material powers, but theory can become a material force once it gets through to the masses" (p. 126). There is the whole weight of the past, the accretion of social habits, which must be undermined, for "oppression is the past itself congealed by history, a take-over by dead memories" (p. 130). Nizan will respond to the "intellectuals' betrayal" (in *his* use of the term, antithetical to Benda's) by another betrayal: the abandoning of his own class and the embracing of the demands of the proletariat. All the old postures advocated by previous philosophers are played out: the "sage," the "citizen," the "intellectual." The new type must aim at the ideal of the professional revolutionary, as outlined by Lenin. The tasks of these new men are: "to overturn the habits of mind they grew up with, to kill in themselves that self-satisfied arrogance which characterizes the bourgeois intellectual. They must contribute all the technical resources of the intellectual but renounce all the intellectual's bad habits" (p. 164). He acknowledges that such renegades from the middle class must of necessity remain for a long time very suspect to the workers. But there is no masochism in such an outlook. A dose of humility will be a tonic to these refugees from the elite, these critics of the bourgeoisie's watchdogs, who will become willing watchdogs themselves, in the other camp.

Nizan thinks for himself. But no man is an autarky; all need foreign aid. It is Marx and Lenin who provide most of it for Nizan. What he collects from them he invests with the unmistakable pulsation of real anger. *Les Chiens de garde* is highly repetitive. Similarly, Marxist propaganda and criticism harps in order to combat the all-pervasiveness of the more diluted and "subtle" bourgeois ideology. Is such reiteration merely self-gratifying? At times it is; the pleasure of playing variations on a basic theme occasionally leads the young pamphleteer astray. But it is doubtful that he really succumbs to the temptation to which he accuses Politzer of yielding in his anti-Bergson pamphlet, *Fin d'une parade philosophique*: that of not going deeply enough into the social motivation of a given philosophy, and of trying to seduce the reader by a display of cleverness and charm. It is in fact obvious to the reader of Politzer's essay that he is building up a fine head of steam about very abstract questions which he makes little attempt to place in their social context, and that he is too busy parading himself to pay proper attention to his professed object of criticism: Bergson's philosophical procession. The true pamphleteer, for Nizan, "does not bother trying to interest people in himself. He wants to fix their attention on the object of his attack."[28] One such object of derision in Nizan's essay is clearly Brunschvicg, against whom Nizan never lets up (a half-hearted pamphlet, after all, is self-defeating), unlike Lefebvre, who backpedals. (After castigating the old master in *L'Existentialisme*, Lefebvre apologizes in *La Somme et le reste*: "We were completely unfair to him. . . . The lofty bearing of his intellectualism included a rather abstract but pronounced love of freedom.")[29] By judicious and no doubt unfair quoting, Nizan creates a character for Brunschvicg, so that the thinker seems to figure in a satirical novel: "I am a taxpayer who likes to be protected by our policemen. . . . I have the exterior of a bourgeois, of a taxpayer, of a professor, but there is something else beneath. There is myself. I try to strip off that exterior and it would perhaps be unfair to judge my inner self by my exterior" (p. 162). It is a prize example of what Nizan means by "alibis."

Nizan's *Les Chiens de garde* might be usefully compared with J-F. Revel's *Pourquoi des philosophes?*, which, though

[28] Nizan, *La Revue marxiste*, no. 2, 1 March 1929, p. 238.
[29] Lefebvre, *La Somme et le reste*, p. 276.

from a non-Marxist angle, sets out to demolish many of the pretensions of post-1945 French philosophy. Revel's main enemy is Heidegger, and his heroes, Plato, Rousseau, Nietzsche, Montaigne, and Proust. From Proust he quotes the same passage, noted earlier, on the worldly greed of idealist thinkers. He attacks gods Nizan did not live to see installed: Lacan ("the Sacha Guitry of psychoanalysis"), and Lévi-Strauss, for extending unconvincingly to advanced societies his persuasive studies of primitive societies. Revel lays about himself with hefty swipes. Contemporary French thought, he states, "oscillates between hypocritical humanism, eclecticism made up of secondhand knowledge, the etymological jugglery of a Heidegger, pedantic platitudes, and theology ashamed to show its face."[30] Amidst the general onslaught, much of what he says has the ring of truth (e.g., that we get more *usable* psychological information from Stendhal, Dostoevski, or Proust than from Bergson, Brentano, or Merleau-Ponty). But the great lack is of any solid ground supporting him. He is forced to be eclectic himself, so as not to appear totally self-supporting. He does not take sides; neither is he neutral, hence the wanton, often ill-directed, splenetic violence of his language and the attitudes. Revel tries to be a freelance sniper, whereas Nizan, without losing his identity, joined a brigade. So often Revel appears a *licensed* satirist, a purveyor of chic rudeness. Besides, Nizan was always hostile to verbal exhibitionism for its own sake. In a review of Alain and Benda, he deplores the autobiographical urge of many thinkers who seem to feel that a *pretext* for thinking must be provided, along with a character reference. In this review, he quotes Descartes' remark that people seemed more interested in his face than in his ideas and that this was like being treated as a zoo animal. Nizan concludes: "It appears that our philosophers have agreed, more readily than did Descartes, to please their public after the

---

[30] Jean-François Revel, *Pourquoi des philosophes?*, p. 183.

44

fashion of elephants and panthers than with hard thinking."[31]
It is against such *monstres sacrés* that Nizan aimed his *Chiens
de garde*.

The English reader might feel alienated by such a vigorous
attack on idealist philosophy and wonder what the fuss is all
about. Such a reader might ask himself what would be the
English equivalent, the English philosophical and pedagogical
alibi camouflaging conservatism. (Such an alibi would be even
more perfidious in Albion.) Imperialistically slanted history?
Emphasis on outdoor activities at the expense of indoor meditation? The cult of amateurishness in all walks of life? The
refusal to act, or even to think, unless there are long-established
"precedents"? The English philosophical stress on uncertainty
and the French philosophical smugness might not be all that
far removed from each other. And Nizan's criticisms, suitably
translated, might be seen as still valid on this side of the
Channel.

What of the critical reaction in France to this challenging
pamphlet? An erstwhile fellow student, Guterman, in the review *Avant-Poste*, commented: "All Nizan has succeeded in
doing is to make Berl's light touch heavy-handed." Nizan, of
course, was not primarily concerned with stylistic niceties in
this essay, and we have suggested already that Berl could have
done with some serious ballast. The comments of Albert
Thibaudet were more thoughtful.[32] Thibaudet himself had
written in his *République des professeurs*: "Anyone who has
prepared for the *agrégation de philosophie* . . . has at some
time entertained the idea, as seminarians do, that the acme of
human endeavour is a life devoted to the service of the spirit."[33]
For him, Nizan's book bit hard, but it lacked a coherent argument and the indication of what might be "a philosophy growing out of a communist society" (i.e., not Marxism, but some

[31] Nizan, *Vendredi*, 1 January 1937, p. 6.
[32] Albert Thibaudet, "Un nouvel anticléricalisme," p. 1083.
[33] Thibaudet, *La République des professeurs*, p. 139.

faith evident in every fibre of national life). This was a tall order, for how could Nizan suggest something not yet visible even in the only viable communist society of that time, Russia? Gide, in his *Journal*, was impressed by Nizan's book, though naturally he felt unable to second the proposal for "a specifically proletarian philosophy." With his usual flair for the weakness of another writer, Gide said: "Nizan takes care not to include art in his indictment, or poetry. He is well aware that he would lose all sympathy if he made out that Béranger must be placed above Baudelaire. But is it condemnation of Mallarmé or Einstein to say that their work is accessible only to a minority?"[34] In *L'Humanité*, René Garmy notes the survival of stigmata from Nizan's class of birth, but has hopes for a future eradication of such flaws.[35] Garmy's tone is fraternal, not yet that of Big Brother.

Nizan's next book was to be *Antoine Bloyé*, where he writes: "Antoine lived in a world where the word 'philosophy' implied laziness and cowardice." It is this lazy use of "philosophical," in the sense of "fatalistic," that he always worked to destroy, and nowhere more cuttingly than in *Les Chiens de garde*.[36]

[34] André Gide, *Journal (1889-1939)*, p. 1140.

[35] René Garmy, *"Les Chiens de garde,"* p. 4.

[36] In her book *Le Destin littéraire de Paul Nizan*, Jacqueline Leiner, who had privileged access to private documents and rare periodicals, provides excellent information on Nizan at school, in university, and on his first writings in ephemeral magazines.

CHAPTER TWO

# AN ALIENATED MAN
## *ANTOINE BLOYÉ*

ARAGON saluted *Antoine Bloyé*, when it appeared, as a novel born not of naturalism but of socialist realism. Presumably he had in mind not the notion of a "positive hero," for Antoine Bloyé is the very antithesis of that, but rather the methodological matter of "the operative principle." This was the theory that, to guarantee authenticity, the would-be socialist-realist author should live what he describes, for example by working for some months in the factory or on the farm which was to be the context of his book. This theory clearly secretes a strong dose of self-punishment for the sin of being bourgeois and having unscarred hands. Closely linked to it was the practice of encouraging "Rabcors" (proletarian correspondents or aspiring novelists) to describe their place and conditions of work in Party journals, and to vent workers' claims. The ultimate aim was to marry culture and economics, the superstructure and the infrastructure. The result was, as might be expected, a leveling-down of the former to the latter.

Nizan did not, in fact, go to work on the railways for the purposes of documenting himself to describe the life curve of a railwayman. His method of fact-finding was closer to that of Zola: extensive reading, discussion with those involved, and, in Nizan's case, personal reminiscences of his own father and grandfather, who both worked on the railways. And Nizan reflected on the general problems of "proletarian literature" in a heavily polemical article he wrote the year before the publication of *Antoine Bloyé*.[1] In this article, which fluctuates between dogmatism and nuances, Nizan repeatedly makes the point that proletarian literature is seldom revolutionary. Henri

[1] Nizan, "Littérature révolutionnaire en France," *La Revue des vivants*, p. 393.

Poulaille, for instance, with the best will in the world, often writes "employers' literature" because his stance and his pitying tone towards his human material is condescending. In addition to such populists, there are those representatives of "the most French kind of literature of them all": the upholders of a leftist tradition (Chamson, Guéhenno, Alain, Duhamel, Prévost) who are still tempted by old dreams of an intelligentsia. Nizan goes on to slate those classy bourgeois writers attracted by the "exoticism" of proletarian subject matter. "M. Gide will write A Journey to the Michelin Factory, A Return from Genevilliers" (Nizan's prophecy was not far out: Gide wrote, a few years later, *Retour de l'U.R.S.S.*). "Men can be born into the proletariat and still betray it." There is no automatic salvation (nor damnation) dependent on circumstances of birth. An interesting case is that of Eugène Dabit, a writer who had fewer enemies than most in the France of the 1930s. Nizan says of him: "Dabit's deepest urges push him towards the party of revolution, but he is held back in a vague literary world by umpteen bonds and formal scruples." Dabit, in fact, had "adopted" a worker, Henri, and exhorted him to write his life story. Dabit described himself as "a man who expects others to make the choice for me."[2] To use a paradoxical phrase, Dabit seemed to be in search of *genuine copy*; he was living vicariously. At that time, a good many writers appeared to feel the urge to enjoy the experience of being a worker, but rather after the fashion in which a hovering maiden might like to be an ex-virgin without going through the possible distress of defloration. It is the *state* that is envied, some kind of supposed quintessential experience, and not the continuous and painful process of laboring.

Nizan rarely seems to have experienced such fond desires. At the École Normale Supérieure, he confessed to a longing to give up words and to become a cinema projectionist. (It

[2] Eugène Dabit, *Journal intime*, Gallimard, 1939, p. 27.

should, however, he recalled that all his life he was a passionate filmgoer.) And, later, as a journalist, he admitted to some envy of typographers. But intellectual suicide was not his meat. He realized that he could not become another man, but that he could identify himself with the deep motivations of other men. Converts from the bourgeoisie, he wrote, must work to associate themselves "by constant practice, by a kind of emotional, intellectual, and political training, with the aims and values of the proletariat whose spokesmen they are."[3] Description of the proletariat, he goes on, is not the sole object of such literature, which can be written on any subject provided that the point of view is that of the oppressed. He recognizes, too, that the reading public for such books has yet to be created, and that the vast majority of workers read, if anything at all, the sports pages of newspapers, detective stories, and pornography. He mocks the critics who consent to scenes of Mauriac's families discussing a will, but who flinch at descriptions of syndical meetings. This kind of reality has yet to find a proper place in literature.

Receiving *Angélina*, a novel by a fellow Breton, Louis Guilloux, for whom he had an affectionate admiration, Nizan rebuked him on several counts: for not situating his novel in a definite time and place, for his prodigiously artificial "popular style," and for the view of revolution he presents as "a poetic fable for unhappy solitaries." Nizan concludes with a phrase which helps illuminate the reasons why he wrote *Antoine Bloyé*: "We're living in an age when children no longer repeat the lives of their fathers."[4] But, to support this new age, Nizan had first to understand the old age it was due to replace. And to do this, he had in fact to rehearse his father's life in order to explain his own different option. In *Antoine Bloyé*, Nizan makes a deep and patient effort to get into his father's boots, under his skin, and into his head. But he aims also to judge

[3] Nizan, "Littérature révolutionnaire en France," p. 395.
[4] Nizan, "Angélina," *La Littérature internationale* 2, 1934, p. 161.

his father, and, through him, a whole class of people. In order to judge, Nizan has first to sympathetically reinvent his father: what he must have been in order to end up what he was. *Antoine Bloyé* is a double indictment, of an age (1864-1927) and of a man. The foreign aid Nizan welcomed in his effort to comprehend includes Freud (for the man) and Marx (for the age).

There was an unmistakable chain between father and son. Nothing is ever lost or forgotten; it is relived differently. But, equally, there is the difficulty of knowing those closest to us: "Il n'est pas dans la coutume des hommes que les fils pénètrent toutes les pensées qui se forment dans la tête des pères comme de grosses bulles douloureuses, et les fils ne sont pas des juges sans passions."[5] In Sartre's *Les Séquestrés d'Altona*, we see the heavy father. Nizan was a heavy son.

The epigraph is taken from Marx's *German Ideology*: "If communism wants to do away with both the worry of the bourgeois and the poverty of the proletarian, it is obvious that it cannot do this without doing away with the cause of both, i.e., 'labor.'" In Marx's 1844 manuscripts can be found a passage which explains what is meant by "labor" in this context: "There is the production of human activity as labor,—that is, as an activity quite alien to itself, to man, and to nature, and therefore to consciousness and the flow of life,—the *abstract* existence of man as a mere workman, who may therefore daily fall from his filled void into the absolute void, into his social, and therefore actual, nonexistence."[6] The reader is warned, then, that this novel will deal not with the stock theme of *difference* (the bourgeois individual's often euphoric sense of uniqueness), but with *alienation* (the concrete plight of the worker). But, as its central figure deserts one class for another,

[5] Nizan, *Antoine Bloyé*, p. 57. "It is uncommon for sons to have access to all the thoughts formed in their fathers' heads like large and painful blisters, and sons are not dispassionate judges."

[6] Karl Marx, *Economic and Philosophical Manuscripts of 1844*, Moscow, 1961, p. 86.

his problems partake of both "poverty" and "worry." The epigraph puts the whole novel under the sign of dialectical materialism, and such signs can illuminate obscurity.

Nizan presents us with the physical setting and its telltale objects, before he introduces the people (cf. Marx's stress on the primacy of the material world, either natural or manmade). This novel begins and ends with the death of Antoine Bloyé; death is its framework. As Nizan says in his blurb: "Antoine Bloyé is not an exceptional case; the whole of bourgeois society is under the shadow of death." In this opening section, the vocabulary, the details of death are precise, almost suffocatingly so. The corpse as it transforms itself into rigor mortis elicits stiff formalized behavior from the mourners. Nizan is saying, in effect: why do funerals involve so much fuss when death itself is so unceremonious? The widow weeps. Her sobs sound now like hacking laughter, now skimpy, almost dehydrated. They are genuine, but she continues living: "Anne wept but went on bargaining" (p. 18). As she checks the dropping temperature of her husband's body, Nizan's consistent care to note *progression* is underlined. The corpse is undergoing its final reification after an alienated life. His coffin is chosen for him by his wife: "Solid, simple, unfussy" (p. 20). This is no doubt how she would summarize his life to outsiders, who would agree. But the son Pierre, in his early twenties, feels anger at the whole performance.

He thinks of all the pseudoreligious fuss as an insult to his father, who did not give a damn for his immortal soul. And Pierre is equally angry with his father for allowing himself throughout his life to be duped by his wife's hidden persuasions. The undertaker's men and the balletic priests strike him as the pimps of death. Pierre wants to touch his father, but the smell, almost willfully, wards him off. Though Nizan's tone is curtly sarcastic, he does not dismiss all the behavior at the funeral as pure mimicry. He is always alive to the weight and automatism of traditions and superstitions. None of the

51

visitors is described as utterly blind to the shocking meaning of the event which has summoned them; some think of their own coming deaths, some even of Antoine. This opening chapter conveys the interminable time scheme of funerals.

In the cemetery, Pierre's eyes fasten on the class distinctions visible in the type and size of graves. Listening to the graveside speech, a potted official biography, Pierre thinks: "Voilà l'écorce de la vie de mon père. . . . C'est comme un rapport de Prix Montyon, un rapport de police."[7] He is led to ask himself what kind of man his father really was. After the funeral, the death odor gradually leaves the house, Antoine's clothes lose the creases his movements imprinted on them, his watch stops. "This is how a life just evaporates" (p. 32). The rest of this novel devotes itself to animating this petrified flesh and giving substance to this fleeing shade.

The house where Antoine was born in 1864 was overshadowed by a railway line for which his father worked. This father is a poor, confined man, resigned to an eternally decreed place in the hierarchy—at the bottom. He lacks projects and revolt. Nizan provides several receding views of the Bloyé family: extension in time always matters to him. At the same time, he sketches the forward movement of society in that period, the growth of the railways in the mid-nineteenth-century, the change of styling of the carriages as the new steam age gradually drags clear of the age of horse-drawn transport, the exodus of labor from the land to the railways (the exchange of one back-bent posture for another). Echoing Marx's harping on the metamorphosis brought about by the invention of the steam engine, Nizan declares: "human beings and the world are transformed more by inventors than by generals or statesmen" (p. 39). Antoine is born into this world of accelerating tempo, beneath "the railway signals which will rule his

[7] "That is the shell of my father's life. . . . It's like a good conduct medal, or a police file" (p. 30).

life" (p. 39). His first contact with trains is magical: an engine to him is a monster. His Breton locale itself is the scene of a conflict between surviving superstitious beliefs in miracle cures and prophetic oracles, and the material changes brought by the railways. But, although the trains have come, world news relayed by the capital still rarely filters through to this reactionary region: "Le dernier cercle amorti des événements vient s'éteindre au pied des Montagnes de la Séparation."[8]

Nizan makes a simple but evocative conjugation of Antoine's childhood world: walking to school along country lanes, intimately concerned with animal life at firsthand rather than with its stylized representation on classroom walls. Up to a certain age, children, in Nizan's view, draw few social comparisons, do not add, subtract, or divide, but merely multiply themselves. But this "naïve equality" gives way to "conditionings." The theme of *Antoine Bloyé* is this taming of freedom, this socialization of the natural man. Yet it is a two-way process, and earlier parts subsist in later ones; all experience is indelible. Something of the coarse child will remain in the grown man.

When Antoine's family moves to St. Nazaire, Nizan once again blocks in the historical context. In 1878, St. Nazaire was expanding rapidly. Guizot's earlier slogan—"Make your pile!"—had acted as a Sermon on the Mount for the grasping young bourgeoisie. The growth of the town is conveyed by intransitive or reflexive verbs: buildings rise up or propagate themselves, as if the human agency were missing or distant. The town is the locus of a linked quest: "men in search of work and investments in search of profits" (p. 52). Antoine, still a boy, is caught up in this industrial exaltation. At this stage of his life, he is not condemned for his weaknesses. Nizan asks numerous rhetorical questions, such as, how could the boy be expected to resist such-and-such a pressure? The schoolboy

---

[8] "The last dying ripple of national events fades out at the foot of the Mountains of Separation" (p. 42).

sees himself "ingenuously in the guise of a leader" (p. 53). His industrial environment conditions him into an industrial imagination. Though he can hear the freewheeling sea wind from his prison-classroom, the sea and foreign parts appeal to him less than do machines, and he has an atavistic peasant mistrust of water. He starts to be aware of his parents' situation. He feels a sad anger at the condescending charity shown to his docile father by his "superiors," whose cast-off clothes Antoine is wearing.

At school he wins prizes: "Antoine was good at being a performing monkey" (p. 58). With a scorn less raw but no less fierce than that of Vallès in *L'Enfant*, Nizan rehearses every detail of the ludicrous prize-giving ceremony. He has no fear of restating the well known: he seeks to underline common experience, to make us *see* what often we do unseeingly. The book Antoine wins is *Le Devoir*, by Jules Simon, from which Nizan quotes: "Man is free: he knows he has the right not to do what he is doing, and to do what he is not doing" (p. 61). In other words, man has the "psychological" or "moral" freedom Rousseau talks of in his *Rêveries*, a highly jesuitical and illusory notion, as Antoine guesses in his lumbering fashion. Is his father free not to go to work, not to be poor? Antoine goes on to misinterpret Simon's "subtle" ideas, but his ingenuousness is something of a saving grace. Meanwhile, his life is being directed from above. Via a chain of recommendations from teacher-deputy mayor-*député*, Antoine is channeled towards technical higher education. The liberal humanities are denied him, though Nizan implies that he is missing little. Antoine goes to the École Nationale des Arts et Métiers at Angers. This is one of the State's training establishments for the sergeants and subalterns of industry. Promotion is offered, like a baited trap: "At that time everything was done to encourage young workers to enter into the employers' conspiracy" (p. 65). Industry needs subordinate leaders to directly supervise the workers, while the overlords stay at a distance. Nizan, swinging regularly between high-level decisions and the action of the individual, presents Antoine as launched "on a path which he perhaps believes he has chosen for himself" (p. 67). But the path leads downward: not a climb, but a degradation.

The engineering school, organized in military fashion, turns out apprentices as if they were rolling stock. It subjects them to a heavy load of studies and physical labor. Though his body is powerful, Antoine barely has time to realize that he is being sold, or is selling himself, short. He has a dim awareness of a conspiracy against the self-development of boys of his class, and at odd moments feels the urge to burst out of the corsets of discipline tightly laced around him. One day, he rises to a brief instant of would-be demagogy. He climbs on to a pile of planks at the workyard as all the apprentices are leaving after work, and calls out the need for a strike against their oppressive conditions of life. It is a call to unity and action. But his companions stream past, ignoring him. This event acts as a trauma in Antoine's life. Later he thinks of it at a crucial moment. He never repeats the experiment, and this first instance of not being taken seriously is his first real alienation. It is an instinctive revolt, for he knows nothing of syndicates or socialism. When he receives his diploma at the end of his course, it is clear that he is qualified but not educated: he has no perspective on himself or on the world around himself. It is true that his subsequent military service in the Languedoc yields him plenty of free time, a kind of truce, but this vacation period is essentially one of numbness and not of self-discovery.

When he goes to Paris as an apprentice-driver, he moves to a city which was still at that time a conglomeration of separate communities. The area he lives in, with its dirty streets and sickly children, arouses in him a pitying anger, but a distancing is already taking place: "Il se divisait et sa sympathie venait comme du dehors, elle semblait se détacher de son corps."⁹ For the first and only time in his life, he integrates himself into a group with his fellow drivers. They are linked by their common knowledge and language, their pool of shared experience. With them he unbuttons himself when off duty. They go in for long rambling night walks around the sleeping city, enjoying the freedom of movement. Yet, as Nizan hints, their behavior is mainly a shoddy copy of rich youth's pleasures. (The big "event" of their night lives occurs when a girlfriend rises to urinating in the street.) Nizan displays in these pages a genuine feeling for and acquaintance with period detail: clothes, furniture, the books people were reading, the conditions of work and play. He is also helped by memories of his own night prowls when a student.

Antoine's first initiation into the lower levels of bourgeois society, when he is invited to dinner by the parents of Anne, begins to instill in him the art of "behaving himself," though on the whole he bows to social graces without truly adopting many of them himself. He is tugged in another direction by Marcelle, the widow of an engine driver who runs a café with her mother in a particularly desolate and almost apocalyptic sector of Paris, where a whore offers herself savagely to passersby: "la reine de ce pays, une Hécate des carrefours. . . . Elle était au plus creux repli des abîmes de la misère."¹⁰ The second phrase deflates the epic pretensions of the first; or perhaps the woman has both mythic and factual dimensions: there is a certain realistic mythology of whoredom in Nizan's work. With Marcelle, Antoine revels in a diverse and rich sexuality. She understands his work, can speak his language, shares his prejudices. But the bedroom, while it temporarily blots out prim, petty bourgeois sitting-rooms, cannot erase the network

⁹ "He was becoming divided against himself, and his compassion came from outside him, as if it were not part of his constitution" (p. 80).

¹⁰ "The queen of this area, a Hecate of the street corner. . . . She was in the deepest recess of the abyss of poverty" (p. 90).

of railway lines proliferating across France. In the early days of his work, these "transport" Antoine even more forcibly than Marcelle does.

Antoine establishes with his engine a kind of working animism: "Les hasards du métal et de ses assemblages combinent une personnalité difficile à saisir."[11] His pride in a well-maintained machine and the excitement of hectic teamwork are described with real sympathy. The alienation lies not in the work itself, at this stage, but in the exploitation of willing workers by their bosses. Antoine shares his workmates' anger at the long hours they have to put in. He almost achieves "workers' thoughts." If he were really conscious, he would notice portents concerning his own future in the person of M. Guyader, the father of Anne, the girl whom Antoine starts to court. Now in charge of the engine sheds, M. Guyader had earlier in life given up seafaring for the sake of his fiancée (just as Antoine turns down the chance of a job in China later on). His fiancée from then on had the value "d'une femme à laquelle on s'est sacrifié: que de femmes possèdent cette seule force."[12] As always, Nizan notes acutely here the manner in which we accept, and justify, the second best. Though he himself has "got on," M. Guyader is hostile to workers' demands for higher wages and improved conditions. He is proud of being *middling*—neither an insolent employee nor a distant superior.

Antoine is gradually snared in the trap of petty bourgeois comfort, "comme une mer montante qui étale sur le sable ses protoplasmes doucereux."[13] Although physically tough, Antoine is impressionable, pressurable. Nizan analyzes without tenderness Antoine's self-delusion that he would be able

[11] "The way metal parts happen to be put together makes up a baffling personality" (p. 95).

[12] "of a woman for whom one has given up something. So many women rely on this one source of influence" (p. 104).

[13] "like a rising tide depositing on the beach its sickly-sweet protoplasms" (p. 108).

to exert his will in major moments but that he is weak in minor questions of choice. He abandons Marcelle for the "better bet," Anne, and his remorse will last a lifetime. They are engaged in 1889, a year of plenty and of civic commemorations of 1789. Antoine thinks of his coming marriage as "sa première ascension sociale, sa première mutilation."[14] The happenings of this dialectical novel are always similarly two-edged. The best of a man, Nizan implies, is so often shoved aside into a corner, censored. But it cannot be altogether killed off.

The second section of the book opens with a summary of Antoine's journeyings with his wife in the first few years of their marriage, and his slow climb up the ladder, more heavily laden with responsibilities at each step. As in the period at the engineering school, Antoine still has no time to ask himself the big existential questions about the validity of the life he leads, or which leads him. "L'élan du capitalisme entraînait de gré ou de force les machines ou les hommes qui travaillaient pour lui."[15] Nizan supplies the telling technical data of increase in freight carried, in speeds achieved. To pin down Antoine's position, he resorts to a Zolaesque image: "il était pris comme un insecte dans cette toile vibrante des voies ferrées, que surveillaient à distance des araignées calculatrices et abstraites."[16] The highest echelons of the railway hierarchy are always imaged as nonproductive, nontechnical, abstract policy makers. Antoine is "a serial man," a prisoner of the network he helps to operate. Schedules haunt the life of this man and begin to dehumanize him, by compelling him to pay more attention to material than to men. The material is strained as much as the men. In parallel fashion, Nizan flogs *his* material hard; he writes exhaustively of exhaustion. Antoine's little

[14] "his first climb up the social scale, his first mutilation" (p. 111).
[15] "The onward rush of capitalism dragged with it willy-nilly both machines and workers" (p. 121).
[16] "he was trapped like an insect in the vibrating web of railway lines, supervised from afar by abstract, calculating spiders" (p. 123).

victories conceal his general defeat. His is a life of instant decision making, except in essentials, but not of exercized freedom. Antoine copes, permanently at bay, and remains unfulfilled. He is a hard overseer, unforgiving of slipshod work, and his own technical skill grants him authority over his men. He is not blind to injustices, imposed on others or on himself, but his ideas are like mental reservations.

One night an accident shocks him awake. A train is derailed and keels over into a garden. In this brutal conjunction of nature and antiphysis, the train looks utterly out of place, a stray meteorite from another world. The fact of death is brought home to Antoine when he has to carry the dead body of the driver to his widow. He feels guilty, by association, in the face of "des femmes aveuglées par le poivre de la douleur."[17] As in the opening pages, Nizan here dwells on the weight of death, both that of the corpse and the symbolic weight of death-in-life, "comme si toutes les années vécues par lui se mettaient brusquement à se rassembler, à s'alourdir, à se coaguler comme du plomb qui refroidit."[18] Antoine takes the corpse in his arms—a gesture, Nizan say, which men fight shy of making when both are alive. This accidental death is a scandal; it is in no good cause; it is the result of industrial inefficiency. Antoine feels himself to be, not the direct enemy of his men, but the accomplice of their enemies. Going home, he repeats to himself: "I am a traitor, then. And he was one." It is, Nizan adds, "a word which could be applied to his whole life."

Antoine acts, but his actions do not derive from his own mainsprings. For a long period of his life, "no man was less self-aware, less aware of the real world, than Antoine Bloyé" (p. 137). It is at this point that Nizan interposes elegiacally

[17] "women blinded by the pepper grief has thrown in their eyes" (p. 133).
[18] "as if all the years of his life suddenly began to contract, to increase in density, to coagulate like lead as it cools" (p. 134).

the view he shares with the younger Marx: "L'homme ne sera-t-il donc toujours qu'un fragment d'homme, aliéné, mutilé, étranger à lui-même? Que de parties en friche dans la personne d'Antoine."[19] Antoine has inklings that he could be other than he is, could be something he cannot clearly picture. Despite his hard working-life, he is imaginatively and emotionally underemployed. He turns down an "exotic" post in China, to please the sedentary Anne, and out of his own fear of novelty: "Se révolter contre la figure présente de sa vie pour mettre en liberté le double qu'on enferme peut-être . . . ? On craint de ne plus être pareil à n'importe qui."[20] It is true that there is "nothing special" about Antoine. "There were millions of men in France just like him" (p. 233)—a rare admission, even in democratic literature. Yet his biography is not a Life of a Simple Man. He is ordinary, and complicated, unfulfilled and yet deserving to be described. He is not specially gifted, not specially deficient. Although average, he is a nonpareil. He stands out, as almost any man would if enough intelligent sympathy were paid him. "Who will dare to decide that somebody is completely empty?" (p. 146). Nizan's study speaks up for, not "ordinary folk" in the usual sentimental sense, but, simply, a man. Speaking up, however, involves judgment. Antoine lacks quotidian courage, the hardest of all to sustain. It is a failure of nerve: he is a man of velleities. When his doctor tells him that he is "neurotic," Anne repeats the formula: "And then everyone was able to handle Antoine like a coin whose value has been established" (p. 141). Years later, Antoine would confess to his grown-up son: "You see, I don't think I've shown what I was capable of" (p. 142). One of the explanations for this short measure is the influence on him of

[19] "Will man forever be only half a man, alienated, mutilated, a stranger to himself? There is so much lying fallow in Antoine" (p. 137).

[20] "Should we rebel against the present shape of our life so as to release the other self we perhaps conceal . . . ? But then we're afraid of no longer being like everybody else" (p. 139).

his marriage, in its own way as mutilating and devouring an experience as his job on the railways. There too division of labor operates: Antoine earns the money; Anne rules the home. Nizan voices strong sarcasm at "good" marriages such as Antoine's is supposed by others to be. It is in fact only an imitation of real love between the marginal, virtual Anne and the restrained Antoine: a shared convenience. Real love would be expansive and demanding: "Il faut un amour presque parfaitement inhumain pour perdre toute la pudeur, risquer les gestes que se permet seule l'activité des rêves."[21] Sartre recounts how the married Nizan "sang me the praises of the *entire* female body. . . . He couldn't imagine love unless it went on from dawn to dusk."[22] Simone de Beauvoir adds: "Nizan and his wife claimed that a married couple should enjoy complete sexual abandon."[23] *Antoine Bloyé* concerns itself with constriction, on all levels, including the marriage bed, where Antoine experiences "the need to keep a watch on himself," a kind of sexual decorum. The couple lack curiosity about each other: "They do not think of the partner as someone with his own private reality" (p. 145). Nizan is scathing towards the cliché, "we're not animals": "Ces animaux savants rougissent des animaux qui se révèlent à eux avec tant de cynisme sous la tente chaude des lits."[24] In all, their marriage reflects "the conventions of a society which detests love" (p. 144).

Yet this marriage is pulled together when a sickly child is born into it. The girl has incurable heart trouble, and, for the six years of her life, Antoine and Anne are lifted above themselves by the depth of their concern for her. It is the first genu-

---

[21] "Love has to be almost superhuman before it stops being embarrassed and risks the gestures we usually allow ourselves to make only in dreams" (p. 143).

[22] Sartre, "Paul Nizan," p. 154.

[23] Beauvoir, *Mémoires d'une jeune fille rangée*, p. 410.

[24] "These household pets are ashamed of the real animals suddenly revealed to them under the warm tent of the bedclothes" (pp. 146-47).

ine and concentrated emotion of their marriage. For once they live attentively, with presence of mind, obsessed with stratagems to ward off death; they are wedded to the girl's spasmodic breathing. The usual parent-child positions are reversed: it is they who appear naïve and she who seems wise, before her time, "saving her energies with all the miserliness of an experienced invalid" (p. 151). But, as Nizan adds, it is an illusion. What the child invalid utters is "ces jugements faussement sages comme des inventions poétiques, ces jeux que l'enfance fabrique avec des syllabes."[25] Nevertheless, her "poetic windfalls" include little made up songs, incomprehensible to her parents: "Quand on tue les oiseaux la nuit, Les oiseaux noirs se forment en pluie."[26] From her birth she is pregnant with death. When she dies at six of a clot on the brain, she groans like a woman in labor, "and she gave birth to her own death." Life and consciousness of death have been coexistent in her. Her father will achieve this consciousness only late in life. Antoine's grief is maladroit and unsharable: "Grief cannot be borne between two people like a basket with two handles" (p. 154). At the funeral, he would welcome some event which might shatter the death spell, someone laughing or refusing to bare his head, "and then someone would have slapped this unpatriotic mourner" (p. 155). Nizan widens out from one individual sorrow with its ambivalences (the conflict of emotions and decorum) to a view of the national idolatry of the dead: "the powerful but enervating temptation to worship the dead" (p. 157). It is a complex matter, for it also involves the question of fidelity to the past. Besides, Antoine is soon reimmersed in work. It has been dinned into him by his father, his teachers, and his superiors that "the only heresy was to wonder whether work had any meaning" (p. 156). His wife would certainly never back any revolt on his part. With her

[25] "Those apparently wise sayings, those poetic windfalls, those games children play with the sounds of words" (p. 151).
[26] "When birds at night are slain,/Black birds fall as rain" (p. 153).

insidious and enveloping tactics, she is far more of a "femme fatale" to her husband than a mistress could be. She traps him in a well-kept nest, a cocoon from which she never encourages him to develop. Her petty but continuous emotional blackmail adds up to indirect tyranny. She invalidates Antoine, who learns to tell her small lies: "He was secretly building an escape hatch." But this is not a project, only a shelving, a gesture of economy rather than of self-expenditure.

A second child is born in 1905 (the year of Nizan's birth). The chief reason why Nizan so often dwells in this work on the well known, the common place we all inhabit, is his desire (learned from Marx) to begin at the beginning, to inspect roots. For instance, if the notion of "human nature" is often used as a convenient pretext for laziness or stasis, the individual human body contains elemental banalities which link it with all other bodies, allowing for the difference of sex. (Perhaps because Nizan views life mainly from a proletarian standpoint in this novel, he frequently distinguishes between the capacities and duties of the sexes. Perhaps the bourgeois is more androgynous, as Valéry remarked of the [bourgeois] artist.) Antoine hopes to find in his son, Pierre, a friend, and even more a compensation for himself: "My son will make up for me." He tries to conduct the current of his own bodily strength across the bridge of the baby's wrist. As if sparked off by thoughts of his child's future, Antoine takes time off for once to draw up a balance sheet of his own past, present, and future. To image it, he telescopes a lifespan of forty years into one day. The idea of dying "at midnight" instead of in some vague "thirty years from now" has a real Pascalian flavor.

Antoine settles into a period of some comfort and of peace; but it is the peace of attrition. After various promotions he can afford to live in a sector distinct from the working-class quarter of the town. In 1910, society was still as divided, as compartmentalized, as those, in Homer, who pass through the gates of ivory were from those who pass through the gates of horn. Antoine now belongs to a true *middling* position, integrated into "la sagesse du juste milieu, la modestie des violettes, la philosophie de l'honnête et de la médiocrité dorée."[27] His neighbors are born pontificators ("They spouted about the seasons of the year and public events, because they were all meteorologists and politicians") and myth-makers. They mistrust the demanding workers, and they cultivate, with a mixture of distaste and prurient envy, legends of the debauched lives of their own social superiors. Though reassured by stable prosperity and blind to the deeper meaning of world events, they cannot feel altogether safe, for "these men loved the police." Foreshadowing Sartre's scornful term "ignoble marmalade" (one of the emblems of the viscous), Nizan's phrase "the sticky jam pot of habits" renders very well Antoine's sinking into his social context. The paradox is that the very people who claim to be "social animals" should in fact lead lives, with their emphasis on the home as an impregnable castle, which are reminiscent of Leibniz's monads. Anne has graduated to the level of holding a monthly gathering, at which the local bourgeoises reveal themselves through their lexical preference for words like "distinguished" over words like "common." They engage in "good works," while disliking workers' claims. Occasionally, Antoine feels personally wounded by some of their snobbish chatter, but his rare outbursts are futile, for they change nothing. Anne is often annoyed at his clinging to his origins. Her fund of proverbs, which is the whole extent of her thinking, produces remarks like "what's bred in the bone will come out in the flesh." Although, like Swann in the Verdurin salon, "Antoine had a built-in resistance that stopped him going too far," he still benefits from his contacts; and he joins in the Sunday Walk, the hat-doffing ceremony, like the bourgeois of Sartre's *La Nausée*. In his work, he is by now mainly an overseer, rather than a manual operative. When the

---

[27] "the philosophy of the happy medium, shrinking violets, the whole business of the golden mean" (p. 183).

railwaymen go on strike and the army is called in to take over the manning of trains, Antoine experiences a decisive split between his inner self and his outer behavior, and feels that he has finally passed over to the enemy camp. He knows in his bones that the living unity and right is on the side of the finally unsuccessful workers, but he connives at the breaking of the strike. "We licked the bastards," comments his boss. Antoine hates and envies his men.

He takes refuge in the pleasure of Sunday walks with his growing son, who waits expectantly for a lead from his father. Perhaps Antoine is recapturing some portion of his own boyhood, just as his annual visits to Paris take him back to his adolescence. On his holidays, he leaves himself vacant, "at the disposal of nature," open to its rhythms. Some peasant atavism remains in him. But, before the holidays end, Antoine is already impatient to rejoin his industrial world. He tells himself that his life has reached its definitive shape. Yet there is in him some cranny filled with suppressed anxiety, recalcitrant to smugness.

The famous splendid weather of 1914 does little to alter the mindless apathy of the majority. A few workers believe that socialism will brake the coming war. Antoine himself is devoid of political ideas. His railway works is converted for the production of munitions, which involves him in the war effort. As in Guilloux' *Le Sang noir*, Nizan's sarcasm is leveled against the frivolous posing of civilians in the face of the war-wounded, though, again like Guilloux, he includes without sarcasm the civilians hit hard by the war: an old man who has lost his sons, baying at the moon in his grief. Antoine's factory dispatches a consignment of faulty shells. He falls under suspicion of inefficiency, even of sabotage—especially ironical as this was the declared aim of some socialists. He has outlived his engineering skill. When he is transferred, he listens to the official speech of farewell, and even to a poem written in "primary-school alexandrines," with accelerating disgust, both at the pomposity and at his own hypocrisies. He is ashamed at being to all intents and purposes sacked. The "smell of defeat" in the home anguishes his young son (though in ways different from Sartre's interpretation). Nizan sums up with a Homeric metaphor—"C'est ainsi que des traits partis du nuage même de la guerre allèrent frapper au loin un homme qui croyait être heureux"[28]—applied to a nonhero.

Antoine now starts on the real decline. He has lost his contact with and responsibility for the machines which once provided him with a sense of really living. He is transferred to a store to look after consumer goods. "A wholesale grocer," he is now as nonproductive as the typical bourgeois. He is marginal, and feels superfluous. The pile of years suddenly stoops his shoulders. He loses the nameless hope which had earlier supported him, in some area of his consciousness, as he moults from man to old man. His father dies in 1917, after his daughter and Anne's parents. "A chaque mort, . . . cette sorte de défaite . . . toute une partie de l'être est *mortifiée*."[29] He remembers his infrequent visits to the family home, and the process of growing apart—another alienation—between generations who live on fictions of each other. He has been his parents' "imaginary son." (Perhaps, similarly, Antoine Bloyé is Nizan's imagined father?)

As he becomes less active, Antoine's dreams grow in importance. Now, according to Koestler: "Socialist doctrine leaves out of the picture the subconscious, the older half of the brain, the archetypes, the world of the dream, . . . the id,—that is, ninety per cent of what constitutes the real Homo Sapiens."[30] Whatever the general truth of this remark might be, it cannot be applied to Nizan's work. Nizan uses the notion of "la

---

[28] "Thus arrows fired from the clouds of war itself pierced a man who thought he was happy in his isolation" (p. 202).

[29] "As each death occurs, . . . a feeling of losing the battle . . . a whole area of being is *mortified*" (p. 255).

[30] Arthur Koestler, *The Yogi and the Commissar*, pp. 122-23.

vie privée" in its double sense of "deprived" and "private": the outer influence on the inner man and his response to it. What Nizan seems to respect in dreams is their indirect honesty: the parables, the puns, the derision of respectability. For the first time, Antoine yields to this "absentmindedness" after years of being conditioned to value "presence of mind" (i.e., attentiveness to the job in hand, not true self-awareness). Men, Nizan feels, separate their sleeping and waking lives, and the day life censors the night existence. For Freud, we are all distorted substitutes for, or indirect allusions to, our "real selves," and therefore we need to be interpreted, to be read between our lines. For Nizan, dreams are a kind of resistance movement—antisocial, anarchist—that compensates for an incomplete and unfree life, and that might also be the first stage of practical revolt in somebody less exhausted than Antoine. Some of his dreams Antoine cannot decode, and he forgets them, but Nizan dismisses none of this oneiric activity. In them all, pride (a social phenomenon) figures far less than sexual drives, for "his sexual life was sadly depleted" (p. 263). (Nizan shared Freud's belief that Western-European culture had been built up at the expense of the erotic, and he would have appreciated the following climatic metaphor: "People . . . do not wear their sexuality freely, but to conceal it they wear a heavy overcoat woven of a tissue of lies, as though the weather were bad in the world of sexuality."[31]) Anne's body has thickened, yet she remains at heart a silly, sentimental, and sexually timid girl. In Antoine's dreams, libido sweeps through. Antoine is plagued by glimpses of the vast diffuse body of Woman. Another unsavory and truthful feature of this novel is this analysis of old-age eroticism, a fact few choose to mention. Lust combines with desire for power: Antoine dreams of massacring, surrounded by worshipping women. In all, men, in dreaming, are for Nizan "ignorant beasts whose knowledge is confined

[31] Sigmund Freud, *Two Short Accounts of Psycho-Analysis*, London: Penguin, 1962, p. 121.

to the oldest secrets of mankind" (p. 266). At times, Antoine nearly sinks into total mental debauchery, but, again, some portion protests against this invasion.

In 1920, walking in the street one day, he suddenly feels, in every fibre of his being, that he is going to die. Nizan is obsessed with death because he is appalled at the number of men who allow themselves to fade out without having truly lived. This brusque sense of death rushes into Antoine's bored vacuum. It is no longer a matter of secondhand knowledge, but "a fundamental anguish, an anguish attacking his roots" (p. 273). He recalls an image of puppies he once shot: mouths wide open to breathe as they died, exactly like himself at this moment. But he knows that death is in reality wordless and imageless: "We cannot be both really dead and see ourselves dead. . . . All we can manage is vertigo" (p. 275). It is the anguish of Sartre's later Pablo Ibbieta in his death cell. Physically, Antoine senses "an icy spider which had seized hold of his lungs and his heart" (p. 274). The presence of death fills him, involves him totally, and yet it is also "cette vaste et indifférente *aspiration* du néant":[32] he is occupied by something seeking to drain out of him what remains of life. He hates his fellows who walk past as if nothing were happening. "Can there be people planning for the future?" He is thinking individually, but negatively. He is being simply existential in the Sartrian sense, angry with those who act as if they were eternal, as if futures could be constructed at will, and as if they were made of "des matériaux incorruptibles, de diamant, et non de sang, de graisse, d'albumine, de mémoire, de choses qui pourrissent."[33] Angry with Anne and her "Everyman's philosphy" (Flaubert spoke of the "eternal and execrable 'one' "). Angry also with himself. All his defenses, his public faces,

[32] "an endless and chilling sensation of being sucked down into nothingness" (p. 280).
[33] "inviolate substances like diamonds, and not of blood, fat, albumen, memories, all those things which rot away" (p. 277).

flake away: "Ce bon mari, ce bon travailleur, tous les bons 'personnages' qu'il avait été."[34] He is rejecting "the conspiracy in favor of life." His social pride has collapsed, leaving him naked and honest in the face of death. Nizan stresses that Antoine is "a man with only a small vocabulary," and so Nizan articulates for him, while admitting that words, at this level of anxiety, are only buffers or bluffs.

The son, Pierre, guesses, via animal intuition, his father's suffering. Unable to sleep, Antoine escapes at night to wander the streets for hours, convinced that he is superfluous and regretting that he will leave no concrete object behind him to mark his passage. He cannot even feel that he has been useful, a fact which Nizan acknowledges. Those around him, disturbed at his night forays and his "gloomy ideas," get him to visit a psychiatrist. This specialist, keeping his head firmly in the sand, prescribes mixing with crowds, joining a club, and visiting a brothel. Antoine goes to a reunion of Old Boys of the Arts et Métiers. It turns out to be a gathering of displaced persons, of middlings who have tried to sit on the fence (between bosses and workers), pathetically indulging in half-hearted nostalgia for an esprit de corps that had never really existed. As Sartre would say, they have had "lives-for-others" (for their superiors and the shareholders), but they had created nothing personal and had formed no real links amongst themselves. Antoine is made more lucid by his withdrawal from this attempt at integration. When he tries to immerse himself in a crowd, he sees the disaggregated mob of Parisians straggling past, many of them twitching with tics or talking to themselves. He returns from these excursions "comme un bouchon qui a tourbillonné pendant des heures au fond d'un ruisseau avec des pailles, des papiers, des épaves."[35] There can

[34] "The good husband, the good worker, all the good roles he had played" (p. 279).
[35] "Like a cork that has swirled around for hours in a sewer next to bits of straw, paper, and other refuse" (p. 297).

be little solidarity amongst flotsam. He has a Céline-type vision of mankind routed under darkening skies. His visit to the brothel is a similar fiasco. He can no longer communicate, even with his son, for Pierre is "cet adolescent taciturne enfoncé déjà dans les aventures de la jeunesse, qui désertait l'enfance avec une sorte d'avide exaltation."[36]

As Anne wishes, in their old age, to live near the graves of her parents, she and Antoine move to Nantes for funereal and perverse reasons; it is a town Antoine never liked. It is the time for final accounts. Antoine has been weighed and found wanting. There is the weight of years, but also the lightness of his achievement and of his human connections. "Antoine ne se posait pas très clairement ces demandes, il ne les habillait pas de paroles bien coupées, mais il sentait bien qu'elles existaient, qu'elles étaient menaçantes, qu'elles comptaient par-dessus tout."[37] Besides, words are not all-important when the physical evidence of impotence is there: "un lambeau de chair, un passage de l'urine et non une source de puissance et de joie, une affirmation de l'homme."[38]

As his daughter had been in labor with her death, so Antoine is big with his angst. He is less afraid of death itself than of "the anonymous shape of his entire life, this useless image of himself" (p. 310). Like a hen continuing to flurry when dead, he is, he feels, beheaded. He sees his room one day. His eyes make their last registering of its unusually distinct objects. He takes a last step, tries to cry out, but his voice is frozen. No blood pearls out when Anne cuts his earlobe to check that he is dead.

[36] "a tight-lipped adolescent already caught up in the excitement of youth and racing away from childhood in a kind of greedy exaltation" (p. 299).

[37] "Antoine did not make these demands on himself in any very clear way, he did not doll them up in neat phrases, but he felt strongly that they were real, menacing, and mattered above all else" (p. 302).

[38] "a scrap of flesh, an outlet for urine, and not a source of strength and joy, or a way of asserting himself as a man" (p. 305).

*Antoine Bloyé* needs appreciation more than deciphering, for its virtues are patience and honesty—paired qualities often overlooked by the impetuous reader that each of us mostly is. The author's gaze, almost palpable throughout, is unblinking. This book lacks events: we read of periods, states, rather than moments or days. But the strategy of the pile-up, the undifferentiated mass, is chosen by Nizan, for it is part of his theme. The reader who grows impatient is perhaps corroborating Dostoevski's judgment that "man cannot bear too much reality." It is true that Antoine signs himself away to his employers (and to his wife) and then, like frozen capital, cannot reclaim himself. His life is a permanent transaction. It is fitting that the funeral speech over his corpse should take the form of an account rendered, a balance sheet of his measurable life effort. He is exploited. He is not dehumanized by technology itself (in one part of his life, it is his real passion, and a *Life of George Stephenson* remains his bedside book to near the end), but rather by the soulless relationships between the distant employer and the employee. The further Antoine moves away from being a manual worker, the more abstract he himself becomes. Like Frédéric Moreau, he is finally consumed without being consummated. His biography is the story of a failure dispersed over a whole lifetime and not often split up into particular moments of choice or climax. Nizan once made a distinction between "problem novels" (which hope after analysis of a situation to encourage action in the present or future) and "balance-sheet novels" (historical novels which seek posthumous comprehension).[39] *Antoine Bloyé* bridges this gap. If only implicitly, it suggests, after a study of a historical situation suffocating in its comprehensiveness, that the only remedy to the problems involved is group action: "Quel homme sait triompher de sa division? Il n'en triomphers pas

[39] Nizan, review of Roger Martin du Gard, *Été 1914, Nouvelle Revue Française*, p. 95.

*tout seul* car les causes de sa division ne sont pas en lui."[40]
*Antoine Bloyé* is a "historical novel," which was still relevant to the society of the time in which it was written. "Nobody can be saved nowadays by private thoughts or private passions."[41] Just as Malraux was fond of quoting Napoleon's saying that revolution was the modern form of fate, so Nizan repeated Marx's dictum that the world market had taken over this function. We see, in Antoine Bloyé, a man at the end of the chain instituted by that modern destiny.

There were several dozen reviews of this novel in 1933. It was put up for the Prix Goncourt, which was awarded in fact to Malraux's *La Condition humaine*. It may well be that Nizan's version of the human predicament in the person of a singular average man is more truthful and to the point than Malraux's exotic shadow play of suffering elites and largely unseen masses. On the extreme right, J.-P. Maxence, in *Gringoire*, wondered whether Nizan might well become "the Paul Bourget of Marxism." At the other extreme, Jean Fréville, in *L'Humanité*, measured praise out grudgingly, suspecting Nizan of not having emancipated himself adequately from his bourgeois background. The orthodox no doubt refused to accept Nizan's picture of an amorphous, unguided proletariat, though, in the period he describes, this version was undeniably truer than the Party stereotype of a revolutionary working class. Aragon distorted the whole book by making out that the real drama lay in Pierre, who suffers over his father's rupture from his class of origin.[42] The liberal Catholic P.-H. Simon fell back on Pascal and the line of "the wretchedness of man without God."[43] *Antoine Bloyé* had to wait until 1960 before it received, at the hands of Sartre, the kind of intelligent analysis it deserved.

[40] "Can any man surmount his inner divisions? He cannot do it alone, for the causes of these divisions are outside him" (p. 26).
[41] Nizan, "*Été 1914*," p. 97.
[42] Louis Aragon, "*Antoine Bloyé*," p. 824.
[43] Pierre-Henri Simon, "*Antoine Bloyé*," pp. 695-96.

For Sartre, "the individual at birth finds his life sketched out in advance."[44] He believes that Marxists tend to neglect the whole dimension of childhood: "Reading them you would think that men experienced their alienation and reification first of all in their work, whereas each man first experiences it, as a child, via the work of his parents," and the family mediates between the class and the individual.[45] Also in 1960 appeared Sartre's preface to *Aden-Arabie*, which seems to depend for its biographical information on a special reading of *Antoine Bloyé*. There again Sartre puts the stress on the child-family relationship. He does not stoop to tell us where he got his knowledge of Nizan's parents. I doubt that it came from Nizan himself, for it suits too aptly the Sartrian train of argument to be other than a working hypothesis of the kind that Sartre practices in his studies of Baudelaire, Genet, and Flaubert. In his view, Nizan, "the child of aging parents," begotten in a truce period between quarrels, interiorized "from his earliest childhood this silent conflict between a childish old-bourgeoise and a renegade worker," and made of it "the future foundation of his own nature."[46] According to Sartre, Nizan was first a witness to a strong father and later an accomplice in his decrepitude. "This constant double presence is a sign of what psychoanalysts call identification with the father."[47] The old man's death-in-life gnawed away at the young man's life-in-the-making. The result, for Sartre, is that Nizan saw "everyone's life through the cold windowpane of death: these lives become in his eyes mere account sheets; his basic alienation is his instinct which has a keen nose for any kind of estrangement."[48] This last phrase seems nearer the truth than most of the others. The great danger of Sartre's neo-Freudian analysis of Nizan's father and the effect of his example on his son is that it chimes too well with the view,

---

[44] Sartre, *Critique de la raison dialectique*, p. 289.
[45] *Ibid.*, p. 47.        [46] Sartre, "Paul Nizan," p. 155.
[47] *Ibid.*, p. 158.        [48] *Ibid.*, p. 168.

perhaps most prevalent in the United States, that the revolutionary is basically a special type of neurotic who displaces his family aggressions on to the public level. This psychology of domestic institutions neglects the impact of extrafamily pressures and demands on the individual: we live in the streets, and in others' rooms, as well as in the home.

Nizan was tackling alienations more universal than his father's, or his own, in *Antoine Bloyé*. As he asked in a review of Martin du Gard's *Vieille France*, is what is wrong with society the fault of "eternal man" or of "man as a private property-holder, alienated man?"[49] In *Antoine Bloyé*, Nizan has translated the dilemma of the young thinker who feels crushed and starved by abstract systems of thought into that of the worker whose life and labor are stolen from him. For Marx, the unalienated man is the intellectual who has *chosen* his vocation and enjoys some freedom in setting his own goals. Nizan does not waste time drooling over his own personal problems. He scorns "confessional" writing. He writes of a whole body of men who are robbed of their rights. It is probable that he sensed in his father a deeper failure camouflaged by the man's ostensible success, and that he exaggerated this for the sake of both art and propaganda. Freud could only help him so far, for Freud distrusted all enthusiasms, and so could only be antiradical. Even Marx could not bring salvation on a plate. Sartre himself, though at times he appears to think otherwise, recognizes this when he says: "Men are not changed by theories; it is not enough to understand the mainsprings of a passion in order to repress it; it has to be lived through, countered by other passions, combatted doggedly. In other words, we have to labor at ourselves."[50]

For Sartre, Nizan, anguished by his father's failure, feared he himself might, even as a university product, be caught in

---

[49] Nizan, review of Martin du Gard, *Vieille France*, in *Commune*, July 1933, p. 74.
[50] Sartre, *Critique*, p. 20.

the bourgeois trap; the exercise of literature, too, might be just another form of self-prostitution. As a result, Nizan began to rehearse his father's frantic follies: "I think he exaggerated his tragic view, for he lacked the flawless and sinister sincerity of a fifty-year-old."[51] Sartre goes on to interpret Nizan's progress from the inevitable initial stage of individualism, via the study of Spinoza and the realization of the need to "act on the causes," and finally to Marx: "Nizan adopted Marxism as a second nature, or, to put it another way, as a reason." Marxist doctrine reconciled for Nizan his parents' contradictory outlooks: the father's engineering was legitimized but so was the mother's concern for end things: "Nizan sank everything into Marxism: physics and metaphysics, the passion for action and the passion for calling his acts his own, his cynicism and his teleological hopes." Where Sartre's hypothesis breaks down is in its insistence on Nizan as uniquely a negating force: "The time was ripe for ripping things apart; other people would stitch everything up afterwards; he enjoyed smashing everything to bits for the good of mankind."[52] Now that he felt *supported*, Nizan could concentrate on laying bare the sophisms of the enemy, and, if need be, to invent countersophisms. Merleau-Ponty assents to this part of Sartre's interpretation by quoting Lenin; as a writer converted to Marxism, Nizan could now feel consecrated, as if he had been summoned to "steal back from the bourgeoisie what it had stolen from others."[53]

This account by Sartre melodramatizes, and thereby falsifies, Nizan's reasons for choosing to become a Marxist. Sartre's family position cushioned him, as a child, from the harsher aspects of social reality. We might wonder whether he has ever really caught up with them, except on the level of ideas. Like Malraux's intellectuals at their Altenburg colloquium, Sartre's political thinking takes off more often from other thinking than from concrete facts and personal experience.

[51] Sartre, "Paul Nizan," pp. 164-66.     [52] *Ibid.*, pp. 173-74.
[53] Maurice Merleau-Ponty, *Signes*, p. 39.

Without going to the lengths of a Simone Weil, Nizan studied the hardships of the French proletariat in his own age with a thoroughness and an understanding Sartre has yet to achieve. One of the real advantages of Nizan's Marxism is that he thinks it out for himself, as well as on behalf of inarticulate workers. He felt personally mutilated by the conditions of Western social life. He wrote no articles of Marxist theory; he did not rewrite Marx; he applied him critically. He did not join the Communist Party on the crest of one of its periodic waves, but in one of its regressive stages. This suggests that he was not seeking instant salvation but a place of work and a challenge.

Like Marx himself, Nizan never held that the economic factor determined all social behavior. Habits of life, religious or superstitious notions, family traditions, educational conditioning, the individual's idiosyncrasies, all of these enter into the equation. Nizan is in tune with several present-day interpretations of Marx which put the stress on the concept of "alienation" as a general sociopsychological state of estrangement rather than as a principally economic or political theory. In such versions, alienation is seen mainly as a failure to realize potential. Marx's famous notion of "commodity-fetishism" is often now translated in more general terms, especially as Marx himself, on the first page of *Capital*, insisted that a commodity "is a very queer thing, abounding in metaphysical subtleties and theological niceties." Thus, we might say that Antoine Bloyé makes a fetish of his work, in that it grows to govern *him*, to make *him* dependent on *it* (though we must acknowledge that in his working life there were good times before all went rancid). As Marx put it: "The worker puts his life into the object; but now his life no longer belongs to him but to the object."[54] For Marx, "object" often simply means work. Antoine has sold his soul to the modern devil: industry. He has helped to create his own wasteland. *Antoine*

[54] Marx, *Economic and Philosophical Manuscripts of 1844*, p. 68.

*Bloyé* is a Marxist novel, in that it is built on dialectical materialism, but not yet a communist one, for it lacks the idea of a revolutionary group. In all, Nizan uses Marxism as an aid to vision rather than as a substitute for sight.

"From the outset Nizan knew that childhood, the body, social experience, all weigh heavily on us, and that family ties and our connection with public events are all interwoven into one big source of anxiety."[55] The result of this knowledge in *Antoine Bloyé* is that density of physical detail, of texture, perhaps more commonly found in Russian or Anglo-Saxon fiction, combined with the analytical gifts of the French literary tradition. A lucid confrontation of what is obvious but mostly ignored produces at times well-worn metaphors, as in the comparisons of Antoine's life span to a river or to a landscape. And yet a kind of courage is needed to restate, to pile it on thick. Writers like Gide can afford the economic luxury of allusiveness, of "skeletal characterization." For Nizan, such shortcuts are short measure. And short measure is the very crime against life which Nizan wrote this book to denounce. Sartre's summing-up of *Antoine Bloyé*, "the most beautiful and lyrical of funeral orations,"[56] while misleading as a total statement of this book's content and purpose, does touch on one of its prime qualities: a sustained and patterned rendering of a deeply felt emotion, a bitter lament for the wastage of a man.

[55] Merleau-Ponty, *Signes*, p. 37.
[56] Sartre, "Paul Nizan," p. 188.

CHAPTER THREE

# MEMBER OF A WORKING PARTY

"The state takes charge of education so as to uphold certain state beliefs and doctrines which are important for its protection."[1] Thus Jules Ferry, quoted by Nizan in proof of the state-orientated nature of French pedagogy. In 1931-1932, teaching philosophy at the lycée in Bourg and finishing *Les Chiens de garde*, Nizan had direct experience of interference in education by its administrators and by local pressure groups. By all accounts, this young teacher (who stood out by not wearing a hat as was *de rigueur*) treated his pupils like younger brothers. Instead of remaining confined to the rostrum in the traditional French way, he walked among the desks, smoked, and offered cigarettes to the boys. His lessons took the form of conversations. All his class passed their "baccalauréat de philosophie." He made no attempt to preach politics to his students, but concentrated on urging them to think critically for themselves. He opposed the Marxist, as well as the bourgeois variety, of brainwashing the young. He once said: "Teaching must not be allowed to function like a machine dispensing ready-made opinions." (This approach contrasts markedly with that of Simone de Beauvoir as revealed in her autobiography, where she narrates with relish her curious zest in deviating and unseating the attitudes of her young girl-students.) Though Nizan kept his teaching and his militant functions quite separate, he quickly upset local sensibilities by his out-of-school agitation, his efforts to persuade the unemployed of Bourg to affiliate with the central workers' syndicate after forming their own union. A local newspaper demanded that this "Red Messiah" be transferred elsewhere; and the municipal council reported his activities to the regional

[1] Nizan, *Les Chiens de garde*, Maspero, 1965, p. 158.

inspector of education. Nizan remained uncowed. He decided
to stand in the 1932 legislative elections. He held meetings, not
in the traditional context of a room in the town hall but in
barns or cellars. His manner was nonviolent, and he impressed
a good many workers and peasants as a man of good faith.
Funds were scarce, and so he traveled about by bus or in
market vans, accompanied by his wife wearing her shocking
red gloves. When the elections came, he polled 338 votes on
the first round and only 80 on the second. The deputy of the
"radical left" was reelected. The 1932 elections were in fact a
national disaster for the Communist Party, which obtained a
lower percentage of the votes cast than it had in 1924. Nizan
had never had any hope of winning. Simply, he wanted to
involve himself in the concrete process of politics, to see for
himself what were the obstacles to radical renewal. But can-
didacy was only one part of his effort. Journalism and various
forms of teaching were others.

Three years after his spell in Bourg, Nizan resumed his
criticism of the abuses practiced in French education in a
series of articles entitled *L'Ennemi public numéro 1*, published
in the Communist-run illustrated periodical *Regards*. The title
is ironical. It refers to the way primary and secondary school
teachers were regarded in France by the forces of reaction:
the ministry of education, the church, and the army. Many
teachers were suspect to the authorities by reason of their refusal to kowtow to the government's attempt to lower the level
of political and cultural awareness. Speaking from his experience at Bourg, Nizan can declare: "There is in French education an extraordinary atmosphere of spying and informing,
with police superintendents joining forces with inspectors of
education." He explains that there used to be a tradition
whereby a teacher could also function as a normal citizen with
political interests, but that this was dying out. He cites several
cases of teachers sacked for making antifascist speeches in
their free time. He notes how the Catholic Church infiltrates

the lay state schools, via movements like "Les Davidées," whereby state primary school teachers swear to preach religion to their charges. "Action Française" colonels are permitted to lecture on military leadership at the Sorbonne, while Pétain pleads for the militarization of education. All in all, the bourgeois state hopes to utilize the teacher as the feudal ages had used the priest: as a spiritual guide and watchdog. Eloquently, Nizan argues the case for vigorous resistance to all such maneuvers aimed at indoctrinating the young. This was to attack the enemy at the base, and also to counteract the gulling of the future adult.

On his return to Paris from Bourg, and in addition to his journalist's work on *L'Humanité*, he became associated with, at the time of its founding, the "Université Ouvrière" directed by Georges Cogniot and Marcel Prenant. Elementary science courses were provided for workers by Prenant, Politzer, Jacques Solomon, and Jacques Decour (the last three of whom were executed in the Second World War by the Gestapo). Friedmann lectured on sociology, Nizan on Soviet literature and the history of materialist philosophy. The aim of the whole set-up was "a proletarian countereducation," and, from what can be deduced from published courses, much of the teaching was of excellent quality and nonpatronizing in character. Later, Nizan ran courses at the Party's "École Centrale" on Marx, Lenin, the history of Ireland and of Russia. He was for some time in charge of the *Humanité* bookshop with the aid of his wife. He was continuously and enormously busy.

In the *Revue marxiste*, he had already written knowledgeably on economic rationalization in the capitalist state, distinguishing it from Communist planning, and yet stressing the need to watch for pointers which could be annexed by the latter from the former. His analysis is refreshingly down-to-earth: family allowances, birthrate, sick pay. He makes a detailed and cool attack on the methods by which workers in France at that time were progressively bonded to their employers for

80

reasons of stability in the labor force. His documentation is thorough: technical and syndical reports, speeches by directors of firms. It is French economic conservatism he is criticizing, with its "evangelical capitalism which promises salvation as a reward for docility."[2] In his early years as a Marxist, he sees his task as one of delineation, of demarcation, as when, for example, he resists some theorists' attempts to assimilate Sorel or Nietzsche with Marx. He mocks bourgeois historians who make only a timid recognition of the role of economics in modern history. Reviewing Seignebos' *Histoire sincère de la nation française*, Nizan comments on that naïve faith in progress which sees no class struggle and envisages the gradual accession of the workers to the living standards of the bourgeoisie. But what of his own Marxist optimism? In *L'Humanité* (January 1936), he wrote a series of articles praising Stakhanovism in Russia against those who maintained it to be no more than Soviet Taylorism. His interpretation of the phenomenon is questionable, especially when he asserts that the production figures achieved by Stakhanovites derive from a method in which "the mental functions of inventiveness and inspection increase, but in which physical effort does not increase." His general argument is that such a method yields workers a greater chance to develop and integrate themselves in a more controlled and humane way. No mention of the exploitation that necessarily figured highly in the Soviet scheme. Nizan has chosen to accentuate the positive and to eliminate the negative. A similar distortion can be seen in the regular book reviews he contributed to Communist journals in the early thirties. There were times when Nizan was undeniably, and willingly, a Marxist journeyman. The tone of his reviews in *L'Humanité* (read, obviously, by a less sophisticated audience than *Commune* or *Europe* could address) is often crude, harsh, the imagery often excremental. Readers are warned (like the servants in Rousseau's *Lettre à d'Alem-*

2 Nizan, "La Rationalisation," p. 90.

81

*bert*) against opening certain reactionary books. (Among these were detective novels, said to exalt the police as the guardians of society.) The difference from the Catholic Index is not great. On the affirmative side, Nizan sometimes showed himself to be oversanguine about the usefulness of applying Marxist methodology to disciplines such as biology and psychology (he praised, for example, Dr. Lacan's theories on paranoiac psychosis, inspired by Marxist dialectics). Yet, equally often, he could be critical of his colleagues' efforts. He rebuked a compendium entitled *A la Lumière du marxisme* for its omission of ethnological studies: primitive societies, as well as future societies, must be understood. His own coverage of current affairs was both wide and intense. In *L'Humanité* (on which the Communist deputy Gabriel Péri was the principal foreign affairs specialist), Nizan wrote incisively on Hitler's regime, Spanish politics, Italy and Ethiopia, British elections, Egypt, and Austria.

Though he wrote no Marxist theory himself, he worked hard to promote it, by publicizing and translating the work of others (e.g., Louis Fischer's *The Soviets in World Affairs* and Theodore Dreiser's *An American Tragedy*). Dreiser's book analyzed in great detail the effects of the powers of wealth and persuasion operating in the United States (unemployment, low salaries, subverted unions, police brutality), praised Marx for his correct prophecy that capitalism produces its own crises, and pointed to the example of the U.S.S.R. as worthy of imitation. In 1934, Nizan shared in the publication (by Gallimard) of a *Morceaux choisis de Marx*. His montage of Marx's philosophical texts contained extracts on Hegel, history, the infrastructure and the superstructure, the movements of history, monopolies, competition, crises, class struggle, and revolution. Because of the still scanty availability of Marx's writings in France at that time, Nizan translated all the excerpts himself. Lefebvre, who edited the collection with the aid of Guterman, later wrote: "Paul Nizan put in a colossal amount of work on the translation and arrangement of the philosophical texts. His selection never met entirely with my approval nevertheless. He does not explain his methods of classification, which are part historical (the works of the younger Marx, which are still not well known, are placed at the beginning but also near the end) and part theoretical, with interpretations slipped in without warning to the reader."[3] The complaint is justified from an academic standpoint. Nizan, however, certainly conceived this publication as a weapon of propaganda, and thought that a philosophy he believed to be valid could be reshuffled to that end.

He flung himself into the public disputes of the day. When Denis de Rougemont invited a cross section of young radical thinkers of various persuasions to take part in a "Cahier de revendications," Nizan's contribution stood out from the rest (including Lefebvre, Robert Aron, Mounier, and Thierry Maulnier) by the uncompromising vigor of its denunciations.[4] Called "Les Conséquences du refus," it listed all the powers of reaction at work in France, and called for a total and collective refusal of compliance with them. This refusal must take the form of positive action, and not that of private meditation or public words without any practical follow-up. There is no naïve utopian vision of a once-and-for-all holocaust. It will be a matter of hard-won smallish victories: "strikes, syndical action, anti-militarist propaganda, recruiting new members and general activism." Only one commitment is thinkable: enrollment in the ranks of the Communists. The tactic in this piece of polemical writing is sweeping and categorical. More subtlety was necessary when Nizan joined battle with Julien Benda, perhaps the leading spokesman in France this century for the case against committed literature or thought.

[3] Henri Lefebvre, *La Somme et le reste*, p. 46.
[4] Nizan, "Les Conséquences du refus," *Nouvelle Revue Française*.

Benda's famous *La Trahison des clercs* is an eloquent on-slaught on the politicization of *clercs*, i.e., intellectuals. His main thesis is that, whereas in the Middle Ages (which he evokes with some nostalgia) there was a well-established cor-poration of thinkers and writers who worked in isolation from the temporal world, from about 1890 onwards their descend-ants have been squandering their energies more and more exclusively on the affairs of the everyday world. The result is twofold. They have lent the force of articulate persuasion to political movements, and they have in this way, without fully realizing it, become the slaves of the "realism" they have espoused. For Benda, the *clerc* is not or should not be, to use Sartre's term, "in situation." Benda owes allegiance to the Hellenistic tradition and opposes the post-1800 German tradi-tion of philosophy. He sees the latter as the fount of all the ills in modern thought: exalted nationalism leading to bel-ligerence, stress on the individual and his sensibility at the expense of humanity and the mind, pride taken in political realism. His chief enemies in France are Barrès, Maurras, Sorel, and Bergson. Although he states his loathing of all forms of concerted class hatred, he makes little mention of *left*-wing political realism and authoritarianism. Despite his myth of a vanished "intelligentsia," he despises all groups, all gregarious thinking. His greatest faith lies in disinterested and unapplied thought. He admits that he is "a man not very interested in feelings." While aware that modern life militates against the existence of *clercs*, he continues to the end to plead for abstract thinking and an abstract humanism.

Already, in *Les Chiens de garde*, Nizan had confessed to a grudging respect for this stiff-necked thinker who presented radicals with more of a problem-case than did most of his ilk. But, while admitting Benda to be an acute diagnostician of a sick class, Nizan also saw him as a symptom of its ailment: "M. Benda lui-même . . . annonce le jour où les penseurs se livreront à l'onanisme de l'intelligence miroir."[5] In 1935, at the Congrès des Écrivains pour la Défense de la Culture in Paris, Nizan took up in his speech elements from Benda's contribution at an earlier phase of the proceedings.[6] The main burden of Nizan's speech was a denunciation of cowardly thought, the ivory-tower complex so common amongst philosophers. Benda's speech, in the line of his *Trahison des clercs*, had attempted, Nizan claimed, to sever the mind from all the other factors of human experience. In his eulogy of Greek philosophy, Benda had presented Greek thought as antitechnical. For Nizan, if this were true, it was due to the labor-saving device of slavery, which enabled thinkers to meditate in freedom from practical concerns. The spiritual descendants of such Greek philosophers (from whom Nizan as usual exempts Epicurus, the ally of the underdog) are nostalgic for the days of slavery. In the modern world, however, it is machines which will free men and give them time to think. In his eyes, Benda is an Eleatic thinker (one who distrusts movement and prefers to think that stasis is the essential law of all phenomena). Replying to Benda's either/or question (is the Communist society an extension or a replacement of Western values?), Nizan says, in Hegelian fashion, that it is both, that it is a *selective* change. Rejecting Benda's emphasis on the mind, Nizan points to those thinkers who share with Marx an interest in the revolutionary ideal of the total individual: Rabelais, Spinoza, Diderot. There is in Nizan's speech, when compared with those of Benda, Guéhenno, and Malraux at the same congress, a smaller amount of official rhetoric. His attack is violent, he proposes no rosy visions of an easy future, but there is a positive will to change the situation. Benda

[5] "M. Benda himself . . . is preparing the ground for philosophers to indulge in the onanism of narcissistic intelligence." *Les Chiens de garde*, p. 70.
[6] Nizan, "Sur l'humanisme," *Europe*, pp. 452-57.

called Nizan "an intelligent and fair-minded opponent," admitted that his own objections to Marxism were mainly intellectual, and conceded at the end that "classical humanism will have to gird up its loins; today it's got practically everybody against it."

One organization with which Nizan was concerned from the outset was the "Association des Écrivains et Artistes Révolutionnaires" (A. E. A. R.), founded in 1932, directed by Vaillant-Couturier, and assisted by Aragon, Nizan, and Malraux. It produced the leading Communist cultural periodical, *Commune*, beginning July 1933, and was one part of a wide front designed to create study groups in schools and universities and to encourage play productions, films, concerts, and art exhibitions. Speaking on behalf of the A. E. A. R. about the already mentioned "Cahier de revendications," Nizan denied all solidarity with the other groups represented in that hotchpotch manifesto. Hyperattuned to the maneuverings of such groups, Nizan declared: "We will not make common cause with just anybody."[7] At this point, Nizan was clearly resolved that the Party he served should have no truck with hybrid organizations or individuals. Writing an open letter from Russia in 1934, he urged the A. E. A. R. to beware of "left-wing fascists" like Berl or Drieu la Rochelle, and, in general, to shake itself up.

The year in Russia (1934-1935) was clearly a major event in Nizan's life as a militant. Before he went there, he had been actively engaged in Paris in the work of the "Cercle de la Russie neuve" (to be renamed in 1936 "L'Association pour l'étude de la culture soviétique"). He went to Russia to see for himself what he was supporting, to edit some issues of *La Littérature internationale* in Moscow, and to be present at the 1934 Soviet Writers' Congress (together with four other French delegates: Aragon, Bloch, Malraux, and Pozner).

[7] Nizan, "Sur un certain Front Unique," *Europe*, pp. 452-57.

While there, he received payment of author's rights for Russian translations of his books, and this financed his stay. He spoke some Russian, and lived with his wife at an "intellectuals' hotel" alongside Russian engineers. He wrote reassuring letters to his mother, describing the comfortable living conditions of the Russians (though we will see later the other side of the medal). He worked at the Marx-Engels Institute, in a "splendid atmosphere of security and hard work"; he traveled extensively; he contacted theatre directors and actors. With Malraux he appeared to get on very well; they shared some basic preoccupations: death, the "new man" who might one day evolve in this new society. As Clara Malraux put it, "There was something clean-cut about Nizan's personality."[8]

The New Economic Policy period in Russia (1921-1928, the time span between Lenin's initial proclamation and the final revocation of measures of individual freedom) was probably the most liberal period of Soviet literature. Trotsky's attitude, in *Literature and Revolution*, was that "proletarian literature" was a nonstarter, for the proletarian regime would be only a transitional stage on the way to a classless society, which would be the first society ever to have a truly human art, freed from class determinisms. Two of the key works of this era were Nizan's favorites among the new Russian literature: Zamyatin's *We* and Olesha's *Envy*. Both books, in varying ways, denounced the misdeeds of a bureaucratized and dehumanized society (cf. Orwell's *1984*). Before Silone, Koestler, or Malraux, Olesha conceived communism as a *moral* problem, and asked the question: are *all* the old values to be jettisoned? *Envy* is ambivalent and perplexing, and can be interpreted, deviously, as supporting the regime. "Olesha is just like Sartre," Nizan told Simone de Beauvoir. Zamyatin's book has been described as "the first émigré book by a non-émigré writer,"[9] though Zamyatin in fact later petitioned successfully

[8] Clara Malraux, "Le Voyage à Moscou," p. 64.
[9] Gleb Struve, in *Literature and Revolution in Soviet Russia*, p. 6.

to be allowed to go into exile, after being hounded as a sub-versive writer. In the years 1930-1932, the R. A. P. P. (the Russian Association of Proletarian Writers) dominated the Soviet literary world. But it was discarded in 1932 by Stalin in favor of the Union of Soviet Writers, which organized the great literary jamboree of 1934: the Soviet Writers' Congress. Over a fortnight, twenty-six sessions took place, at which nearly six hundred Soviet delegates and forty foreign guests listened to two hundred speeches or reports. It was at this congress that the doctrine of "Socialist Realism" was first put forward by Zhdanov, who, ignoring Marx and Engels' general reluctance to dogmatize about literature, referred to a less familiar pamphlet by Lenin: *Party Organization and Party Literature* (1905). Lenin himself had made it clear that he did not mean creative writing but propaganda, when he wrote that "literature must become a cog and screw of one single great social democratic mechanism, brought into action by the whole conscious vanguard of the whole working class." He added, however, that "comparisons are odious" (cf. the mechanist metaphor above), and that it was undeniable that wide scope must be left for "individual initiative, individual tastes, fantasy." All he felt sure of was that neutrality of standpoint was impossible. Marx himself never renounced his own preference for Greek literature, despite his theory of the dependence of art on economics. He scorned those critics who could view fictional characters only as concentrated embodiments of social types. Engels was more ready to bend with the wind and to adapt his literary judgments to prevailing political exigencies. But even Engels was hostile to *overt* partisanship on the part of an author, whose message, he felt, should act like a delayed-action bomb, timed to explode the optimism of the bourgeois world.[10] These doubts, contradictions, and qualified assertions by his famous predecessors were ironed out by Zhdanov into a theory according to which the inescapable aim of socialist

[10] Peter Demetz, *Marx, Engels and the Poets*, pp. 129-30.

realist writers must be to infect readers with class ideology and to fabricate a hortatory art designed to support the goals of the state. There had been few "positive heroes" in nineteenth-century Russian literature, but writers were expected to create them to order in the 1930s. Such party-mindedness owed more to pre-Marxist publicists like Belinsky than to Marx himself.

Nizan once wrote: "A rounded whole was always the main ambition of art, which is more at home in endings than beginnings, as can be seen in the teething troubles of Soviet literature."[11] At the congress, great hopes were expressed about the future upsurge of a new literature. There were deluges of clichés, but delegates also raised crucial questions of form and style, and of borrowings from past or from foreign literatures. Olesha made a moving and embarrassingly frank speech, which must have appealed to Nizan in its concern both for personal and for collective needs. Olesha declared that his rediscovery of his own youth (and he was fascinated by the way in which trivial childhood experiences provide the images of the grown-up writer) coincided with his realization of the strength of the new Soviet youth. From this coinciding he hoped to find the means of connecting inner and outer worlds, which in his work thus far had been in conflict. (Unfortunately, Olesha's creativity appeared to dry up in subsequent years.) Babel, too, with whom Nizan was in frequent and close contact, confessed to his unproductive spells, but showed himself to be very concerned with a problem that was close to Nizan's center of interest: the need for a fresh, less loud-mouthed style and vocabulary; the need for "fire, passion, strength, fun." Above all, Babel defended the artist's right to *surprise* his readers. Some of the spokesmen revealed cultural illiteracy, as when Radek accused James Joyce's *Ulysses* (set before the First World War) of omitting the 1916 uprising in Ireland! On the other extreme, the sophisticated Malraux

[11] Nizan, "*Été 1914*," p. 95.

reminded the audience that "the photograph of a great epoch is not great literature," and that "the task of culture is to conquer the unconscious, to reduce experience to conscious thought," the dimension of psychological depth being essential to any literature: sentiments with which Nizan would wholeheartedly concur. Ehrenburg was the only Soviet writer to express similar views, and to state that the proposal of group writing was nonsensical. On the whole, no clear defense of the author's individuality arose during the congress. The age of literary politics was being installed. A century before, Tocqueville had complained that in France political life was dominated by literary standards. The reverse was now happening in Russia. In this situation, however, Nizan's good taste drew him to the lasting works of Olesha, Babel, and Zamyatin, rather than to the hacks. When he edited three issues of *La Littérature internationale*, he published translations of Chinese literature, of John Strachey's *Education of a Communist*, some Saroyan, and part of Pasternak's poem *Childhood*.

On the prompting of the Communist film and theatre critic Léon Moussinac, Nizan adapted, for the State Jewish Theatre in Moscow, Aristophanes' *The Acharnians*. This vigorous antiwar play had lost little of its relevance. Nizan's version preserved the essential: a violent indictment of all war, its profiteers and its dupes, and "an almost continual surge of poetry inspired by nature, farm work, and a straight-forward kind of eroticism."[12] What attracted Nizan in addition was the idea of Greek theatre as a perfectionist spectacle for the masses (cf. the revival of the Greek chorus in left-wing avant-garde plays of the twenties and thirties in order to represent the collective voice). Nizan believed, like Meyerhold, that author, actors, and audience should be linked in an active communion, whereas the twentieth-century theatre provided amusement for solitaries or fashionable little cliques. In the

---

[12] Nizan, *Les Acharniens*, Introduction, p. 8.

90

play itself, the hero Diceopolis makes a private, but exemplary, stand against war and warmongers of every variety. He resists his persecutors both verbally and physically. He declares peace, and opens his market to his state's enemy. The play ends with the triumph of peace. Nizan succeeds very well in conveying a rough peasant lust for life, yet this naturalism is conveyed elegantly. The play is frequently funny (when a stranger asks in the market for a genuine Athenian product, he is offered a police spy). There is surprisingly little sense of anachronism in Nizan's version when it is compared with Aristophanes' original. The only regret is that, owing no doubt to puritan official policy, Nizan omitted Aristophanes' fruity double meanings on the pretext that these had dated badly. Luckily, he was never so priggish when writing his own books.

During his year in Russia, he visited Soviet Central Asia, which he evokes with great force and beauty in "Sindobod Toçikston" and "Le Tombeau de Timour."[13] This was a pioneer region and gave Nizan a chance to see for himself how the vaunted technical transformation of Russia was progressing. Throughout his account of his travels, he keeps a balance between descriptions of work and leisure-time activities; he notes with delight that the writing of poetry is accepted as a job like any other. His insistence on the rich diversity of the Soviet peoples counteracts the usually stereotyped Western view of Russia. No longer was he looking at the fatalistic and docile Arab laborers, as at the time of *Aden-Arabie*, but at "nomads taking up pickaxes so as to wage war on their own past." He is enthralled, yet still critically conscious, at the spectacle of the taming of nature—the antiphysis in action: "A la sortie de la montagne, les hommes qui n'aiment pas laisser les fleuves descendre tranquillement vers la mer, pas plus qu'ils n'aiment voir l'énergie se dégrader en chaleur, et qui rêvent

[13] In *Europe*, 15 May 1935, and *Vendredi*, 22 January 1937.

toujours de renverser le sens de la dégradation de l'énergie, le sens du nivellement et finalement le sens même de la mort—et c'est la principale raison qu'on a d'aimer l'homme—à la sortie de la montagne, les hommes ont entrepris de construire des barrages, de percer des canaux et de faire tourner les turbines des hydrocentrales."[14]

What he is saluting here is the signature of human presence and effort, the mark men make on the physical world. It is a conscious rejection of the anti-industrial visionaries of the thirties: prose poets like Ramuz or Giono (two writers whose lyrical works Nizan admired but whose prophetic books irritated him as potentially reactionary). In a review of Ramuz, Nizan declared: "Pour le paysan solitaire, la nature est une grande puissance étrangère, qu'il n'arrive pas à dominer. La science et le travail socialiste ont la puissance de la comprendre et de la vaincre et même *de l'aimer*."[15] The last phrase is important, for Nizan was no exclusive urbanite. As Sartre said: "Although a town dweller, out of faithfulness to his origins Nizan retained a kind of rural naturalism."[16] Sartre himself, with his notorious (metaphorical) "allergy to chlorophyll," resisted the thirties cult of open-air escape, hiking, camping. And, with his man-centered vision, Sartre naturally believes that nature is mute and deaf without the presence of man. Nizan's view is more dialectical: man marks, and is marked by, nature. Sartre, on the other hand, is so taken up with

[14] "Where the mountains end, men reluctant to let rivers wend their uninterrupted way to the sea, and loath to see energy wasted, and always eager to reverse the pattern of wasted energy, of contours and most of all the pattern of death itself—and it is the main reason why man is worthy of affection—where the mountains end, men have undertaken the construction of dams, the cutting of canals, and have started operating hydro-electric turbines." In "Sindobod Toçikston," *Europe*, p. 58.

[15] "For the isolated peasant, nature is a huge and alien force which he cannot control. Science and socialist effort *can* understand it, overcome it, and even *love* it." Nizan, *Monde*, 22 March 1935, p. 6.

[16] Sartre, "Paul Nizan," p. 169.

demolishing the myths of nature cultivated by "the righteous bourgeois" that he forgets to have a positive attitude himself. He describes the bourgeois holidaymaker's "sweet, mute ecstasy in the presence of plants," and concludes that what such people imagine they see in nature is in fact a reflection of their social consciences: "Solitary self-enjoyment in the bosom of nature is a ritual part of life in society; sky, water, and plants merely reflect back to the righteous man his easy conscience and his prejudices."[17] For Sartre, then, the countryside is infected with bourgeois ideology. For Nizan, it can be described from a technical and a revolutionary viewpoint, and still be admired as a source of awesome beauty. This consciousness of nature, of how deeply and ubiquitously it influences, thwarts, and at times yields to, men's actions, remained strong in Nizan, and prevented him from wandering about, like so many French intellectuals, in some cerebral hothouse insulated against the weather.

In the vast Asian steppes, Nizan recognizes that in these early days of progress the imprints of man on the landscape are still tiny. The deserts are still inhabited mainly by animals. But the thought of the coming conquest excites him: "It's bad enough that we can't control the sea." In this rough domain, he is impressed by the only slight disparity in living conditions between the bosses and the workers; and he notes the psychological difficulty experienced by the settlers in adapting to their new, remote, and uncomfortable home. As he watches the successive waves of workers assigned to the projects, the realization that he is in on the birth of a world encourages hope. He takes care, all the same, to dwell on the hope-less areas he also visited—"a desperate region where people leading end-stopped lives would have to spend the rest of their days."[18] His presentation, as a whole, is cool and balanced. On the one hand, "weak but cunning little monsters who had managed to

---

[17] Sartre, *Saint Genet, comédien et martyr*, Gallimard, 1952, p. 250.
[18] Nizan, "Sindobod Toçikston," p. 96.

survive the revolution were fleeing towards these peripheral towns of Central Asia. A lot of old scum was still slopping about in this human warmth." On the other, "hydraulic engineers from the depths of the desert talked to each other about irrigation and the conquest of the steppes."[19] Altogether, it is a portrait of an incipient land, still messy, but which can make its inhabitants and visitors glad to be alive. Nizan's report certainly does not merit Caute's description of it as "a panegyric on Soviet education and construction."[20] Nizan knew that in order to denounce France it was not necessary to eulogize Russia. He did not join the Party out of sycophancy for its leaders, nor to allow a new clergy to do his thinking for him.

It is time to study two critics of the Soviet experiment: Georges Friedmann and Gide. Friedmann, a specialist in industrial and agricultural sociology, visited Russia three times between 1932 and 1936. He praised its polytechnic education and the efforts to rationalize work and to reduce the workers' isolation from decision making. But he criticized the scarcity of consumer goods, the low wages, and the escalating prices. Like other Communist writers, he neglected to mention the vast and often homicidal deportation of the peasantry in the process of collectivization. His main argument, in *De la Sainte Russie à l'U. R. S. S.*, is that the surviving Holy Russia was not yet ready to put Marxism into practice. Friedmann was subsequently ostracized for his criticisms, since, as a formerly sound and devoted Marxist, he was now considered more subversive than a Gide. Nizan's review of Friedmann's book, while praising much of what his old friend said, attacked his "intellectual's kind of criticism, typical of those who feel justified in giving personal advice to history and deciding what direction it should take."[21] Nizan, who had never failed to do exactly this when writing on capitalism, held back from extending the

[19] Nizan, "Le Tombeau de Timour," *Vendredi*, p. 5.
[20] David Caute, *Communism and the French Intellectuals*, p. 126.
[21] Nizan, *Commune*, May 1938, p. 1124.

practice to a study of communism in action. Until late 1939, he clung to the tactic of benefit of the doubt.

Gide was a different kettle of fishiness. His *Retour de l'U. R. S. S.* stated the classical, liberal humanist case against a totalitarian society, even a would-be radical one. Gide claims his approach is based on psychological criteria. There was no doubt that, emotionally, Gide had been increasingly tempted to lend his support to communism, from a discreet distance at first, and then finally by plunging into the Russian people as if into a pool ("I am immersing myself in my fellow-man"). Quickly, however, he was disturbed to find in this crowd a kind of depersonalization, and in the regime as a whole a loathsome stress on conformity and mind bending. He was re-discovering the bourgeois mentality that he had hoped to leave behind in France. (The Russians' harsh treatment of homo-sexuals as "counterrevolutionaries" appalled him in particular.) He was clearly worried, also, about the lack of freedom for artists. Even some of his pats on the back are more like stabs (e.g., of a town run successfully by reformed criminals he said: "I suspect that in other countries men would not be quite so malleable"). Gide's case, especially when he quotes statistics from *Pravda* to support it, is often telling. In the follow-up to his first book, addressing defenders of the U. S. S. R., Gide de-clares roundly: "If you had not built it up so much, my dis-appointment would have been less profound and painful." With Gide, the disappointments created by *friends* are the most influential. His trip followed the characteristic Gidean pattern of preconceived ideas, intoxication, contact, disintoxi-cation. As Gabriel Marcel once forecast: "For a mind like his, communism could only be a more or less protracted holiday."[22] Gide's own version of communism, a nostalgic myth about primitive Christian societies, clearly could find no reinforce-ment in Stalin's Russia. Yet he had warned his Communist

---

[22] Gabriel Marcel, *Gide et son temps*, Gallimard, 1935, p. 33.

friends from the outset that "I will never be a docile recruit." Before the publication of Gide's work, Nizan had written warmly of Gide's antidogmatism and his readiness to evolve in a changing world. After *Retour de l'U. R. S. S.* came out, Nizan's chief complaint was that Gide describes Russia, after admitting that it is a nation in a state of flux, as if it were completely finished. This was due, according to Nizan, to Gide's having met with too much dead wood, too many survivals from the past, and his not having ventured far enough afield on his travels. Nizan's conclusion is: "Il juge l'économique, le social, à travers une enquête psychologique extrêmement courte, qui a laissé échapper les singularités, les différenciations, les diverses 'époques' psychologiques d'un pays où elles sont plus nombreuses que partout ailleurs."[23]

All of Nizan's writings on Russia are marked by such care to avoid hasty generalization. This, of course, led also to his feeling obliged to silence many of his own disappointments and worries. On the question, for instance, of the purges and trials that came to a climax a year after he had left the U. S. S. R., Nizan could not, naturally, criticize this brutal phenomenon while remaining in the Party. By the dubious virtue of our hindsight, we may condemn him for not condemning the trials. Perhaps we should be grateful that he at least did not defend them in the hectoring fashion adopted by Aragon and others. In his book *De la Sainte Russie à l'U. R. S. S.*, Friedmann, even when in the process of disintegrating himself from the Party (which he left a year later), still accepted the thesis of the opposition's guilt. At least his view had the merit of willingness to concede that erstwhile supporters of

[23] "He judges the economic and social context by means of an extremely short-sighted psychological inquiry which missed out on the idiosyncrasies, the variability, and the different psychological 'epochs' of a country where they matter more than anywhere else." Nizan, "Un Esprit non prévenu," *Vendredi*, p. 5.

the revolution could (from the orthodox standpoint) be thought to have gone rotten—a more plausible line than that favored with such superficially compelling brilliance in Koestler's *Darkness at Noon*. Koestler's explanation of the astounding confessions issuing from former Bolshevik leaders at the Moscow trials has perhaps the widest popular currency. Yet it is a hypothesis as mistaken in terms of historical probability as it is on the level of artistic discrimination. For Koestler, the old Bolsheviks caved in because they had signed their personalities away to the Party, and, when the Party needed scapegoats for tactical purposes, they could only, logically, offer themselves up in a final act of self-annihilation. As Harold Rosenberg has said, such an argument is closer to metaphysics than to politics, or even to observable human behavior. After shaking off the meretricious symmetry of this hypothesis, we might find Nizan's refusal to pronounce on the trials an act of honesty, the honesty of agnosticism. Nizan was always convinced of the complexity of human motivation. The one public comment on the Moscow Trials he allowed himself was that there was no question of truth drugs, totally fabricated confessions, or "Slav soul": "Les héros des *Possédés* paraissent infiniment faibles quand on les compare, du point de vue du romancier, aux personnages politiques qui jouèrent leur vie contre l'histoire et la perdirent."[24] In this final clause there can be felt a tone of respect for the losers, but also a recognition that national issues take precedence over individual fates. This statement, moreover, dates from 1938. When Nizan was in Russia in 1934-1935, he seems to have felt that as the purges at that stage were aimed mainly at military personnel (a body of men for whom he experienced little instinctive sympathy),

---

[24] "The heroes of *The Possessed* are nothing, from the novelist's point of view, when compared with the political figures who wagered their lives against the course of history and lost." Nizan, *Ce Soir*, 21 April 1938, p. 4.

the persecution was a matter of internal policy in which he had no say. He was conscious also of the differences between national temperaments and of the difficulty (as today in matters of Chinese affairs) of acquiring the true facts of the situation. At a later stage, when it became clearer what was happening, it seems likely that he forced himself to swallow the trials, but not to stomach them. In 1939, at the time of the Hitler-Stalin Pact, he would disgorge his feelings about them.

He never gave way to that long-winded and automatic lyricism about the Russian achievement that was such a characteristic feature of foreign Communists' writing in the 1930s. He was as convinced as his colleagues that the vigor of this new nation contrasted markedly with the decadent West, but he asked the same questions of the Russians as of everybody else. By Sartre's account, Nizan had hoped to find in the Russian people a sense of communion and continuity, of men passing on their identity through time because they were joined in a long-term common enterprise. He did see some evidence for this faith, but was bitterly disappointed that the revolution could not cure, nor even alleviate, the individual's fear of death. Koestler tells an anecdote which helps to illustrate Nizan's anxiety (shared by Malraux): "At a Communist writers' Congress, after hours of speeches about the brave new world in construction, André Malraux asked impatiently: 'And what about the man who is run over by a tram-car?' . . . The only answer which Malraux, after a painful silence, received was: 'In a perfect socialist transport-system, there would be no accidents.'"[25] Nizan knew as well as Malraux that no system would ever be that perfect. Where he differed from Malraux was in the degree of patience with which he was willing to wait while Russia blundered on its way to a possible and distant improvement of men's lot. His one public statement about Stalin is couched in the woolliest of terms: the person of Stalin

[25] Arthur Koestler, *The Yogi and the Commissar*, p. 126.

bears, he said, "aujourd'hui le maximum de signification quand on parle de l'humanité"[26]—"humanité" in the sense of "mankind," not of "humaneness." He never indulged in the panegyrics of Stalinism, as did Barbusse or Aragon. (Aragon wrote in 1935: "When my dear wife gives me a son, the first word I'll teach him will be 'Stalin.'") One of the distinctive features of Nizan's performance in the Party is the way he managed to draw the line and to keep his distances, without thereby getting himself expelled.

On his return from Russia, Nizan was immediately in the thick of militant activity, as a journalist, as a lecturer engaged in exhausting tours of the provinces, as a liaison agent (for the Popular Front was in the making) with other sympathizing groups, in particular Catholic radical groups like Emmanuel Mounier's. From October 1935, Thorez had instructed Communists to practice the policy of "proffering the hand to Christian workers." But it was when he addressed the listening public in April 1936 on Radio-Paris, a few days before the legislative elections, that this notion was popularized, and debates in the press began. This was clearly in good measure an electoral strategy. But for some time various forms of cooperation on the ground level had been taking place: priests helping strikers with food and clothing, Communist and Christian youth groups meeting for discussions. At the summit, dignitaries like Cardinal Liénart fulminated against any gesture of friendship with the archenemy, communism. (In 1937, the Pope was to declare communism to be "intrinsically perverted.") In July 1936, at the Maison de la Culture under the chairmanship of Malraux, the Catholics were represented by Jacques Madaule and Louis Martin-Chauffier (later to prove one of Nizan's firmest friends), and the Communists by Vaillant-Couturier and Nizan. As always, hostile to the blurring

[26] "the highest importance when we talk of humanity," Nizan, *Monde*, 13 June 1935, p. 7.

of boundaries, Nizan stated firmly that the divergences between the two doctrines were enormous and probably irreduci-
ble. He was fond of quoting the words of his friend, Father
Maydieu, whom he enjoyed accompanying to the Dominicans:
"The really serious thing separating you and us is that we're
both banking on the certainty of victory."[27] Mounier had considerable respect for Nizan's clarity and frankness, whereas he
loathed Aragon's attempts at seduction: "Aragon fusses around
me like a young socialite."[28] Altogether, Nizan's approach
seems preferable to that of a Garaudy today, with his efforts
to institute a Marxist-Catholic "ecumenical movement." In
1933, Nizan had closely examined the program of Mounier's
"personalism," which he valued for its antibourgeois sentiments, but which he found inadequate as a philosophy of action. What Mounier's *Esprit* condemns, he says, is the "im-
purity" of bourgeois values, and it recommends the removal
of this false carapace, leaving the kernel untouched, "the
almond, the eternal part of man." While the personalists acknowledge the force and right of the workers' demands, they
secretly fear them. When they talk of "the full development of
the person," they mean a bourgeois person. It is, in short, another elite movement, and Nizan concludes: "Il n'est pas question de sauvegarder la 'singularité' de la personne, mais de créer
l'individu en le plongeant dans les rapports de masse."[29]

Of other Catholics, he preferred Bernanos, the aggressive
questioner, to Mauriac, the sly soother. For Nizan, Mauriac
creates impasses and interposes God as the only exit. In addition, in Mauriac's world, money brutally simplifies the human
predicaments on show there: "Dieu et Mammon mutilent
l'homme, parce qu'ils ne lui donnent jamais que des dimen-

[27] Quoted in Ariel Ginsbourg, *Nizan*, pp. 51-52.

[28] Emmanuel Mounier, *Oeuvres*, vol. 4, p. 573.

[29] "It is not a matter of safeguarding the uniqueness of the person,
but of creating the individual by plunging him into contact with the
mass of men." Nizan, *Commune*, October 1933, pp. 105-11.

sions imaginaires."[30] Nizan's real complaint is that Mauriac seems amazingly out-of-breath when not talking of damnation. Mauriac waited for his revenge. In 1960, reviewing the republished *Aden-Arabie* with Sartre's long preface, he quotes Sartre's anecdotes about Nizan's juvenile religious velleities and insists, against Sartre, that Nizan was seeking Christ. Such presumption drew forth the deserved response—from Nizan's widow, who argued with calm plausibility that Nizan's adolescent anguishes gave Mauriac no right to pontificate on the grown man's attitude to religion, which was one of complete and unhysterical rejection. Sartre himself maintains that at the lycée, while saying that he did not believe in God, Nizan confessed to a desire to enter Protestant holy orders, because Protestant ethics appealed to him.[31] Elsewhere, however, Sartre tends to present the stages of Nizan's life as if they all stemmed from some central "religious" need: "His flirting about with Calvin, the metamorphosis of his Catharism into political Manicheanism, his royalism, and finally Marx."[32] It was a case of the friend (Sartre) proving himself as much an infidel towards the real Nizan as the adversary (Mauriac). There is no justification for believing that every profound and lifelong motivation is somehow "religious" in character. We have only to see Nizan explaining pagan philosophy to be convinced of this elementary truth.

In 1936, he published *Les Matérialistes de l'antiquité*, a collection of excerpts from Democritus, Epicurus, and Lucretius, with an introduction which has lost little of its cogency today. One of its chief merits is that it does not present philosophy in a vacuum as a "pure" activity of the isolated mind, but rather as a choice of existence motivated and shaped by social conditions. Epicurus thought and wrote, Nizan stresses, against an

---

[30] "God and Mammon both mutilate man because the only dimensions they allow him to have are imaginary ones." Nizan, *Monde*, 1 February 1935, p. 7.
[31] Sartre, "Paul Nizan," p. 146.      [32] *Ibid.*, p. 156.

intrusive background of civil violence, and his goal was the acquisition of security in an unstable world. Whereas Plato spoke for the aristocratic class, Epicurus addressed people of humble means. At his point in time, *collective* solutions to problems were not yet feasible. Only the immediate salvage of the individual (and Nizan accepts, like Stendhal, that man's deepest urge is towards individual plenitude) was possible. Epicurus' greatness lay in his belief that this salvage could take place here and now; his was "a materialist wisdom, relying on the virtues of the body to prevent dying from desperation."[33] In *Les Chiens de garde*, Nizan had already saluted Epicurus' radical disrespect for pundits. He continues here the account of the actions deriving from that welcome rudeness: the secession from a society which thwarts individual fulfillment, driven by a belief in the nonviability of social life. Epicurus had no revolutionary urge to change the social order, and it might seem strange then that Nizan should be so enthusiastic about this antique philosophy. Possibly, Nizan accepted that despair can reach such a pitch that it may come to seem the very essence of social life, and not just an accidental stage, and that therefore in such a context all thoughts of revolt die before birth. The result is a private philosophy, an artifice of self-preservation that channels its energies elsewhere, so that "an optimism about nature takes over from social pessimism." After freeing himself (and those who listened to him) from society, Epicurus went on to liberate them and himself from the gods, by extirpating man's fear of these shadows. With his belief in the primacy of the external world, against which man reacts, and his demystification of false gods, Epicurus can be seen as an ancestor of Marx. His goal of autarky (self-sufficiency in a fear-free and god-less world) anticipates the classless state. For Epicurean retreat was collective and not hermetic. Epicurus warmly praises the virtues of friendship.

[33] Nizan, *Les Matérialistes de l'antiquité*, Maspero, 1965, p. 18.

Under his inspiration, there grew up a kind of finer society which did not obstruct "the goals of natural man." His disciple Lucretius was more positive in that he expounded Epicurus' ideas both as a cure for private ills and as reinforcement for an attack on the ruling class. As Nizan remarks, "the frankness of materialism has always been unpopular," whether it speaks of God, science, society, or sexuality. Perhaps what Nizan responded to most in Epicurus was the frank recognition of the impossibility of complete serenity, as when he quotes Epicurus' belief that peace of mind can be reached concerning all matters except death, for in face of death men live in a city without walls. Yet what matters even more is the effort to conquer this fear of death.

It is appropriate to mention at this point Nizan's lasting admiration for another man devoted to the endless task of freeing men's minds from the wrong objects: Spinoza. This admiration is a further indication that Nizan, as a militant, never committed intellectual suicide. Spinoza was a favorite before Nizan encountered Marx or Lenin, and he remained one afterwards. At the E. N. S. Nizan worked on a study of Spinoza, none of which has been published; but it is possible to guess at what attracted him to this retiring yet powerful mind. Like Epicurus, Spinoza lived in seclusion and tried to cultivate self-sufficiency, whereas his opposite number Leibniz (one of Nizan's bugbears) was a gregarious and power-seeking man. One of Spinoza's basic beliefs could describe Nizan's general existential strategy. Spinoza believed that freedom lay in concentrating one's passions on a proper object, and that the only way we can conquer an undesirable emotion is by attaching our thought to another and stronger emotion. Nizan swung his fixation from the luxurious anxieties of individualism to the collective strivings of the underprivileged. Spinoza's theory of the "conatus," the effort towards self-maintenance, would also attract Nizan, who supported the collective only insofar as it sought to benefit the individual. He could not, of course, have accepted Spinoza's acquiescence—partly due to Spinoza's lack of any idea of historical change—to existing social laws and conventions. But the "conatus," which has been likened to Freud's concept of the libido, and the insistence by both these Jewish thinkers that the cure of mental illness lies in making the patient more self-conscious—these theories provide real backing for some of Nizan's deepest convictions. "A free man thinks of nothing less than death." Epicurus and Nizan would agree with Spinoza on this point, and Spinoza would recognize with them that the problem is how to free men from this obsession. The solution is to teach them the proper use of the mind and the emotions. The obstacle to this education is the lazy preference for that secondhand knowledge, which Nizan frequently claims to be the mark of many writers of his own era who fail to think for themselves. Altogether, Nizan must have found Spinoza less shallow than Descartes and his rather facile optimism about the powers of human reason and will, and his relative lack of interest in the less conscious sources of human weakness. No doubt Nizan admired not only Spinoza's interest in this weakness, but also his open mind on the question of human potentiality. Spinoza refused to dogmatize on the limits of possible action of the human body. This "most ambitious and uncompromising of all modern philosophers"[34] kept company with Epicurus and Marx in Nizan's grateful mind.

Nizan had joined the Communist Party in 1927, when it was sunk in one of its periodic troughs of unpopularity, and was laboriously working to organize itself properly for the first time in view of the coming 1928 elections. A new tactic was ordered: the theme would be not left versus right, but class against class. "Opportunism" was discredited. Nineteen twenty-seven was the year of Sarraut's declaration: "Communism is

<hr>

[34] Stuart Hampshire, *Spinoza*, London: Penguin, 1967, p. 11.

the Enemy!" Sarraut went on to harry *L'Humanité*, which had called for French troops and sailors to fraternize with Chinese revolutionaries. Communist deputies were persecuted in and out of the Chamber. Several were continuously on the run, arrested, released, rearrested, in the period 1927-1929. There was little hope of any cooperation with the Socialists, and the Party developed the mood of "we will go it alone." Sarraut's successor Tardieu (whom Nizan insults so frankly in *Les Chiens de garde*) translated Sarraut's slogans into increasingly repressive action, and with the aid of the police chief Chiappe extended the policy of preventive arrests of agitators. Party numbers dropped drastically in 1929. The Party suffered serious setbacks in both the 1928 and 1932 elections. It was, then, with this struggling, confused organization that the young Nizan allied himself. We have seen already that it was his contact with the European microcosm in Aden, and his readings in Marxism, which led him to the Party. On the level of intellectual appeal, Edmund Wilson describes very well the import of Marxism for a young radical: "The triad of the Dialectic has had its real validity as a symbol for the recurring insurgence of the young and growing forces of life against the old and the sterile. . . . It conceives revolutionary progress as an organic development out of the past, for which the reactionary forces have themselves in their way been preparing and which combines the different resources of both sides instead of merely substituting one thing for another."[35] It is this eclectic brand of Marxism that Nizan believed in. He never became that kind of Marxist whom Wilson describes as putting himself "in the state of mind of a man going upstairs on an escalator," in other words, the kind who convinces himself of some automatism in history which will guarantee success. The leitmotifs of Nizan's communism are those of dubious battles, ignorant armies clashing by night, painful transitions, and

[35] Edmund Wilson, *To the Finland Station*, pp. 197-98.

cruel sacrifices—and the warm enjoyment of human communion. He has no mechanistic belief in foregone conclusions. All depends on the action, or inaction, of men. The proletariat, as the antithesis, is seen as initially destructive. But an antithesis is also a thesis; demolition clears the ground for reconstruction. He had a much firmer sense than Malraux of the enemy as a concrete obstacle. For Malraux, the enemy tends to dissolve into some mythical "fate"; he once declared, gnomically: "Opposites do not exist." Nizan was too involved in the real problems of the everyday world to ignore the obvious fact that the opponent is very much alive.

Nizan was temperamentally averse to the elitist sentiments of Auden's poem *Spain*: "Today the expending of powers / On the flat ephemeral pamphlet and the boring meeting"; and incapable of the self-wounding jauntiness of Sartre: "When Communist intellectuals try to be funny, they call themselves proletarians: 'We do manual work at home.' A bit like lacemakers."[36] By all accounts, in his contacts with workers Nizan never affected "proletarianitis," nor went in for that abject prostration before the workers that some Communist bourgeois intellectuals practiced by dressing scruffily, showing off black fingernails, and indulging in what linguisticians call "the mucker pose" (the affectation of substandard speech for the purposes of currying favor with lower-class speakers). Nizan did not talk down, and he dressed neatly. He was angry at the sight of Doriot (then still a Communist) elaborately shaking the hand of an elderly worker in a great show of comradeship. Nizan's lack of pandering won him the respect of the workers he met, and he was able to contribute without awkwardness to the discussions and activities of his Party cell at Clignancourt.

Membership, of course, did not solve Nizan's anxieties, but it gave them a center of operation. In Caute's opinion, "The

[36] Sartre, "Paul Nizan," p. 179.

communist intellectual, unlike most others, tends to speak his mind only within the context of a wider corporate mind."[37] The same could be said of government officials or partisans of any group. Was it more of an effort for a Communist intellectual to subjugate himself in this way? Koestler confesses to having lived in the thirties "in a mental world comparable to the self-contained universe of the medieval Schoolmen. . . . Euphony, gradations of emphasis, restraint, nuances of meaning, were suspect. . . . A process of dehydration. . . ."[38] It is tempting to reply: Speak for yourself; these limitations the later proselytizing anti-communist refused to accept. Orwell, never a Communist, believed that a successful totalitarian society would set up "a schizophrenic system of thought, in which the laws of common sense held good in everyday life and in certain exact sciences, but could be disregarded by the politician, the historian and the sociologist"; and that "the direct, conscious attack on intellectual decency comes from the intellectuals themselves" by a process of self-censorship which can easily create a "mental slum." Yet, Orwell granted the appeal of communism: "It is the patriotism of the deracinated."[39] Nizan had uprooted himself from his class. It is true that he silenced many of his objections to communist methods until he could hold them in no more. It is true that such a mental constipation cannot have left him unharmed. The question is: did he therefore become one of those intellectual slum dwellers described by Orwell?

Henri Lefebvre, who joined in 1928, analyzes in his post-expulsion book, *La Somme et le reste,* the process whereby Party members who were "philosophes" or writers came to accept certain unwritten laws (e.g., that psychology was a bourgeois individualistic pseudoscience and that sociology resembled reformism because it concentrated on established bour-

[37] Caute, *Communism and the French Intellectuals,* p. 205.
[38] Koestler, *The Invisible Writing,* p. 26.
[39] George Orwell, *Collected Essays,* pp. 145, 315, 322.

geois societies).[40] People like Politzer virtually renounced the work for which they were gifted. Of himself, Lefebvre comments: "I started off naïve, then became disingenuous, and I didn't protest." One of the chief problems for intellectuals was the constantly shifting nature of the party line: "I've suggested the terms 'pseudodogmatism' and 'ultradogmatism' to characterize this opportunist tactic of the Party which lacked the coherence of a genuine dogmatism like Thomism and which conceals its fluctuations behind the facade of codified 'principles,' like the Jesuits."[41] The favor that the French Communist Party increasingly won in Moscow, after the advent of Thorez as leader, derived mainly from its willingness to perform about-faces every time Russian interests seemed to require them. Nizan was perhaps lucky to be mainly concerned with cultural affairs, for, whereas *L'Humanité* kept its staff on a much tighter rein than did *Commune, Europe,* or *Ce Soir,* in general Moscow seems to have been less demanding on cultural and ideological issues in the thirties than after 1945. Zdhanov's doctrines did not become really virulent until the time of the Cold War. In the 1930s, Moscow appeared to recognize the need for different varieties of strategy in a bourgeois democracy and in a pioneering nation.

In France, the leading spokesman on cultural affairs, Paul Vaillant-Couturier, kept up a reasonably liberal program. Nizan respected him for this, and for his beautifully written autobiographical fiction. Vaillant-Couturier once declared: "We want to fight but we must avoid like the plague turning the fight into a bureaucracy." Two sentences might give a small indication of the reasons why Nizan could be attracted to this man. In his autobiography, Vaillant-Couturier tells how, as a boy, he once offended a peasant woman who washed for his family by calling her "clodhopper." Her response was to force a handful of the nearest bit of nature through his lips: "Then he had felt the force of those who work on the land and ex-

---

[40] Lefebvre, *La Somme et le reste*, p. 41.    [41] *Ibid.*, p. 45.

perienced once and for all the bitterness of class vengeance in a mouthful of cow dung."[42] Such a trauma helped later to put him on the side of the servant against his family's class. The other sentence comes after a dialogue between a Bolshevik intellectual and a Russian émigrée, in which the man puts up a feebler display on the side of the angels than the aristocratic lady does on the side of the dispossessed oppressors: "If he could have seen his conscience in a mirror at that moment, he would have run away."[43] Such criticism of defective allies and understanding of the enemy was in key with Nizan's own preferences. As a member of the Political Bureau, Vaillant-Couturier had some real power of direction. His personal qualities lift him far above his post-war counterpart, Laurent Casanova, just as Nizan and Politzer were much superior as hatchetmen to Kanapa or (in his earlier Stalinist phase) Garaudy. "Nizan and Politzer, of course, had not shrunk from the 'guilt by association' technique, but they had done so with greater spontaneity, conviction, and, above all, relevance."[44]

We can further define Nizan's position, negatively, by comparing him with his colleague Aragon, who also joined the Party in 1927 (and tried to commit suicide in Venice the following year). It can be doubted whether Aragon the Communist differs all that much from Aragon the surrealist; in both cases, it is a matter of "automatic writing." Aragon once wrote of "the poetic power of advertisements." He has swiveled between plugging the party line and advertising himself. Orwell's term "the good party man, the gangster-gramophone" fits him very well. By Koestler's account, Aragon toured the front during the Spanish Civil War in a loudspeaker van, dispensing poetry to the militiamen, and threatening to resign when another writer was mooted for the job. This winner of the Stalin Prize indulged in some neo-Malherbian eyewash

[42] Paul Vaillant-Couturier, *Vaillant-Couturier écrivain*, p. 318.
[43] *Ibid.*, p. 231.          [44] Caute, *Communism*, p. 271.

about the educative value of contact with the proletariat, whom he often presents in his fictional works as a collection of noble savages: "I have learnt some most valuable things from French workers, who as teachers are more than a match for standard grammar books." It is impossible that the author of the ultra-sophisticated *Traité du style* could really believe this. Nizan worked with Aragon, but they were never friends. Nizan was attracted to the best of the Party intellectuals: Politzer, Gabriel Péri, Vaillant-Couturier. However haughty and verbally cynical he often was, it would never have occurred to Nizan to say, as Aragon once did, that "there are days when I wished I had an eraser with which to wipe out the filthy presence of humanity."[45] We will see later Aragon's attempts to erase Nizan from the collective memory of French Communists. His early praise of Nizan is as inaccurate as his subsequent denunciation.

By not having an elevated post in the Party, Nizan was probably spared most of the endless intrigues about promotion, favoritism, and incestuous backstabbing. He was used principally as a liaison agent (as he was by the military in 1939-1940). He made contact and argued with the Catholics, he carried out various cultural duties in Russia, he taught proletarian students, he ran a bookshop, he went on lecture tours, he linked up with the liberals of the weekly paper *Vendredi* (Chamson, Guéhenno).

Is Koestler correct in affirming that, to the Party, intellectuals "were no more trusted or respected than the so-called 'useful Jews' in Hitler's Germany?"[46] If so, was Nizan able to stand being suspect, for the sake of being useful? The answer must be yes. Besides, there were individual benefits. One of these was the sense of purpose and of support he must have felt to

[45] Quoted in Maurice Nadeau, *Histoire du surréalisme*, Seuil, 1945, p. 200. From "Un Cadavre," *La Révolution surréaliste* 1, 1 December 1924.

[46] Koestler, *The Invisible Writing*, p. 31.

be in a Party and still able to write creatively. With typical hyperbole, Sartre says: "The writer was the Party's creation." Moreover, Sartre tends to stress the negative aspect of Nizan's writing: "Calumny had just been born, and it was full of high spirits; it got close to being poetic."[47] This is true of *Les Chiens de garde*, but far too limited when applied to *Le Cheval de Troie* or *La Conspiration*—books which Sartre in his study of Nizan does not mention, for fear perhaps that they might interfere with his thesis that "Nizan accepted willingly to be the negator, the literary demoralizer."[48] This view leads Sartre to define Nizan's anxiety in purely metaphysical terms: "When he had gone, all that would mean was the disappearance of a negator. A very Hegelian kind of demise, in effect: the negation of a negation."[49] The pedantic joke in the last sentence is perhaps Sartre's attempt to conjure away the uneasiness his friend never ceased to provoke in him. Sartre's naïveté about his friend's actual activity in the thirties can be seen in his confessing that he believed Nizan had been a spokesman for the Political Bureau, a confidant of all its secret decisions. The same ingenuousness is visible in Simone de Beauvoir's autobiography. She says, in explanation of her own and Sartre's hostility to engineers (to which group Nizan's father belonged), that from their individualist aesthetic viewpoint engineers were the epitome of the mechanical socialist planning that they both found repellent. She and her companion were forever disconcerted by Nizan's sibylline menaces and prophecies. They lacked his saving grace of humor, and they failed to see the creative side of his endeavors. They failed also to see the complexity of his antifascist attitudes, which we must consider before passing on to a study of *Le Cheval de Troie*.

Throughout the 1930s, Nizan collaborated in the concerted movement of "antifascism." It was a strange phenomenon that

[47] Sartre, "Paul Nizan," p. 175.   [48] *Ibid.*, p. 176.   [49] *Ibid.*, p. 180.

had the obvious and desirable aim of combating any form of totalitarianism, and yet was itself more than somewhat neurotic in character. According to some students of the process, the ideology of antifascism sprang up *before* the advent of organized fascism and in fact helped, if not to create, at least to magnify fascism itself.[50] The French Communist Party, the Socialists, and Frossard's Parti communiste unitaire were denouncing in their journals from 1923 onwards the fascist threat to and in France. This campaign could be seen as a tactical means of unifying the left prior to the 1924 elections and, as such, a prelude to the later Popular Front strategy. The left was inventing a bogeyman, since fascism, in the Italian style, hardly existed at that time in France.

It was Georges Valois' "Faisceau," created in 1925, and rejecting as fainthearted much of Maurras' theory and organization, which came nearest to being a fascist movement. Mussolini's "Fascio" professed to be attacking liberal capitalism and Bolshevism (judged to be the last stage of decadent capitalism), and to intend setting up a truly efficient industrial society. In 1923, Valois had gone to Rome to meet Mussolini. He was bowled over by the Duce, "as we would have been won over by Lenin," as he later confessed. (In return, Valois' skill in political economy was recognized by Lenin.) Valois was a proletarian autodidact who, until he joined Maurras' organization in 1906, had worked in the anarcho-syndicalist movement, in many ways the movement of the elite of the working class. Influenced by Proudhon and Sorel, he would clearly have some points in common with Marxist theory. He founded a "Cercle Proudhon" to enable syndicate members to meet Maurras' intellectuals. One of his main ideas was that an organized proletariat would compel the separate segments of the bourgeoisie to shape themselves into a coherent *class* and from this useful antagonism the nation as a whole would benefit. There would

[50] Jean Plumyène and Raymond Lasierra, *Les Fascismes français*, p. 21.

be no need of parliament, for the monarchy would link the whole of society. It was in 1925, the year that Nizan (then a student at the E. N. S.) briefly joined it, that Valois' movement broke with the Action Française, after battles between Maurras' gangs and Valois' newly started "Faisceau Universitaire."

Though Valois considered the Slavs to be barbarians, he wanted to ally with the anticapitalist proletariat and persuade it to forget its internationalism and to share his nationalism, which would be, syncretically, socialist. The Faisceau grouped together ex-servicemen, members of the "Ligues," syndicalists, and some communists. But its political effect was nil: not one deputy was elected in its name. (Later, Valois would denounce Italian fascism and come back full circle to his original anarcho-syndicalism.) In many ways, his basic program offered to those dissatisfied with contemporary capitalism a quite attractive alternative to the Marxist option. His efforts to find a system which would cut across class differences between boss and workmen must have had a real appeal. But, essentially, he was trying to divert working-class unrest from socially destructive ends. Nevertheless, like Sorel, he was drawn to the vision of a *heroic* revolutionary movement. Valois died in a German concentration camp.

What could this man, who in some ways resembles a less stylish Ernst Juenger, have had to offer to the twenty-year-old Nizan? Nizan was intellectually precocious, and had clearly despaired prematurely of democratic solutions to the problems of the day. His intelligence lacked the acumen it would later acquire. Though he belonged for a few months to Valois' "Chemises Bleues," in the same year he wrote from Florence to his future wife that he was heartened to see scrawled on the walls there "Long live Lenin!" Henri Lefebvre reports that Nizan came to his *Philosophies* group from a reactionary organization (that of Valois), and that Nizan claimed to be spying on those he had left.[51] The grim Lefebvre was evidently

[51] Lefebvre, *L'Existentialisme*, p. 17.

113

not in tune with Nizan's quirky humor, which vents itself in letters he wrote to his fiancée in July 1925 from an aristocrat's country residence where he was tutoring the son. There he met the Princesse d'Orléans et Bragance: "How ironical for a member of the *section française de l'internationale communiste*, in favor of the Bolshevization of the Party." He met the Radical Socialist candidate for the local elections ("I prefer royalists to supporters of the left coalition"). He wrote tongue-in-cheek speeches for his royalist host, who won the election: "In them I defend the idea of private property, the Church, the Republican Union and religious peace." An industrial magnate asked him whether the ignoble present government persecuted him for his religious opinions. Some of this material was to be used for satirical purposes in *La Conspiration*. All these indications suggest that Nizan's brief adherence to the "Faisceau" stemmed from impatience with the establishment, the urge to be provocative, the need to feel part of an activist group, and a good measure of undeceived playfulness. For J.-A. Bédé, who was a friend of Nizan both at Louis-le-Grand and the E. N. S., Nizan was "attracted to extremes because they were extremes"; it was significant, Bédé goes on, "that the first extreme he thought of was an outrageous excrescence of bourgeois values."[52] Yet at the same time, that short stay might help to explain why Nizan later devoted so much energy to studying the fascist phenomenon, both in politics and in literature. His instinctive desire to understand the enemy, so as to combat him effectively, was always one of the mainsprings of his activity.

He was especially interested in comparative fascism, particularly the idolatry of warmongering, as in Japan. This militarist bent was pronounced in the works of "exoticist" writers like Kessel, Peyré, and H. de Monfreid.[53] Men like these fore-

---

[52] Jean-Albert Bédé, letter to the author, 8 March 1968.
[53] See Nizan's reviews in *Commune*, October 1933, pp. 141-44.

shadow the Lartéguys of today: in their works, rebels in the colonies are dismissed as savages; the heroic troops who fight them are worshipped by native girls. The market for such novels, Nizan suggests, is "the bourgeois who owns colonial shares," who rejoices in the "tricolor murders" committed in the colonies by his defenders. Men like Monfreid have cultivated a myth around their own persons in the Middle East; theirs is "boundless individualism." All in all, Nizan sees the progression in such writings as one which goes from "adventurous colonialism" to "gaga colonialism." He attacks not only French imperialism, but also Dutch, particularly when it is extensively backed up by missionaries who induce the idea of death in natives not previously overobsessed with such anguishes: "It is a spiritual violence supported from beneath by the material violence of traders."[54]

He wrote in 1933, in an article in the periodical *La Jeune Révolution*, that "we cannot talk of a fascist ideology, but only of a series of fascist themes." In articles for *Monde*, he examined this "series of themes" as they occurred, blatantly or latently, in the works of Colonel de la Rocque, Maurois, the *Revue française* group, Drieu la Rochelle, and Céline. Of de la Rocque, Nizan wrote that he was closer to the Corsican inspectors of the French *Sûreté* than to Mussolini, and that the program of the "Croix de Feu" gang was so nebulous as to be virtually nonexistent ("Political pataphysics had never before achieved so pure a level of abstraction").[55] But Nizan stressed that this "demagogy of woolliness and dead ends," in that it appealed to some traditional nationalist demands, contained a real threat. On a more sophisticated level, but no less pernicious, was the "polite" literature of an André Maurois which flattered its numerous upper-bourgeois readers' self-estimation. This supporter of de la Rocque creates a literary world of smooth

[54] Nizan, review of Jacques Viot, *Déposition de blanc*, in *Europe*, 15 March 1933, p. 443.
[55] Plumyène and Lasierra, *Les Fascismes français*, p. 53.

pebbles where nothing clashes or grates. Well-bred society fosters such "fake great writers" as Maurois or Lacretelle, whose impact is one of lulling consolation. This is the posh wing of the conservative counterrevolution. Nizan would have shrugged aside the rejoinder that writers like Maurois have no political significance, for he believed that every style and tone contains an ideology. Not that he often (except in *L'Humanité*) sets himself up as the agent of some Communist Party Index, consigning to the flames all those writers with whom he politically disagrees. Nor were his criteria always purely political. The Rumanian writer Panait Istrati, for example, is criticized less for coming to terms with antisemitism than for allowing his old love of life to degenerate into peevishness.

It was probably the collection of young, right-wing anti-capitalists, including Maxence, Brasillach, Bardèche, Thierry Maulnier, and Drieu la Rochelle, who most engaged Nizan's attention. These men were attempting in various ways to provide for the diverse "ligues" a syncretistic theory to fill their ideological vacuum. In *Commune*, Nizan wrote of these young right-wingers, and of Heidegger's backward-looking vision of an artisan society: "All these philosophies are those of disappointed 'elites.' They are terrified when they learn that 'success' is no longer possible."[56] As such, they are ripe for fascism.

Standing out from such company, Drieu la Rochelle was a special case. In a review of Drieu's *Socialisme fasciste* and *Journal d'un homme trompé*, Nizan applauds Drieu's effort to "think about the most important constituents of human life": politics, love, and war; but regrets that he does not face up to death. And, ultimately, Drieu comes to convince himself that all these subjects are "unthinkable." While acknowledging that Drieu's style is probably the best of any contemporary French essayist, Nizan sees in him an example of the bankruptcy of the bourgeoisie, which is losing itself in the mazes of fascism.

[56] Nizan, *Commune*, November 1933, pp. 310-15.

116

(Nizan ironically hints that France is not yet worthy of true fascism, as the French are too timorous to desire a genuine Leader.) On the whole, Nizan stresses Drieu's attempts to destroy phantoms he has engendered himself by his "fake profundity." Once again Nizan quotes Spinoza's category of "secondhand knowledge" when he says: "Drieu's thoughts are based on gossip and sentimentality. He doesn't really think at all." Despite his wriggling, Drieu has not escaped the coils of his class. The very women he chooses to write of are jetsam, like himself. He lives a life of dispersion. Nizan's final verdict is: "What his life lacks is anger, and the seriousness that entails. His life is made up of a forty-year-old man's vexation at being still entangled in the disappointing experience of a rather protracted sentimental education. . . . He will die utterly alone, as he always expected he would. He'll cry for help and it won't come."[57] Nizan's lucidity about Drieu was both cruel and prophetically correct. But he also laments the waste of a man who could have served a much more useful function, if he had not doubted his self so deeply and had not tried to take refuge in various forms of collective anonymity. For Nizan, Drieu typifies what is often thought to be the *suicidal* essence of fascism. Lange, in *Le Cheval de Troie*, has overtones of Drieu as well as of Sartre. As in this novel Bloyé is a friend of Lange, so Nizan felt affection for Drieu. The peculiarly incestuous nature of intellectual society in France, particularly the writing fraternity, provided a context in which a Nizan could respond to a Drieu's plea for a total physical reaction to life, and to his disdainful tone, his sweeping dismissals. Whether their elective or involuntary affinities go any deeper than this is unlikely, though an erstwhile friend, Emmanuel Berl, writing in 1960, chooses to see a good many more resemblances.[58] As we have seen already, Nizan grew out of his early friendship with Berl

[57] Nizan, in *Monde*, 25 January 1935, and *Vendredi*, 13 December 1935.
[58] Emmanuel Berl, "Deux contemporains," p. 35.

and directed some harsh criticism against him, which might explain Berl's attempt years later to bracket Nizan and Drieu as two fascinating but fundamentally juvenile rebels against the bourgeoisie. Berl fuses their antipodal differences and constructs a two-headed creature which does justice to neither of the two men. "The style of the age they lived in superimposes itself on individual characteristics. . . . A communist romanticism makes a pair with fascist romanticism." Nizan would undergo a similar treatment after 1945, when the Communist Party practiced on his reputation their notorious technique of "the amalgam."

Nizan's own custom is more honest: the delineating of difference, the art of demarcation, with considerable room left for overlap. Of Céline's *Voyage au bout de la nuit* he said both: "This pure revolt can lead him in many different directions," *and* "But he rips the masks off everything." Nizan was convinced that there is no such thing as innocuous writing—that a writer chooses a side to support, or a midway state to get bogged down in, or a hovering position, and that all these options are to be judged from the angle of the critic's own choice of viewpoint. A stating, and not a melting, of differences. Nizan was a logical critic of the fascist tendencies he sniffed out in his contemporaries. In *Le Cheval de Troie*, he shows fascism and antifascism in action.

# CHAPTER FOUR

# POLITICS AND THE NOVEL
## *LE CHEVAL DE TROIE*

GEORGE ORWELL once wrote: "On the Continent, during this century, things have been happening to the bourgeoisie which in England do not even happen to the working-classes." He was underlining two phenomena: the inescapable fact, for a European this century, of violent politics as part of the stuff of everyday living, of everyday concern; and, as a counterpart, the difficulty, for an insulated English reader, of understanding this alien fact of life. For those on the receiving end, "politics" means those areas of experience in which the authorities have the power to interfere with and to manipulate the mass of people. These areas include conditions of employment, wages, education, information services, and legal systems. Obviously, the English have experienced severe problems in such areas, but their response has differed in kind and style. Nizan's *Le Cheval de Troie* springs from and responds to a radically different context. As a result, it is a novel which the English reader has to make a special effort of imagination to comprehend.

Why write a political novel? Many writers, as well as readers, would doubt the validity of the exercise, for what can a mere book hope to *change*? What in fact do we know of the effect of politically-oriented literature on a reader's political attitudes or behavior? The probable answer is: as little as we know about the effect of pornographic or sadistic literature on readers. It may well be that books can bolster, but rarely subvert, already formed beliefs. But the question whether they can inculcate beliefs where only a vacuum existed before is wide open. At the least, however, if "effect" contains the idea of a nuancing of understanding, then perhaps this hope can

119

sustain a committed writer in his efforts at communication.

Proust, for one, believed that artistic representation of life could help us interpret reality more acutely. He describes the process as one of *recognition*. Seeing or hearing our own thoughts and feelings externalized, elaborated, and shaped leads us to associate ourselves with the artist's angle of vision, to assent to it. For Sartre, when we identify with a character in a novel, we will what he wills, we espouse his beliefs. The question is: can we emerge from this espousal unchanged? Can a divorced person ever utterly shed a marriage? Although this sounds like wordplay, it is difficult to see how else to explain the intensity of the act of identification except as one of the multifarious forms of love.

Now, if what we are invited to ally ourselves to is a political outlook, what are the problems facing the writer? What resistances must be overcome, even while trying to encourage the reader to be critical and think for himself? First, he should avoid the temptation to provide totally predigested material. "The political novel must absorb into its stream of movement the hard and perhaps insoluble pellets of modern ideology."[1] Howe defines ideology as "a hardening of commitment, the freezing of opinion into system. It speaks of a society in which men feel themselves becoming functions of large impersonal forces over which they can claim little control. It represents an effort to employ abstract ideas as a means of overcoming the abstractness of social life. It is the passion of men with their backs against the wall."[2] Now, even an apolitical writer like Robbe-Grillet complains that we judge twentieth-century novels by criteria learned from nineteenth-century novels, from which we derive our concepts of character, plot, and a dispassionately omniscient stance on the part of the author. Perhaps the chief notion which has disintegrated this century has been "the whole idea of the *self* as something precious and

[1] Irving Howe, *Politics and the Novel*, p. 20.
[2] *Ibid.*, p. 160.

inviolable." As Howe goes on to say, this is "a cultural idea and a product of the liberal era."[3] Nizan believes the self, certainly, to be precious; but he believes even more that it is *violable*, and that, in an age of political urgency, the novel of private sensibility is a luxury. All political fiction should, however, disclose the two faces, the twin faces, of public and private behavior, the individual as well as the group.

But the question remains: does political militancy militate against good fiction? Or is such a view the same sort of pseudo-aesthetic dogmatism that made Sartre say that a *good* anti-Semite novel was unthinkable? Is it an unfortunate fact that literature of disillusion with politics reads better than positive political fiction, just as it is widely believed that pessimism makes better literary material than happy virtue? For a socialist novelist, present society is condemned (like a decayed building), and future society is only optative. Inevitably, the first state is easier to illustrate than the second. Demetz remarks that those who have recourse to the old theory that a work of art reflects society expect this artistic mirror to function also as "an X-ray machine or as a divining-rod."[4] For, how can a mirror "reflect" simultaneously the present and the future? Into socialist art is built a prophetic element: the urge to depict the birth of tomorrow out of today, with all the attendant problems of such a birth. Nizan is aided in this task by his strong sense of painful transitions ("initiation-rites"). Gramsci wrote that politicians are concerned with a world in a state of flux, whereas writers create fixed images of that flux at a given moment; hence, writers always seem to politicians to be anachronistic. But what if a writer chooses the tactic Nizan quoted with praise from Dostoevski's *A Raw Youth*, the attempt to "guess and make mistakes"? As a corrective, Nizan upheld this very demanding ideal: "I would almost go as far as saying that we ought to require of the novelist qualities comparable

[3] *Ibid.*, p. 237.
[4] Peter Demetz, *Marx, Engels and the Poets*, pp. 211-12.

to those of the statesman. . . . If he lacks that total view of the march of events, the novelist will never produce anything except partial snapshots which will soon fade."[5]

Nizan's belief was that, in a rapidly changing world, problems stand out more clearly than do social types. As Howe puts it, "For the novelist to portray nuances of manner or realistically to 'cut a slice of life,' society must not be too restive under the knife."[6] Nizan salutes in the work of Kafka and Malraux the creation of people who are principally incarnations of problems. But it is probably Nizan's reaction to Dostoevski that reveals the several-sided nature of his opinion. On the one hand, Nizan can understand why the Russia of the 1930s should be shelving Dostoevski, whose world is one of unhappy dead ends. On the other, Nizan feels that Dostoevski still has a good deal to say to Western Europe because his descriptions of degradation, for example, implicitly contain a radical protest. Nizan, in effect, is trying to "recuperate" Dostoevski, and, in so doing, to leave room for the realm of solitary misery in revolutionary literature, which he believes must never be "self-satisfied literature" (as, for example, it is in Aragon's *Les Communistes*). In general, he applies to the novel what Marx said of philosophy: that it must force people to be conscious of themselves, even against their will. He was saying in the 1930s in briefer and clearer form what Sartre was to say in 1947: that writers must renounce traditional narcissism; that incarnated problems should replace the traditional idea of "character"; and that the new literature must be one opening on the future and based on will, and not one referring to the past and centered on description. "A novelist tackling the problems of the present day is easily led astray by the confusion of events, the vagueness of human types, the conspiracies of silence, the ideas which have not yet been translated into

[5] Nizan, *Monde*, 15 February 1935, p. 6.
[6] Howe, *Politics and the Novel*, p. 19.

action, and by ignorance of the future."[7] Nizan faced such a risk in *Le Cheval de Troie.*

Searching for a concrete image for the contemporary situation (a mixture of hope and ignorance, the area of the provisional), Nizan decided that politics must, ultimately, come down to street level and be fought out in this common place. Today, thirty years after *Le Cheval de Troie,* we see strikes more often than street fighting, but strikes are only a less direct form of violence and dramatic conflict. Besides, present-day protest movements in various countries are reacquainting us with this European phenomenon of the thirties: street battles between the forces of the old order and the would-be new order.

Nizan set *Le Cheval de Troie* in a town he calls Ville-franche, which is in fact a composite of Bourg and Vienne, two towns he knew well after teaching and agitating at Bourg in 1931-1932. He wrote part of it during his year in Russia. If, like a good communist, he was a tactical opportunist, it was of the anticipatory variety. For this book was written not on the crest of the wave of the Popular Front, but in the troubled eddies that preceded it. In August of 1935, Nizan was sent to Brest by Cachin and Vaillant-Couturier, the editors of *L'Humanité,* in order to report on the explosive situation there and on the condition of the local Communists. During his visit, Nizan saw the corpse of a worker killed by a soldier in the street riots. He wrote to his wife, with a reference to his usual area of inquiry: "Some people deal in diplomatic dispatches, but the only really important thing is the city morgue." The one cheering part of his mission was his meeting with the sailors who had thrown their rifles to the ground on the day of the riots. The incident must have aroused in Nizan memories of Trotsky's account of the day when the cossacks refused to disperse the crowd. There was to be no equivalent scene in

[7] Nizan, "*Été 1914*," p. 95.

his novel, which dwells more on the mortuary and the uncompromising fighting between the crowd and its enemies.

Nizan had been working on his novel for at least two years before its publication in late 1935. Two long excerpts which he did not include in the final version appeared in 1933 and 1934 under the general title of *Présentation d'une ville*. These reveal the considerable spadework Nizan had put into documenting himself on the context for his novel. He once said that the best writer is "the man who is able to base his description of an event on the most complete knowledge possible of its constituents."[8] He justifies his right to speak by stressing the need for patient accumulation of detail, in order to discover in a town "its rhyme and reason." All the statistics and sociological detective work which Nizan had assimilated when he was a candidate at Bourg in 1932 stood him in good stead. In *Présentation d'une ville*, he analyzes not only the business activities, but also the amenities, the individual and group customs, the education, and the religion of a French provincial town. Viewing the proliferation of small, privately-owned shops, he remarks that if Descartes were alive today he would prefer, as more "rational," chain stores. He points to the large numbers of "societies" and clubs in this small town, a sign of its inner fragmentation hidden by its surface uniformity. All his separate findings add up to a grim summary of a mean, hostile, and inbred society where "manias have taken over from life." The workers are described as too cowed to form any focus of dissent; and Communists are still rare in this largely rural and semifeudal area. The Church exercises a repressive authority over all age groups of the population. It boasts a masterly organization that thwarts any efforts at reform of working or living conditions. "God's imperialism" prospers. Nizan quotes from the report of a meeting concerned with the discipline of believers: "Our missionaries have propagated the Christian spirit and prevented the birth of a black proletariat." As a cli-

---

[8] Nizan, *Monde*, 15 February 1935, p. 6.

max to his account of the Church's political contraception, Nizan rises to a denunciatory vision: "Above the stage towers a colonial Christ figure, wearing a legionnaire's helmet, holding in its left hand a Sacred Heart aflame like the tomb of the Unknown Soldier and in its right hand a bullwhip." Every acquisition to the faith is described as espousing "the politics of property owners."[9] Nizan's novel centers on those who refuse such a marriage.

*Le Cheval de Troie* opens with a breathing space. A group of militants have gone out to the country one Sunday "to watch the world breathing." In this singular holiday, this reprieve, they experience life as a suspension: birds hover at great heights, and the whole movement of the earth seems to have slowed down. Six people taking a day off from their struggles lie down, surprised at being disarmed, "unwinding themselves." In Nizan's tense outlook, people knot friendships, knot up in anguish, knot together for collective support; or they untie relationships and unknot into relaxation. He has a strong sense of *bonds*, willing or unwilling, and also of broken ties. It is essentially a dialectical view, and it penetrates everywhere ("les arabesques qu'on noue et dénoue sur les dessins d'un mur pendant les maladies ou près du vertige du sommeil").[10] He is as interested in "homo ludens" as in "homo faber." Lying in a field as if floating on the sea, after years of urban conditioning, his people rediscover neglected dimensions of life. In towns the impermeable pavements insulate feet from the soil. Nizan hints at later events when he remarks: "On ne s'étend pas sans défense sur le pavé des villes, sauf dans la paresse d'un évanouissement, sauf dans le dénouement de la mort."[11] Death, the ultimate casting-off, is present in this peaceful opening.

[9] Nizan, "L'Église dans la ville," *Commune*, pp. 62-63.

[10] "The little patterns we make and unmake on the wallpaper when we are ill or on the dizzy precipice of sleep" (p. 15).

[11] "Nobody lies down completely off guard on city pavements, except when collapsing in a faint or in the final prostration of death" (p. 14).

The present and the absent are intertwined. Though these people lack the vocabulary to name the natural products around them, they can still observe exactly: "Les arbres perdaient ce luisant que possèdent seules au monde les feuilles entre mai et juillet et la robe des chevaux pansés."[12] These fighters in a world divided into Manichean camps have so far known only dispersed encounters and casualties. In such a world even leisure has its climaxes. Their sleep is a warrior's rest and so bears the marks of the past. They are marked, not only by the stones and grass they lie on, but also and above all by their work.

The eyes watching them sleep belong to Bloyé, a teacher. He reckons the sleepers' style of life from their faces. Some are scarred by age and years of resistance. Others are tired but willful. The women have had little time for cosmetic self-defense. Such attractiveness as they possess is only what is called "la beauté du diable," the short-lived bloom of youth and not the chill perfection of the well-off. Varicose veins, calloused hands, slack breasts all tell a tale. But bodies reveal only so much. Bloyé had hoped for a full yielding of secrets from the sleeping faces, but they struggle back into wakefulness. Besides, the group has no corporate soul. One of the couples in the group quarrel peevishly. The pregnant wife, Catherine, is shown no considerateness by Albert, her husband. Bloyé reflects that the underprivileged have to learn to work for things other than economic justice: marital justice and concern; and that this awakening might take even longer. After their sleep, the group become young again, exploring, thrashing through undergrowth, climbing an inland cliff. This is the site of a prehistoric settlement and an antique vantage point for spying out enemies. From the top they can see their common adversary: the town of Villefranche, with its factories, churches, and law courts standing out above all else. As the ancient site has

---

[12] "The trees were losing that glossiness peculiar to leaves between May and July or the coats of well-groomed horses" (p. 35).

rekindled in them a sense of the primitive, the town is described in natural terms, compared to a coral growth: "Villefranche avait grandi comme une colonie de zoophytes, chacun
de ses habitants, de ses propriétaires laissait après sa mort sa
coquille, l'alvéole minéral blanc et rose qu'il avait mis sa vie à
secréter."[13] This notion of secretion recurs compulsively in all
Nizan's work. In this novel, the bourgeois secrete their own
protective shell of housing; Albert and Catherine harbor bitterness toward each other within the group; all men hug their
own secrets to themselves, and all men secrete death. The very
title provides an image of such concealment and, in addition,
of a potential outbreak from constriction.

How do the members of the group relate to each other? Bloyé
gazes at the youngest, Marie-Louise, whom he does not love
but to whom he warms, for although her eyes are enigmatically
out of key with the rest of her face, she embodies a courageous
natural hopefulness. The members have shared memories, and
peasant ancestors from whom they derive fragments of popular lore and superstitions. The memories of the oldest member,
Philippe, provide an extension back in time to before 1914 and
the world of anarchist activism. Some of this anarchist impatience and sporadic violence survives in him. Self-taught, he
cheerfully mingles snippets of Plato and Nietzsche. All of the
group have a firm sense of the obstacles in their path. Bloyé,
as the most educated, is the most articulate and, at times, the
most pompous. He feels that the most they can hope to achieve
would be "to give meaning to the suffering and anguish of
their fellow men" (p. 33). Such moments of Malraux-type
magniloquence are fortunately rarer than down-to-earth description of atrocious conditions. At the end of this opening
section, the view swings down from the heights to the Arme-

[13] "Villefranche had grown like a colony of zoophytes. Each of its
inhabitants and property owners had left behind him after his death
the shell, the white and pink alveole that he had secreted throughout
his life" (p. 30).

127

nian textileworkers in their slum. A real ghetto, for which the only solution would be to blast it, and its official reason for existence, out of existence, in a cleansing destruction.

This context is particularized further the next day when Bloyé walks to work through a poor quarter of the town. He sees the shrunken people of the district. "The people in the street reminded him of the most commonplace of images: ants, wasps" (p. 49). Nizan is forever on guard against such facile, dismissive clichés, but recognizes that to see such dejected people as human beings behind their dehumanized appearance demands an act of faith and will. Bloyé passes groups of unemployed men congealed on street corners and lacking even a stray dog's instinct to roam. The description is not all ideologically loaded. It makes room for the random sights of everyday life (a group of deaf-mutes, whose wordless gestures seem an attempt to conjure their private fate).

In comparison with such bereft lives, empty, but heavy in impact on the sympathetic observer, the world of Bloyé's work at the lycée seems insubstantial, vaporous. Bloyé's role is to act as a link between all the separate worlds depicted in the book. At the lycée, "des fantômes régnaient sur des troupes d'enfants vivants qui redoutaient leurs fantômes."[14] As always in Nizan's work, the enemy manifests itself as an abstraction, but one exercising concrete authority. His view coincides with that of Guilloux in *Le Sang noir*, when he says that a few of the children resist "this ghostly oppression" and are drawn to "the real blood contained in some ideas and men" (p. 52). Bloyé watches the daily ritual of gathering in the schoolyard, with the teachers banded together in the center, linked and defined mainly by their loathing for their charges. Upheld by the hoary myth of a "vocation," the teachers concern themselves solely with the security of their careers and ward off any appeals to engage in a truly human act. Nizan's condemnation is pithy:

[14] "Phantoms laid down the law to real children who were afraid of ghosts" (p. 52).

"Il faut que tout le monde vive. Ils vivaient mal."[15] Even their own deaths they reduce to a euphemism ("a stone effigy somewhere in a park"). They themselves are reduced by the "espionage machine" they serve. "Leur légèreté les rendait malades. Ces solitaires appelaient leur solitude dignité: ils racontaient bien d'autres mensonges à leurs élèves."[16] Nizan is both understanding and pitiless. "Tout comprendre" does not lead to "tout pardonner." On the contrary, he seeks to understand so that his condemnation will have all the more solid a foundation. And so he moves from summarizing the collective sins of the group to the specific ills of two individual teachers, Perrin and Lange.

Perrin is a hanger-on with a whole biography of petty humiliations to his debit, and an inchoate desire for revenge. Lange is far more complex and plays a leading role in the book as a kind of negative pole. His outlook smacks of the early Sartre, of Drieu la Rochelle, of Brice Parain, for all of whom Nizan felt varying degrees of affection but whose ultimate aversion to his revolutionary cause he could not forgive. Lange was at the École Normale Supérieure with Bloyé, but has not grown out of that intellectual context. He lives in a spiritual decadence, "a border country near solitude and death." On this brink he acts his last role: himself ("he put on a private show"). In an antithetical exchange as they walk away from the school, Bloyé asserts the need to change society. Lange, while admitting the scandalous nature of this world believes that it is an ontological and not a social problem, for all that concerns him is "the relationship of man in isolation with being" (p. 59). The Sartre of *La Nausée* is here foreshadowed. Bloyé accuses Lange of nihilism, a form of assent to the status quo. The cause of Lange's angst is the fact of life itself (and

[15] "Live and let live. But these men were only half alive" (p. 55).
[16] "Their lack of substance enfeebled them. These solitaries called their isolation dignity. They told a good many other lies to their pupils" (p. 56).

so he claims to be more *radical* than Bloyé); its manifestation is the ceaseless activity of his mind, ticking over without pause, and building up lustful visions of cataclysms. He is excited by reports of brutality in Hitler's Reich and of the attempts there (as Sartre would later say of French torture in Algeria) "to turn men into vermin while they are still alive." In the streets he behaves like a voyeur; his boredom pushes him into vicarious living. At the end of the scene, Lange and Perrin are suddenly thrust away into the distance, Lange's neurosis visible in the twitching of his hands behind his back. If not the whole truth, the body, in Nizan's world, speaks volumes.

Bloyé leaves his sick-minded colleagues to return to his lodgings at the house of a couple of militants behind a grocer's shop. A political refugee, Paul, arrives from Saint-Étienne. Nizan briefly evokes the large-scale migrations of the unemployed around France. No longer a quasi-heroic age of the company of journeymen, as at the turn of the century, and no longer a merely seasonal fluctuation of work, but a more desperately political problem of hounded men, the economic situation backs up Marx's observation that "these laborers who must sell themselves piecemeal are a commodity . . . exposed to all the vicissitudes of competition."[17] The market, as Marx said, is the modern form of fate. Nizan sums up the situation of many workers, especially those not sustained by political options, in a very condensed reference to suicide: "Le gaz auquel on fait appel la veille du jour où la ville le couperait."[18] After talking with Paul, Bloyé works with Philippe on the setting up of a news sheet for the cable works, where there are as yet no Communists. The actual printing is carried out in the tenement flat of Albert and Catherine. There Bloyé continues to sense the barely pent-up discord between them.

Nizan describes the workers' "cité" as the extreme opposite

[17] Robert Freedman, *Marx on Economics*, p. 17.
[18] "The gas that people turn to as a way out the day before the company had threatened to cut it off" (p. 66).

of "radieuse." It is a whole separate world. Nizan always fastens on to such basic oppositions, such worlds of difference, between one district or one age group or one class and another. From a distance Villefranche had seemed to possess the natural organic shape of coral. But workers' districts lack this order and give no impression of extension in time or of traditions. From his recent Soviet experience, Nizan compares them to nomads' villages in Asia. The workers of Villefranche are the "natives" of industrial colonialism and live similarly in segregated areas. Nizan does not stoop to idealizing such proletarians. In his view, many of them despise themselves. From what Bloyé overhears of the marital row, he guesses that some sexual problem has come up. Sex is yet another separate world, "connected with cunning, belief, magic, and all sorts of secret forces" (p. 73), and one that runs parallel to the political world throughout this novel.

At this stage of their development, the militants still think in local terms, though they feel the need to think more globally. Their immediate task is to counteract a fascist meeting advertised to take place the following Sunday. In this section, Nizan becomes high-strung. Convinced that France is at long last catching up with other politically divided European countries after decades of stasis, he almost gloats over the coming bloodbath in which lives will be risked and lost in the conflict between armed factions. Making analogies with Spain and Germany, Nizan's militants envisage possible torture and wonder how they might stand it. But this section, after an exalted upsurge, drops heavily down to earth again in a description of the noisome work offered to the unemployed: transferring putrescent coffins from one part of the town cemetery to another.

This novel constantly swings between the group and the individual. The following section is given over entirely to Albert's expedition to seek a midwife to perform an abortion on his wife, pregnant with the child they cannot afford. This part is loaded with the idea of judgment in all its forms. Nizan says, in a phrase which might have been his motto: "No one can live without passing judgment on his life" (p. 85). As he pedals across the countryside, Albert thinks of life as a trap—an image which comes naturally to this factory worker always exposed to industrial injury. The verb "broyer" implies mangling by machinery and crushing by injustice. Albert sees the legal system as a machine. But this system is two-pronged. To be tried and sentenced for political acts makes sense to Albert, for in them he is consciously attacking what he loathes. But in common-law cases, like abortion, the enemy is more slippery, for the whole realm of common law deals with the primordial life of men, the area where vision is blinkered and distorted by fears and prejudices. Albert's militant comrades can lend him no help in his private dilemma. When he finally locates the "faiseuse d'anges," the abortionist, he senses that he is no longer in charge of the chain of events. His head is full of popular fallacies about sex and freaks. Though used to a clandestine existence, Albert begins to feel obscurely guilty for the first time. Perhaps his militancy should have helped him not to feel sneaky, but, as yet, he keeps collective secrecy and personal secrecy separate. Albert's anxiety over the possible legal sanctions for his act, as well as representing the private sector of the public/private dialectic and indicating the acute point at which the state interferes brutally in personal problems, might also be referring obliquely to the Party's internal polemics about "legalism." By its very nature, the Communist Party has always had to worry more than other parties about the law. Albert is affected, then, by the situation of the organization he has joined and by his personal constitution. In this novel as a whole, politics are inflated to the level of a life-giving (and death-dealing) myth, and problems like abortion or death are robbed of some but not all of their mythology. Nizan is attempting a redistribution of the passions and fears of men.

Albert returns from his anxious trip to a cell meeting of the local Party. It is just coming to life after years of ineffectual talking ("verbal politics"). It is no longer alone, for in the town Socialists, Radicals, syndicates, and freemasons are also stirring. Bloyé warns his comrades that, after years of being too advanced for the workers, the Party must now take care not to fall behind them. He is very conscious of the difference in temperature between militants and average workers, and of the strong local tradition of anarchism with its apocalyptic visions of a general strike, its hostility to party discipline. But he believes that the Communist Party has proved itself in February 1934. As Lenin pleaded thirty years earlier, workers are now opening their minds to other and wider problems than wage claims.

In order to give body to their enemies, Nizan inserts a description of a dinner party at the prefect's residence, with an ex-mayor, a leading industrialist, the local army commander, and Lange present. Nizan once spoke of the right-wing publicist Henri de Kérillis as "one of our enemies, who must be taken seriously," and added, "M. de Kérillis has a world view; nobody can manage without an overall perspective."[19] Nizan felt the true novelist's intuitive urge to include an opposition as a brake on his own willful optimism. Victory is not sweet without an overcoming of real obstacles. The world view of the local power holders is made apparent at the dinner. The commander confides that the army is ready in the event of any insurrection. The industrialist vents the opinion that recourse to fascist solutions to national problems should be used as a threat, a trump card: "People are not quite so stupid as we might like" (p. 111). In his view, fascism exploits the army, offering it various myths of honor and patriotism in exchange for its material support. He is a cynical realist. For him, fascism, especially in its avowed aim of transforming capitalism, is a series of untenable promises. In fact, he prefers as a political context the woolliness of democracy, where verbal hypocrisy

[19] Nizan, *Vendredi*, 3 January 1936, p. 7.

can work wonders; but he plays safe by subsidizing a fascist organization. In response, Lange stresses that his own stance is apolitical and that, as he told Bloyé, only metaphysics matters. But he is intellectually curious. He is impressed by Nazism, and by Soviet innovations (especially the attempt to "try out a real community of men in which people can believe in something other than death"). For him, communism is better organized than ideological capitalism, but he cannot "get along with workers." There is a kind of desperation in Lange's talk of solitude and nothingness, which is missing from the industrialist's verbal play, prophetic of Sartre's Lucien Fleurier: "Giving orders is a value. Responsibility is a value" (p. 118). But, as Nizan adds, there are limits to this man's play: "He would never take it to the lengths of actually reflecting on himself" (p. 119). And, in Lange's favor, we might say that he is as hostile to this bourgeois boss as he is to the proletariat. While the others enjoy the serenity of the night sky, Lange goes off alone, like Roquentin, into the town.

"C'était son lot d'être seul avec les villes, de se promener au milieu des pierres paralysées comme lui, qui n'avaient pas plus de communications entre elles qu'il n'en avait avec autrui."[20] Lange often dreams of a book that sounds very similar to *La Nausée* and that describes the confrontation of a man with a town whose inhabitants are merely background decor: a book depicting a man as a desert island. Like Pluvinage, who plays a similar "nihilating" role in *La Conspiration*, Lange is drawn to places analogous with his state of mind: a decayed alley, a cemetery of the living. His mistress lives there, but this night he only spies on her from outside. Just as he humiliates himself by remaining a teacher when his social status could have won him a position of authority in commerce, so he is attracted

---

[20] "His lot was to be utterly alone alone in towns, to walk past all those stones which were as paralyzed as he was himself and which had no more contact with each other than he had with other human beings" (p. 121).

134

POLITICS AND THE NOVEL: LE CHEVAL DE TROIE

to "degraded women whom he could wound and treat like maniacs" (p. 125). As Rameau's Nephew said, "Tout le monde a son chien," everyone has got some hound to kick. This self-alienated, spiritually paralytic, book-ridden man is a night bird whose existential angst is fully released by nightfall. He feels separated from others, but as if by glass walls, which complicates matters. He would like to live distractedly, like the majority, but can only live distraught. His favorite bedside reading is an account of a dream that tells of a petrified and manless town, and sardonically repeats the motif "Taste the joy of being alive." Beside the raw and rock-bottom degradation of the underprivileged in this novel, Nizan makes room for this luxury, but equally real, despair.

After Lange's night prowl, Nizan switches to the militants and their nocturnal slogan-painting campaign, their first active step of resistance. As they paint hammers and sickles and "set up Soviets everywhere" on walls, watching out for police patrols, they are boosted by memories of like gestures across the world, and by the sheer schoolboy delight of deflowering virgin surfaces. Caught up in the collective mood, Bloyé feels that he is a "cog with a place in the machine that he could accept . . . a machine generating friendship" (p. 133). At the E. N. S., Bloyé had resembled Lange and had breathed the same death-laden intellectual atmosphere of the twenties, best summed up in René Crevel's idea of "the mysterious drive which is not the life urge but rather its marvelous antithesis, the death urge."[21] Bloyé's uniting with the workers had rescued him from such giddy seductions. Since siding with the workers, his way of thinking has tended to coincide with their lives ever more sharply. He has recovered from his weightlessness, and, though still preoccupied with death, he now considers it a yardstick against which he measures the authenticity of commitment of his co-workers and himself. In terms which

[21] René Crevel, Mon Corps et moi, Sagittaire, 1926, p. 107.

clarify Nizan's own radical conversion, Bloyé thinks that he
has had to "reverse the direction of his thinking, to get rid of
the mental habits of this world of camouflage and evasion
where he had started off" (p. 135).

The smallness of the act of painting slogans is freely admitted, but its meaning is what matters. It is an act of accusation,
a rupture of taboos. The group daubs the prefecture, the police
station, the monument to the dead with its idealized corpses of
soldiers, and the biggest factory, which has been for too long
an industrial forced-labor camp, surrounded by a shantytown.
This factory is their most immediate enemy, since so many of
the local workers rely on it for their inadequate livelihood.
The militants leave their mark everywhere, as a warning.
Their slogans represent a gesture of refusal against the official
falsehoods of government posters. These men are writing up
their own fate on the wall "which is like a piece of virgin paper
simply begging to be written on" (p. 133). The first half of
the novel ends with a vision foreshadowing 1936, though over-
optimistically: "Bloyé pensait au temps où des hommes comme
eux, sortis du grand cheval de Troie des usines et des rues
ouvrières, occuperaient les villes dans la nuit."[22] There is a
force hidden within the capitalist stronghold, ready to take it
by subterfuge and assault. This romantic vision will be cor-
rected, if not destroyed, by the events of the second half.

The townsfolk, on Sunday morning, have an intuition of a
full day ahead of them. "They hoped that this sense of fullness
would not prove abortive,"—a reference to the expected public
clash of workers and fascists, and to Catherine's coming private agony. On this day, all the usual barriers will go down,
even those between the separate sectors of bourgeois and workers who normally keep to their own ends of the town. "Les
deux univers n'étaient pas seulement des univers de raison, de

[22] "Bloyé thought ahead to the day when men like themselves, emerging from the Trojan Horse of factories and workers' houses, would
occupy towns in the night" (p. 144).

discours, mais des mondes réellement coupés, gravitant sur des orbites différentes."[23] In the face of the fascist provocation, Villefranche witnesses the first steps towards a popular front: pacifists, freemasons, and socialists begin to approach the Communists, though Nizan does not refrain from a dig at the socialists' worn metaphors. They all draw closer when the fascist youth groups arrive, with their berets, arm bands, and sticks. When the first left-wing flags are unfurled, the crowd's singing is tentative and ragged. Perhaps recalling his own juvenile adhesion to one of Valois' groups, Nizan bothers to motivate the enemy. Of these fascist youths he remarks: "Pour beaucoup d'entre eux, la politique était un jeu violent comme un sport. Pour d'autres une ruse. Pour d'autres, un effort maladroit pour respirer. Ils élevaient les mots du fascisme comme de grands masques magiques."[24] But such magical reactions to reality have to face the music, the hostile crowd's music. Emerging from their meeting in a dark hall decorated with marine-life motifs, the fascists shrivel together in the sunlight "like a piece of seaweed torn off a rock." It is this sketchy army which focuses the crowd's resentment. The enemy is now no longer a mere abstract idea, but flesh-and-blood men. The crowd, however, is still insufficiently concentrated to react with positive vigor to this materialized adversary.

Before the fighting starts, Nizan once again pans away to the private sector: Catherine, after the abortion, lying in bed with her lifeblood flowing away from her. He follows her death agony stage by stage. She feels herself to be a shell. Every object seems distanced as she enters a new world of muffled sounds and distorted visions. She experiences a kind of de-

[23] "The two worlds were not separated merely by ways of speaking and thinking, but were two totally cut-off universes moving in different orbits" (p. 149).
[24] "For many of them, politics was a kind of violent sport. For some, an exercise in cunning. For others, a clumsy attempt to breathe more easily. They lifted up their fascist slogans like giant magic masks" (p. 159).

tached peace, even as she pours herself away. Nizan's firm sense of gradations enables him to enter into her gradual drifting away from the world of density. There are no barriers between the stages; they are linked only by increasing unconsciousness. Catherine is too physically threadbare to resist. Like Laforgue in *La Conspiration*, she sinks into what is for her the first utter egoism of her life. She casts off all ties. The sounds of bells wash over her: "Elle n'était plus que le rivage où venait expirer le monde."[25] A surge of vertigo comes, and at last biological reflex forces her to resist. What she imagines to be her vast struggle is in fact only the tiny gesture of a blind woman searching for a dropped thimble in the folds of her skirt. Just as earlier Nizan had worked to counter fallacies about sex, so at this point does he try to demythologize death. Death is not, he says, a figure external to us. We *secrete* it, until it emerges from us. In the last stage, this presence of death in the room is compared to a noxious gas. But this is the real death, not the intellectual myth of the twenties that used to haunt Bloyé and still pursues Lange. Death is not a battle, but simply an urge to flee when flight is impossible. It is a shrinking prison which eventually crushes the life out of Catherine: "l'étouffement d'un oiseau par le vide d'une machine pneumatique."[26] Like Antoine Bloyé, Catherine loses her life by asphyxiation—social as well as medical.

Catherine's death is not crudely exploited as a counterpoint to the political action of the novel. The episodes are concurrent, reminding us that, while politics rages, elsewhere life and death in other forms continue. When Albert returns to find his wife dead, he gives way to expansive and violent gestures in the cramped prison of his grief, which is "a stupor against which his whole body protested" (p. 175). The "strange soft statue"

[25] "She was like a shore where the last waves of the real world petered out" (p. 170).
[26] "the suffocation of a bird by the vacuum inside a pneumatic machine" (p. 173).

of the corpse forces him to see that, in his earlier anxiety about the twin prongs of justice, he had failed to account for death itself, which is judge and sentence combined. His grief is not noble for he is thinking of possible legal consequences of the death. He rushes off to rejoin the crowd. For the first time, he ceases to keep distinct his private and his collective passions. But it is now the passion bred of despair, "dead ends, perfectly smooth and impenetrable walls." He struggles toward an open space, and is amazed at his hyperacute vision of tiny surface marks on the suddenly free pavement. Raising his eyes, he sees the police: a concrete object of hatred. On his own, he rushes them, hurling a piece of iron railing.

Nizan swings back to Lange as he listens to and mentally deflates clumsy, abstract antifascist speeches. He is proud to feel alien, impregnable, in his self-chosen apartheid. Like Sartre's Roquentin or Érostrate, he enviously detests the crowd's comradeship, its herd instinct, its mass mind. Although adept at deciphering the monistic complexities of bourgeois culture, he is ignorant of collective passions, and fears being swept away. His life is an intellectual treadmill, but the monad is here caught in the mass. Wishing to be only a spectator and priding himself on his impartiality, he resolves to watch events from the other side. He approaches the fascists just at the moment when they are being routed, and he joins in their stampede. Having changed positions, he is now in a group ruled not by cohesion but by disaggregation. He is a closed atom beside other atoms. Like Érostrate again, he acquires some foreign aid. He picks up a small revolver from the ground, thus adding another histrionic and puny (and phallic) dimension to his pathetic form. The bookworm feels brusquely reconciled with the technical world he normally despises. He is for once empty of thought, a vacuum, as mindless as his co-stampeders. He had often dreamt of the day when the buzzing in his head would cease, the day when "he would not recognize himself, and would give up his presence of mind" (p.

200). Like Drieu, he undergoes the call of the impersonal, the urge of the "I" to change into "it." Like Lucien Fleurier again, he remembers when he and his father were catcalled by workers. A stone hits him. After a life of stasis, he opts. Pointing the toy-like gun at the crowd chasing him and the fleeing fascists, he pulls the trigger. The brain box has acted passionally for once, and feels a delusion of erotic power. The book-bound intellectual has erupted into a gesture of terrorism.

The crowd of workers, heartened by its numbers, assumes it can drown any opposition. But Nizan makes no pretense of total cooperation. There are many nonparticipants: those always present to watch events from a safe distance, to place bets, to be lifted out of the deep rut of provincial boredom. In addition, pockets of normal life function as always on the fringe of the strife: children playing, families strolling, brothels doing business as usual. It is reminiscent of Brueghel's Icarus and of Auden's commentary on "How suffering takes place / While someone else is eating or opening a window or just walking dully along."[27]

In the face of brutal handling by the police, the crowd's contained anger bursts loose. But the riot police are a well-protected and well-drilled machine. They are a different species and cannot be appealed to like the cossacks in Trotsky's account. Little rolls of well-fed flesh peek over the collars of their seemingly armored tunics. Yet, just as the Aztecs stopped believing that Cortés' cavalrymen were immortal once they had unseated one horseman, when the first policeman falls, the crowd suddenly realizes that the police are pregnable. But the contest in an open square is unequal. The police methodically beat up people they cut out from the mass, and enjoy kicking women in the belly. When the police have cleared the square, a few bodies lie inert on it (a scene forecast in the opening section when the militants were relaxing in a field). The pat-

[27] W. H. Auden, "Musée des Beaux-Arts," in *W. H. Auden*, London: Penguin, 1958, p. 61.

tern of the fighting is: first, the routing of the fascists; second, the retreat before the riot police; third, the struggle reengaged in the narrow backstreets, on the workers' home ground. The crowd's moods swivel from bravado to courage to fear to hesitation. They are in a constant state of flux, and are suitably compared to the sea—a hackneyed image here rejuvenated. People at windows join in the battle by dropping makeshift missiles, suddenly ennobled by new uses, on the police, who are forced to retreat. The workers go home in rough orderliness.

After the fighting, the militants add up the balance sheet and judge it a day of which they can feel proud. Bloyé, speaking for the tactical line of his Party, counsels patience and the waiting game and warns his colleagues not to play the enemy at his own (armed) game. The politics comes after the passion and the action. Suddenly distancing the whole sequence of events, Nizan sums up the day as one of great local importance, unlikely, however, to rate more than a few lines in the Paris papers. But, for the local people, a new tradition is being born.

Albert is arrested after his solo charge; Paul, dead. As they go to identify Paul's body, the group feels far less victorious but deeply angry and vengeful. As earlier in the book, here Nizan lets himself rise up on a balloon of apocalyptic words which draw far-fetched analogies with Canton, the Paris Commune, and Oviedo. Such war-mongering language, even though in intent internecine rather than international, reads falsely in this context. Nizan is on more personal and truthful terrain when he speaks of the suffering, rather than the dealing, of death. Men talk, he endlessly repeats, to stave off an awareness of death. The group, especially Bloyé, try to look at it straight. Bloyé maintains that, when some kinds of avoidable death (accidents in badly run factories, backstreet abortions) are canceled, then perhaps "natural" death will come to seem less terrifying. (But Nizan had heard the dispiriting answer of Soviet workers to that wondering hope.)

141

The book ends on a quiet note. Bloyé and Marie-Louise go for a walk and hear an Armenian worker chanting what seems to them an inhuman song, "a song from a dead-end world." For Bloyé, the outlook is bleak but heroic: the choice is either a living death or a life of risking death to make life more livable. The novel ends with a dawn, but a chill one; hopefulness, but hope with a hole in it. Lange and Catherine are as important in this novel's natural balance as are the political issues. For all its dogmatism, it is essentially an open-ended book.

The original title of the book was *Le Jour de la colère* (Day of Wrath). The present title indicates a step onwards from explosion to a long-term conspiracy. In Caute's opinion, Nizan is following "the socialist-realist precept of illustrating the current Party line"[28]—a questionable and unhelpful opinion. Like *La Conspiration*, this novel houses conflicting points of view. It is concerned, like Debray's study, with the "harsh dialectics of the here-and-now," and not with an artificial dialectic in some intellectual empyrean. We see the obverse side of political action and thought throughout the book. The warriors' rest of the opening section, by revealing how a group of militants relax, enables us to measure how involved they normally are in their efforts. It is not a question of either/or, but of both. As Howe says: "The political novel turns characteristically to an apolitical temptation. . . . This, so to say, is the 'pastoral' element that is indispensable to the political novel, indispensable for providing it with polarity and tension, but it matters only if there is already present the public element, a sense of the rigors, necessities and attractions of political life."[29] Nizan always allows for, and underlines, the strong survival in the industrial context of the pre-urban, elemental influences on men's decisions and styles of life. There is no denying that the theses are there, and often nakedly, but they are conceived as

[28] Caute, *Communism*, p. 326.
[29] Howe, *Politics and the Novel*, p. 23.

life patterns and are not merely, as Caute says, "illustrated." In this novel, what people say counts, but words are not at a premium. What really matters is that, after years of cowed acquiescence, a partially prepared but mainly spontaneous upsurge (and not the glamorous exploits of select individuals in Malraux fashion) unites formerly separated people in a collective struggle. The excitement hangs on the *possibility* of cohesion, with all its fluctuations.

The exalted tone of parts of the story are explainable, if not entirely acceptable. The situation in France in 1934-1935 offers one explanation. Fascism, whether a real threat or not, was generally believed by the left to be one. Being in tune with the demands of his time, Nizan was also at times a dupe to its delusions and self-mystifications, for instance, the cooked-up demagoguery of the whole Popular Front period. Nizan's personal situation suggests another explanation. He wrote part of *Le Cheval de Troie* at Stalinabad, capital of the Tadzhik Republic, in the midst of some spectacular developments, and the rest at Grimaud, near Saint-Tropez, where he was recuperating from an exhausting lecture tour that had brought him into contact with sympathizers and militants all over the south of France. As a consequence of such exposures, Bloyé occasionally lapses into axioms like "we must change the world." Apart from the common French habit of striking verbal poses, what is wrong with such bits of dialogue is not that "people don't say things like that." People say anything and everything. Rather, it is a mistake of tactics on Nizan's part, because the action of most of the novel is kept deliberately on a local, grassroots level, and this sudden global vista is out of keeping. But what of the conversation at the prefect's dinner party? Is this the usual parody of capitalists common to left-wing art? Critics tend to make a song-and-dance about the need to avoid pigeonholing people. But the fact is that, if pushed hard enough, most of us do confine ourselves in a definitive category: the reactionary, the soft liberal, the firebrand in us comes out starkly.

143

Nizan is keen to observe people pushed to this point. Under the threat of an insurgency, the prefect's guests align themselves along their chosen axes.

There is a sense of a real dialectic, between the revolutionary projects and the vestiges of previous bondages (Albert's dread of the law), a tug between future and past that begets a troubled present. Like Marx himself, Nizan was always sensitive to the real cost of progress and the nonexistence of miraculous solutions. When Paul dies, the emphasis is on waste, not on glorious martyrdom. (The French Communist Party hymns its "fusillés," its executed martyrs, and slanders many of its living members.) The time factor is always crucial in Nizan's view, whether it is a question of the conflict of age groups, the influence of an epoch, or the timing of a tactic. His conspiratorial view of life coincides with the practice of his chosen party, whose undermining action lends itself to an agonistic world view. In *Le Cheval de Troie*, we see a Communist cell and the crowd. This kernel does not direct the mass; it suffers and fights in its company. There are no tangible results from the street battles. The workers' living and working conditions are not thereby revolutionized. It is an exemplary demonstration, a show of strength, a focusing of awareness. The epigraph quotes from Lenin's journal *Iskra* a letter from a weaver which testified to the influence Lenin's paper and pamphlets exercised on the advanced workers. (Lenin's *Where to Begin* is also used as a rallying point in Silone's *Fontamara*, translated into French in 1935.) The letter ends: "And we should like to write a letter to your *Iskra*, to ask you to teach us not only how to begin, but how to live and how to die."

As Marx lent weight to Nizan's theory, so Lenin inspired his militant behavior. In a review of Mirsky's book on Lenin, Nizan categorized Lenin's strength as "one whose deepest secret lies perhaps in the complete absence of mythology and demagogy, in the precision of concrete thinking which attacks and gives the lie to mythical thinking." Most of all,

"Leninism strikes real hammer-blows."[30] Nizan shared Lenin's firm belief that revolutionary theory must back up revolutionary movements. Reliance on the spontaneous element in crowd psychology is, in Lenin's view, too risky, and needs to be reinforced by induced consciousness of concrete problems, considered from a national as well as a local point of view. There is, then, a positive role for the progressive bourgeois intelligentsia, which has to encourage and to educate the workers into a full awareness of their situation. There was in Lenin none of the later anti-intellectual, cap-in-hand humility in face of the manual workers. "The worker must grasp the meaning of all the catchwords and sophisms by which each class and each stratum camouflages its selfish strivings and its real 'inner workings'; he must understand what interests are reflected by certain institutions and certain laws and how they are reflected."[31] As an intelligent bourgeois renegade, Nizan was in a position to help. From the time of *Aden-Arabie* and *Les Chiens de garde*, he had been well versed in those "catchwords and sophisms." Nizan's attitude to the mass of workers undoubtedly echoed Lenin's: "The average people of the masses are capable of displaying energy and self-sacrifice in strikes and in street battles with the police and the troops, and are capable (in fact, are alone capable) of determining the outcome of our entire movement."[32] The crowd, then, must never be underestimated; but its spontaneity needs channeling from above by the cadres. Yet Lenin's lack of political snobbery leads him to see the frequent delinquency of such cadres. "Are there not advanced people, average people, and masses among the intelligentsia too? Does not everyone recognize that popular literature is also required for the intelligentsia, and is not such literature written?"[33] Nizan could only agree with such an undeceived, tough-minded, democratic leveling of all men,

---

[30] Nizan, *Nouvelle Revue Française*, 1 May 1935, pp. 772-73.
[31] V. I. Lenin, *What is to be done?*, pp. 69-70.
[32] *Ibid.*, p. 107.      [33] *Ibid.*, p. 128.

who must be judged by the criterion: are they pulling the weight they are capable of pulling? The intellectuals are the vanguard, and their responsibility is heavy.

Nizan taught Sartre that all thought is ideological, and that abstention from politics was still a political choice. By Simone de Beauvoir's confession, both she and Sartre, in the 1930s, were "elves." Nizan's harsh view of his friend is clear from his review of *La Nausée*, which Nizan had recommended to Gallimard. In his review, Nizan speaks of this "novel of absolute solitude," and describes Sartre as entirely alien to ethical problems, unlike Kafka, whom Sartre otherwise resembles in his ability to express the horror of certain intellectual vicious circles. It is Sartre's "fear of life" (and not, as with Heidegger, "the anguish of nothingness") that induces angst in him. Even Nizan's praise is demanding: "M. Sartre's gifts as a novelist are too keen and too ruthless for him to avoid taking part in the process of denunciation, or emerging into full reality."[34] But Sartre, alias Lange, as a fascist? Why not? It was a possibility. In 1960, describing his student years in the twenties, Sartre said: "The authors we admired explained to us around that time that existence is a scandal." He and his like cultivated theoretical violence: "It was a sick kind of violence . . . which could well have led us straight to fascism."[35] At the time of *Le Mur* and *La Nausée*, published three years after *Le Cheval de Troie*, Sartre was still sceptical, uncommitted, and his budding philosophy, which would later emerge as *L'Être et le néant*, had a strong nihilist flavor. In all these books, man is seen basically as a "playactor." In *L'Enfance d'un chef*, Sartre's main objection to fascism, influenced perhaps by his aesthetic separatism as much as by anything else, was its gang ethos. At that time, what sustained Sartre was the myth of writing as a vocation. Though a political cypher, he could just about will himself into a sense of justified arro-

---

[34] Nizan, *Ce Soir*, 15 May 1938, p. 6.
[35] Sartre, *Critique*, pp. 23-24.

gance. But it was a tightrope that he walked. Nizan, pushing virtuality to its logical conclusion, toppled Sartre off into fascism.

*Antoine Bloyé*, like Aragon's *Les Cloches de Bâle*, had centered mainly on the years before 1914—from the French standpoint, a pre-communist period. *Le Cheval de Troie* centers on the years 1931-1935: it is a commentary parallel with the times in which it was written. It is an "activist novel," both in that its events are hectic, and in that it contains a call to united action. "The law of literature, like the law of history, is upheaval."[36] In *Antoine Bloyé* and *La Conspiration* politics figures intermittently, like the famous "pistol-shot" intrusions in Stendhal's work. In *Le Cheval de Troie*, however, politics is omnipresent, not dictating all the action but forming (as in the novels of Koestler and Orwell) an inescapable accompaniment to everything that takes place. It was a considerable feat for a French writer of that time to construct a specifically communist work. There had been no revolution in France which might have focused and inspired the literary imagination. This novel is specifically communist in that it displays a violent collective reaction to fascism and brooks no compromise with any variety of enemy.

A colleague of Nizan in the Party, Léon Moussinac, published in 1935 a novel *Manifestation interdite*, which may be compared with *Le Cheval de Troie*. It is set at the time of the Sacco and Vanzetti affair. It makes an extremely sentimental use of Sacco's last letters to his son from the death cell. Throughout, Moussinac keeps up a glaring juxtaposition of good-hearted proletarians and viciously frivolous toffs. At the end, he brings the two enemies crudely together when the crowd storms and sacks a nightclub full of businessmen and socialites. "The crowd of workers silenced the international

---

[36] Nizan, "Ambition du roman moderne," *Les Cahiers de la jeunesse,* p. 19.

brotherhood of high living."[37] The discussions between a Communist typesetter and an anti-bourgeois editor of an avant-garde periodical are very strained and far too well rehearsed. A liberal goes to a protest meeting and is won over by the collective emotion. At the end, he is arrested along with other demonstrators, and his life, we are supposed to assume, has taken a radical turning. In all, this novel relies on the traditional stereotypes all too common in communist literature. Very little effort of the imagination has apparently been made. Press clippings are used to bolster the "authenticity," but they do not generate fictional truth.

What of the personal meaning of *Le Cheval de Troie?* There is in it what Sartre and Simone de Beauvoir call "la fête," an energy which can take the form of exuberant destruction as well as of playful junketing. The ring of personal experience audible in this book resounds from Nizan's encounters in Russia, his years of militating, especially in the provinces. Howe's view that the result of personal political experience "is at once a gain in political authority and a loss of subtlety and range in the traditional skills of the novel"[38] does not do justice to Nizan. Nizan was present at riots in Vienne; he painted slogans; he worked to politicize the apathetic local workers. An eminent doctor praised the expressiveness and the exactitude of Nizan's description of a woman dying of a hemorrhage. He has the true novelist's gift of physical sympathy. In fact, his thoughtful sensitivity to sensations seems to tally with Howe's prescription for the political novel: "Amidst the clamour of ideology—the indispensable, inescapable clamour—*listen to your nerves.*"[39]

Nizan's view is tragic in its repeated insistence on death. But he does not compound fate by adding to it some sense of ontological guilt (Albert's guilt feelings are induced by a

[37] Léon Moussinac, *Manifestation interdite*, p. 261.
[38] Howe, *Politics and the Novel*, p. 206.
[39] *Ibid.*, p. 234.

disproportioned society). "I'm not very keen on this taste for damnation or the idea that each life is merely the payment of a debt that nobody remembers having incurred." Kafka (like Lange) is listened to, and rejected. Stendhal, Dickens, and Tolstoy, those who in their differing ways say yes to life, are called in: "Dickens's courage and Tolstoy's courage were of the only really sublime variety: the courage of lying."[40] Here, "lie" stands for "hopefulness" in a world apparently without hope. *Le Cheval de Troie* is just such a courageous lie.

Although Malraux himself now dismisses it as a "daub," his *Le Temps du mépris*, also published in 1935, is not without significance as a fellow-traveler's attempt to project himself into the mind and body of a devoted Communist (Kassner). Even so, it is worth noticing that, with his flair for high drama, Malraux selects Germany, not France, as his context. And the old Malrauvian themes of "virile fraternity," resistance to torture, and solitude, rather than any specifically political theme, appear in this new setting. Kassner's effort to "disintoxicate himself from nothingness" on being released from prison is perhaps the nearest Malraux gets to a lessening of the metaphysically-slanted anguish. Kassner's comrades risk or give their lives for him. It is a grand gesture. What else? Malraux's reiterated theme of "return to earth" does not imply a return to *normal* life.

Howe defines the political novel as a novel in which "the idea of society, as distinct from the mere unquestioned workings of society, has penetrated the consciousness of the characters in all of its profoundly problematic aspects so that there is to be observed in their behavior, and they themselves often are aware of, some coherent political loyalty or ideological identification. They now think in terms of supporting or opposing society as such; they rally to one or another embattled

---

[40] Nizan, *Vendredi*, 11 December 1936, p. 7.

segment of society; and they do so in the name of, and under prompting from, an ideology."[41] Hence it is a question of lucidity, entailing a certain anticipation, a being-in-advance of general consciousness. In 1935, *Le Cheval de Troie*, inspired by contemporary events and passions, was yet *ahead* of them. The risk Nizan took was worth taking. In this novel he does not always succeed in not reducing ideas to formulae, but at no point does he reduce experience. Politics in a work of literature, said Stendhal, is an intrusion of loudness, and yet a thing to which it is not possible to refuse one's attention. Nizan's whole effort, especially palpable in this novel, is exactly this: to force readers to look when they would prefer to turn away.

[41] Howe, *Politics and the Novel*, p. 19.

CHAPTER FIVE

# A CONSPIRATORIAL WORLD
## *LA CONSPIRATION*

In 1937-1938, freed from a good deal of the hackwork he had
earlier carried out for the Party, and enjoying greater freedom
of expression writing for the broader-minded evening paper
of the Party, *Ce Soir*, than for *L'Humanité*, Nizan was in a
position to reflect on himself and his previous environment
with increased leisure and maturity. After years of cheerfully
denouncing the manic stress on inner life in bourgeois literature, he paused to examine his own, in public. But his standards
of judgment remain the same as they had been during his militant activity. He adopts the viewpoint of the collective questioning the individual on the validity of his private dilemmas. The
process is, however, a literary one. It is the author's control and
judging of his characters which performs the duty of the public tribunal. *La Conspiration* was the product of this stage of
Nizan's development, and, even more than any other of his
works, it demonstrates just how much talent was lost when
Nizan was killed in the war.

Before examining it, we can find some indications of his
new readiness to delve into his personal depths by looking at
his "Histoire de Thésée."[1] He had already referred to this
myth in *Antoine Bloyé*, where Marcelle saying goodbye to
Antoine stands watching him go "like Ariadne standing beneath the sun of Naxos, watching Theseus disappear into the
open sea." Nizan describes how Antoine's memory of his mistress gradually sinks into the "dark pit of censured thoughts,
where human passions are rendered powerless."[2] This notion
of the censoring of a valuable truth, in effect a self-censoring,

[1] Nizan, "Histoire de Thésée," *Commune*, November 1937.
[2] Nizan, *Antoine Bloyé*, p. 114.

151

is taken up in "Histoire de Thésée," in which Theseus appears as a budding dictator. It is a cruel version of an already painful story. Theseus, a novice, commits his first homicide on an ambiguous creature which might be a human bull or an animal man. After killing it in its sleep, Theseus feels simultaneously elated and adrift. On the return journey to the light of day, his squabbles with Ariadne, who has lost the thread, are interspersed with bouts of brief and violent sex. These grand figures of legend are accomplishing their destiny to the accompaniment of undignified sessions of urination in the tunnel. Theseus believes that he will be robbed of his renown for killing the monster if they do not get back to be acclaimed. Ariadne (like Marcelle) pleads that love alone counts and that "a whole life can be concentrated in a few short hours." Theseus, however, clings desperately to the Minotaur's head as evidence of his feat, and, fearing that the other witness, Ariadne, will be able to recount how easy in fact the killing was, thinks of silencing her tongue. He is so obsessed with his public image that he rides roughshod over her feelings and seeks to ignore his own confused motives. Nizan presents him as an anachronism. Theseus has not realized that the old days of slaughtering monsters are over, and that "men nowadays only believe in their interior lions, hydras, or dragons, and that it would be less easy to kill these." When the pair reach daylight and are greeted with questions about the struggle, Theseus suppresses the truth: "I had a long battle with it." He glimpses Ariadne's smile. He strikes her, jumps into a boat, and sails off. At sea, he listens to her despairing cries until he is out of earshot.

"Histoire de Thésée" is a weird tale. Not really an allegory, and yet clearly enclosing a secret meaning. Nizan imposes on the Theseus myth the interpretation currently favored for Racine's *Phèdre*: a Freudian stress on the monsters of the psyche. In denying this inner dimension, the self-deceiving and lie-spreading Theseus is abandoning (just as he deserts

Ariadne) what might have made him a whole man, and choosing a career of falsity in preference to love and self-knowledge. Some of Nizan's doubts about his own home life and his service in the Party may well have found expression in this intriguing variation on the classical myth. One of the central characters of *La Conspiration* visits Naxos, relaxes into something approaching genuineness during his stay there, and, when he leaves it, begins to fall apart as a coherent personality. Marcelle haunts Antoine's memory, where she lies in wait, ready to recur as a regret. In *La Conspiration*, Nizan aimed to pass judgment on some aspects of the Theseus side of his life—his career as a rebel against the bourgeois monstrosity—while integrating into it all that Ariadne stands for. *La Conspiration* brings out for inspection in the limelight what "Histoire de Thésée" darkly insinuates.

Sartre, who loves such loaded conundrums, once asked, in a review of this novel, whether a communist can write a good novel, since he has no right to become the accomplice of his characters.[3] It is a strange query, and will be discussed later. Some of Sartre's best fiction can be found in his critical studies, those splendid novels which have Baudelaire, Flaubert, Jean Genet, or Nizan for hero. In his preface to Nizan's *Aden-Arabie*, while seeking to rehabilitate his dead and envied friend, Sartre confesses with chestbeating his own lack of insight into Nizan's reality during his lifetime. A good many critics, however, still content themselves with viewing Nizan through the powerful distorting-lens of Sartre. In *La Conspiration*, Nizan was trying to see himself straight. He should be emulated by the critic.

The group of young men at the center of this novel are at the awkward age of French youth, between twenty and twenty-four years old. As in *Aden-Arabie*, Nizan here discards the comfortable middle-age myth of youth as a time of

---

[3] Sartre, "*La Conspiration*," p. 29.

adventure and, in its stead, stresses "cette colère ambiguë qui naît du vertige des occasions manquées."[4] Initially, his young men experience themselves as nonentities. Nizan mingles their self-criticism with an indictment of society, which they picture chiefly in terms of their families. The tone is sardonic: "C'est gai cette existence de larves en nourrice en attendant d'être de brillants insectes de cinquante ans."[5] They refuse this readymade future, and conspire against the conspiracy of their parents who try to fob off their demands on life by the provision of a safe career. In reaction, and largely governed by the fear of being swindled, these young men opt for the provisional mode in all things, even friendship. In Sartre's view, youth is here presented as "an artificial age, partly the creation of other people and partly self-creation."[6] In other words, young people perpetuate the choices made for them by their progenitors. This idea is much more applicable to Sartre's own Frantz von Gerlach in *Les Séquestrés d'Altona* than to Nizan's heroes, two of whom manage to break out of the system.

Rosenthal, Laforgue, Bloyé, and Pluvinage are philosophy students whose chosen area of reference embraces Spinoza, Hegel, Marx, and Lenin. But, true to their times, the middle and late 1920s, they retain vestiges of surrealist penchants: moments of solipsism, and that inverted snobbery that prefers local flea pits to the Salle Pleyel. As often happens with novels of French intellectual life, the Anglo-Saxon reader might find risible the degree of venom aroused in these students by that then stronghold of idealist philosophy *La Revue de métaphysique et de morale*. But this would be to underestimate

---

[4] "the ambivalent anger caused by missing opportunities and feeling totally baffled." *La Conspiration*, Gallimard, 1938, p. 20.
[5] "It's a lovely life, being fed like infant larvae while waiting to turn into brilliant fifty-year old insects" (p. 21).
[6] Sartre, "*La Conspiration*," p. 27.

the seriousness accorded by intending radicals on the Continent to the intimate connection between intellectual standpoints and political assumptions. The kind of academic thinking under attack is regarded by the students as a coverup for bourgeois values of conservatism and the burking of social problems. Just as these young rebels conspire against the insidiously tranquilizing plots of their elders, so they decide to found a periodical in order to combat the official philosophy of the Sorbonne.

*La Guerre civile*, its title, was in fact the name of a review planned in the 1920s to pool the energies of the surrealists, the *Clarté* group of Trotskyites, and the *Philosophies* group, which included Henri Lefebvre, Georges Friedmann, Georges Politzer, Pierre Morhange, and, at a distance, Nizan himself. The project flopped. In the novel, Rosenthal is the initiator of a similar review, and at first his policy is one of built-in obsolescence. Ironically, these bourgeois rebels can afford this luxury project thanks to capitalist philanthropy. "Comme ils n'étaient pas pressés par la nécessité déprimante de gagner leur pain sur le champ, ils se disaient qu'il fallait changer le monde."[7] From the outset, Nizan both mocks and espouses their ambition, so that Sartre grossly oversimplifies when he talks of Nizan's lack of indulgence of them. At this stage, lacking any contact with the oppressed sectors of society, "il n'y a au fond de leur politique que des métaphores et des cris."[8] In a passage which anticipates Sartre's image of the viscous, Nizan both ribs their ignorance of the facts of life and acknowledges the trickiness of the obstacles before them: "Ils ne savaient pas encore comme c'est lourd et mou le monde, comme il ressemble à un amas sans queue ni tête de

[7] "As they were spared the depressing necessity of earning their own living straightaway, they claimed that the world had to be changed" (p. 23).

[8] "The basis of their politics was only a few metaphors and outcries" (p. 24).

gélatine."[9] This sets the tone for the whole novel: an intelligent disgust with all hindrances to honest living, and a deep sense of a world of multiple conspiracies, "ces chassés-croisés de trahisons qui se compensent."[10]

While they are not utter dupes of their illusions, the student rebels are convinced that they must express their will to subvert. The aim is demystification. Laforgue plans to extend Marx's theory of commodity fetishism and to construct "a universal classification of deception" (p. 47). The group tend to think of their enemies as more stupid than lethal, and such overreliance on intellectual criteria means that they do not face their dilemmas squarely. Yet they strive to go beyond surrealist anarchism and to "achieve true seriousness." Rosenthal, whose hectoring ways smack of Georges Politzer (that Buck Mulligan of a militant), quotes that saying of Marx which Nizan himself preferred: "Men must be made aware of themselves whether they like it or not." Despite fine intentions, however, Rosenthal, obsessed with profanation of the bourgeois gods, is more in tune with Lenin's boast that after conquest he would build gold urinals in every capital of the world. Soon, he moves from a belief that words can outdo deeds to a hunger for action. Protected by their social status, the group's review undergoes that sanction intolerable to rebels: impunity. Rosenthal dismisses their opening articles as "woman's work": embroidery. Going back on his earlier Gidean cult of "availability," his surrealist visions of pointless holocausts, and his vague nostalgia for the days of anarchist terrorism, he now lusts for some irreversible commitment, and warns (ironically, as he is one of the novel's traitors): "Let us beware of our future infidelities" (p. 64). In fact, he is so involved with the future that he hardly ever coincides with his present. Similarly "existentialist" is his scorn for good

[9] "They were unaware as yet just how heavy and flabby the world is, how close it is to a shapeless mass of gelatine" (p. 23).
[10] "The crisscross betrayals which cancel each other out" (p. 15).

intentions and his insistence on "proof in action." In all, it is a demand for what might be called "punity." As he believes that "the revolution will be a technical one," he organizes a tiny network of industrial and military espionage, in order to contribute, he hopes, to Soviet strategy. (The Sixth Congress of the Communist International in 1928 asked the sections to be ultra-attentive to systematic preparation for war against the U. S. S. R. by capitalist countries intent on an anti-Soviet crusade.) As he wishes both to be useful to the cause and to keep his own conscience clean, he makes jesuitical attempts at self-justification. To Laforgue's argument on the need to officially join the Communist Party, he replies: "Notre fonction consiste à inventer ou à approfondir des mystiques, mais non à les dissoudre dans des politiques."[11] On the whole, conspiracy, for him, is partly a metaphysical and partly an operatic concept, derived from Renaissance Italy via Stendhal.

It is significant that in the plot he devises, passing on information gathered by his agents, he functions in the traditional bourgeois way: vicariously. He exploits Simon, an old schoolmate undergoing national service, in order to procure part of the army's contingency plans in the event of civil insurgence. Simon risks himself so as not to offend those he idolizes. No longer bolstered by Rosenthal's moralizing, Simon feels at sea in the army, unable to mix with the lower ranks as he had hoped, jealous of the effortless insolence of the proletarian privates, bewildered by military codes of discipline, and generally exposed to what might be called "servitude sans grandeur militaire." He has a rather impotent sense that army life breeds mindless servility and, as such, acts as a reductio ad absurdum of capitalist society (like colonial practices as depicted in *Aden-Arabie*): another form of alienation, another feudal setup. Like Sartre's Oreste, he feels pathetically unballasted and cannot conceive that a young man's acts can

[11] "Our function is to devise or to amplify mystiques, and not to adulterate them with politics" (p. 71).

157

have consequences. He is every inch a product of his family, rich Nantais business people who, because of uneasy consciences, worshipped the mind as well as money, favoring diplomats and writers, "all the creators of alibis." Aptly enough, when he is caught copying out secret documents, after cracking with ease the army's naïve security codes, he spins the yarn that he was collecting material for a science-fiction novel. His far-fetched alibi fits in with his superiors' prejudices about dreamy intellectuals. In addition, class solidarity comes into play: the officers simply refuse to believe that this well-bred young man could side with the political underdog. Welcoming his impunity, unlike the other rebels, Simon backs out of the conspiracy. The whole episode is recounted with a deadly comic awareness of this "mad military universe."

Laforgue rebukes Rosenthal for his ruthless handling of Simon. Although all along Laforgue has criticized his friend's Dostoevskian cloak-and-dagger intellectualism, been aware that Rosenthal is seeking above all a cure for some private ill, and repeated that a militant metal worker runs far more real risks than any of the privileged group, he falls in with Rosenthal's other project of industrial espionage. He yields largely because he feels proud to steal secrets from his own father's engineering works: "This act so contrary to all filial duty seemed to me completely natural" (p. 159). This sounds very Gidean, but his father had already asked him to engage in what struck him as a peculiarly base form of spying: time-and-motion study, "acting like a stool pigeon with a stopwatch." His antifamily resentment, then, has a more down-to-earth and less self-centered grounding than Rosenthal's. Like Bloyé, Laforgue's ancestors were peasants. In Nizan's scale of values, without echoing Vallès' belief in the crime involved in deserting the country life, this tradition always contains the notion of fidelity. Laforgue, moreover, is fully alive to "all the seductiveness of families." And, as Nizan ironically remarks, these youths "were forever mistaking grown-ups for capitalists" (p. 55). The family context, there-fore, is of great importance in this novel. (The title of the review, *La Guerre civile*, refers also to the internecine war of children against the family.)

Rosenthal's ties with his family are more sickly. Where Laforgue spoke with mixed bitterness and affection of his family nest, Rosenthal frets over "the family poisons which his liver and kidneys would never be able to evacuate" (p. 110). Though he imagines himself emancipated from his family cell, he is in fact only on parole. In his father's body he reads the portents of his own future aging. (For Nizan, an "urge to surpass" always exists between adolescent sons and their fathers.) His father nourishes himself on the abstract maneuverings of the stock exchange, as does Rosenthal's brother, who differs from the father only insofar as he opposes a pseudoscientific concept of the market, while the old man believes in laissez-faire capitalism. On Rosenthal's terms, they are barely alive. He lives, like Pluvinage (and later we shall see other links between the initiator and the traitor), in a mortuary district, "des rues nettes comme des allées de cime-tières à concessions perpétuelles."[12] This context haunts him and decreases his reality. Life he experiences mainly "via tell-ing rejoinders he remembered from books" (p. 139). Unlike Laforgue, who draws some sustenance from tracing back to peasant forebears, Rosenthal feels only irritated dislike for his fellow Jews, both rich and poor. Yet his very act of keeping everything within the family, even his illicit love affair, seems part of a Jewish tradition, as does his love of writing meta-phorically "Mene, Mene, Tekel, Upharsin on every wall" (p. 88).

In keeping with his clan's conventions, he at first thinks of Catherine, his brother's wife, as a decorative chattel, and feels only a "holy revulsion" at random glimpses of her flesh. Nizan

[12] "streets as neat as cemetery alleys lined with graves on permanent leases" (p. 13).

lists her visible qualities in such a way that all Rosenthal loathed in a woman takes on a cold beauty all its own: "Son éternelle présence d'esprit, cette garde nonchalante, sa dureté de décision, cette connaissance parfaite des rites, sa peau incorruptible."[13] Her very impregnability incites Rosenthal to challenge her as a bastion to be taken by ruse and force. To conquer her, he feels, would be a smack in the eye of the bourgeoisie. The affair starts like a conspiracy, with a few complicities and passwords. He wants her to commit herself to him wholeheartedly and squanders borrowed lyricism on her. But "Catherine resisted like life itself, that is, passively" (p. 155). She is part of that gelatinous magma already mentioned. At times he experiences, as he leans over the depths of her mindlessness, that vertigo that Sartre detects in both Flaubert and Nizan.

Nizan analyzes Catherine and bourgeois society in the same terms: both are afflicted with an atomized consciousness, which produces a short memory, which favors the status quo. Catherine regards the sexual pleasure Rosenthal offers her as a chance occurrence, not as a foundation to be built upon. When they are separated for a time, he begins to construct "autour de quelques signes, de quelques bouffées de mémoire et de quelque insomnies les grandes fables de l'amour."[14] It seems as if Nizan believes that the sons of the bourgeoisie have changed little in seventy years, for Rosenthal, preparing a room for Catherine, planning a trip to Versailles while social upheavals go on around them, repeats Flaubert's Frédéric Moreau. He acts all the great roles. Nizan deflates: "Il se croyait alors sincère, mais il n'était que naturel. Il ne s'apercevait point que rien n'est plus artificiel que la sincérité, et que

[13] "Her unshakeable presence of mind, the nonchalant guard she kept up, the inflexibility of her decisions, her perfect knowledge of rituals, her incorruptible flesh" (p. 129).

[14] "great myths of love on a foundation of a few signs, a few whiffs of reminiscences, and a few sleepless nights" (p. 161).

la nature est le royaume du mimétisme."[15] The final irony is that Catherine never makes head or tail of his disquisitions. The affair, pointless as it ends up, does have the effect of placing Rosenthal in open defiance of his family. When the liaison has been unearthed and the family council summoned, he wonders whether his scandalous act will be absorbed by them or will stick in their throats. This confrontation chimes with his would be tragic preferences: "Il les avait enfin contraints à entrer avec lui dans le monde sans mensonges, le monde impoli de Caïn et d'Abel."[16] But the trial passes off quietly, "un drame bourgeois, du mauvais Diderot, ce moyen terme."[17] And he can never be satisfied with in-betweens. The only area of tragedy left to him, he feels, is the will to die. But even this grave moment is falsified by posing. It is still against his family that he measures himself. He gets drunk and, in a heady mixture of rage and sloth, takes poison. For the first time he sees himself clearly: like the hero of *Antoine Bloyé*, "he was going to die the victim of a robbery." (It seems at times as though he were meant to function as an upper-class Antoine, never attaining full reality, never truly expending himself, and at other times as though he were simply a pathetic fake.) As the poison grips tight, he feels—too late—a last wild urge to live. Of the previously harsh and dehydrated mother, Nizan says: "Nobody is a complete monster. She had wept for hours" (p. 184). His father feels bizarrely guilty, "and he wanted to be forgiven for some drawn-out but deadly betrayal he had perpetrated" (p. 198). With a kind of sarcastic compassion, Nizan has Rosenthal buried overlooking the Mur des Fédérés, where the Com-

---

[15] "He thought he was being sincere but he was only acting naturally. He did not realize that nothing is more artificial than sincerity, and that nature in fact is ruled by imitation" (p. 166).

[16] "At long last he had forced them to accompany him into a world devoid of lies, the discourteous world of Cain and Abel" (p. 183).

[17] "hardly a bourgeois drama even, just a bad play by Diderot, that middle term" (p. 185).

munards had been executed. Rosenthal is in fact a victim of his own imperious urges rather than of any reactionary savagery. A luxury victim, yet his disillusionment is not worthless. Laforgue keeps a photo of his dead friend, "la dernière apparition d'un Rosenthal éternellement jeune, éternellement déçu."[18]

Laforgue survives. After discovering that Rosenthal had done nothing with the stolen information passed to him, Laforgue ponders for some time on the chasm yawning between their ambitions and their achievements. The effect of this shock, however, is to force Laforgue to start growing up. He says to Bloyé that the group's failures were merely limbering-up exercises and that their lives would not be forever subject to the shifty rules of improvisation. He faces the problem of how to bridge the gap between youth and manhood. Always fascinated by "the great ceremony of bourgeois life," he transfers to his own dilemma from his readings in anthropology the notion of the puberty rites in primitive tribes. Though he knows that self-conscious farce enters into such rituals, he values their definitive character. Instead of an accepted roughing-up or the help of a medicine man to ease the passage from one age to another, Western youths have at their disposal only "that filth, mental maladies" (p. 245). While waiting to free himself from his parents, he fears that in his state of noncommitment, he will "faire le ludion," bobbing up and down like a bottle imp, but this philosophy student has been such a "Cartesian diver" long enough, and now longs to shatter the glass encasing him. He is a member of a privileged class who wants to live down this foreign aid. His problem is akin to that of the European who wants to "go native." We might say, on the model of Nerval's "ignorance cannot be learnt," that "poverty cannot be borrowed." Laforgue will move from wishing that he lived in a primitive community

[18] "It was the last appearance of a Rosenthal who would look young for evermore and disillusioned without end" (p. 200).

to working for a society where that simplicity may be re-installed in the place of the needless complexity of so-called advanced society.

When he falls seriously ill, his illness acts as his medicine man. Nizan had nearly died of a clot on the lung in his twenties, and all the precise description of physical agony in his work has the ring of authenticity. Drieu la Rochelle once wrote: "What we must ensure, I feel, is that our characters are wedded to the pattern of our deepest and most ordinary reflexes, tied up in the same difficulties as we encounter in life. They are the temperature charts of the handful of illnesses we've had, and the recoveries as well."[19] Laforgue's vertiginous hallucinations during fevers are seen from the inside: the room around him melts from a thorax into a cellar to a cell. Laforgue enjoys the passivity of it all. He is an empty vessel, a receiving set for febrile perceptions and the pulsations of airwaves. Preternaturally etched details alternate with blurred visions, interspersed with dank nightmares and coma. He is utterly indifferent to all and everyone other than his own experience, in which, no longer dabbling, he immerses himself. One evening he wakes up on the other side of illness. The sheer and simple joy of being alive overwhelms him. As he resurfaces, he rediscovers his own body: he is, for the first time, a living entity. His second life begins, but the price he pays is the knowledge that he is now living towards death after twenty years of marking time. He has found his variety of "punity": "Le grand jeu des tentatives avortées avait pris fin, puisqu'on peut réellement mourir."[20]

Whereas, at the École Normale Supérieure, Sartre by his own admission dreamlessly snored through the nights, Nizan "was the most obsessed of us all; sometimes, when fully awake, he could see himself laid out as a corpse." In reaction

[19] Pierre Drieu la Rochelle, *Sur les écrivains*, Gallimard, 1964, p. 182.
[20] "The great game of abortive enterprises had come to a close, because death was a real possibility" (p. 249).

against this anguish, Nizan developed such a lust for life that
Sartre marveled at his friend's avid acceptance of "the risks
of a wide-open life, unprotected and without any guarantee
of an afterlife."[21] In Laforgue, then, are invested many of
Nizan's basic fears and hopes. This whole episode proves how
cogently Nizan conveys his sense of painful transitions,
whether in the public or the private sphere. At this moment,
Laforgue is that "incomparable monster" that, as Malraux
said, each of us is to himself. "Ce bonheur de se reconquérir
l'absorbait entièrement. . . . Tout autre existence que la sienne
lui semblait inexplicable, indécente et pleine d'une encom-
brante bouffonnerie."[22] The future is open for him. Some of
the elements of Nietzsche's recipe for rebels in an unrebellious
age are already present and active within him: "Objection,
evasion, joyous distrust and love of irony are signs of health:
everything absolute belongs to pathology."[23] Nizan once said:
"Novelists shy away from the necessary ending of any novel:
death, which is alone able to sum up the whole truth of a
man's life."[24] Though Rosenthal (physically) and Pluvinage
(to all intents and purposes) die, this novel in fact ends with
Laforgue's symbolic death and rebirth, his change of life in
an "initiation rite."

*La Conspiration* describes a group as it splinters; *Le Cheval
de Troie*, a militant group clinging together for mutual support; and *Antoine Bloyé*, a group-less person—in many ways
as desolate a situation, for Nizan, as being a stateless person.
But was the group in *La Conspiration* at any time truly unified? Are not these young bourgeois typical specimens of

[21] Sartre, *Les Mots*, pp. 162-65.
[22] "The joy of regaining possession of himself absorbed him completely. . . . Anyone else's life struck him as inexplicable, obscene, and
heavily absurd" (p. 248).
[23] Quoted in Howe, *Politics and the Novel*, p. 50. From Nietzsche,
*Beyond Good and Evil*, Edinburgh, Foulis, 1909, p. 98 (Helen Zimmern,
trans.).
[24] Nizan, review of François Mauriac, *Plongées*, in *Ce Soir*, 10 March
1938, p. 6.

their fragmented class culture? The conflict of generations, in addition, is not only between the student group and their parents, but between them and two sympathizers from the next older generation: Régnier and Carré.

There is a splendid scene of intellectual diamond-cut-diamond when the students first meet the writer, Régnier (vaguely reminiscent of Henri Barbusse). His ideas disappoint them and cause them to overlook the man himself. It is in his *Carnet noir* that we see him as he is to himself: rife with self-questioning. Of the generation that provided the officers in the First World War, ten years later he feels not so much *déclassé* as out-of-place. He refuses the temptation to become, like Duhamel or Gide, a literary pundit and chooses to stiffen his own resolve by reference to Stendhal, who was too hard-headed for such self-delusions. As he begins to "set" with age, he compares Rosenthal's opting for the provisional with his own preference for some longer-term value: "You get ripe for religion or for communism with its sense of destiny and great prospects" (p. 101). This is a term Nizan himself would endorse, with its implications of an open-ended fate, a combination of project and determinism: a kind of tragic optimism. Régnier sounds remarkably like Nizan again when he speaks of the need to "retarder la mort par la fureur. Dans la vie privée. Dans la politique."[25] But his doubts and maxims, cryptic and abstract, keep Régnier on the level of an interesting shadow. He stands for the man of goodwill, somewhat marginal, whose choice of action defines him only questionably.

Carré *has* opted. For Aragon, as might be expected, Carré is "the positive element" amid the shambles of values in the rest of this novel.[26] (Carré is probably based on one of the men Nizan himself admired most in the Communist Party,

---

[25] "Postpone dying by passionate action in private life and in politics" (p. 104).
[26] Louis Aragon, "Le Roman terrible," p. 443.

Paul Vaillant-Couturier. In 1929, he was arrested on a charge of sedition while in hiding in a writer's house, as was Carré in Régnier's home.) For Carré, communism is a total faith in which ethics and politics are wedded in a "life style." He has been a member since the Congress of Tours and his explanation is simple: "I can live with communists," whereas for him socialists are merely political part-timers. His host Régnier asks, as an invincible liberal, the inevitable question: how does an intellectual reconcile himself to the discipline imposed by the Party? The scornful reply is that such a view of freedom is essentially negative. Yet Carré's own blanket acceptance of his political creed could clearly hide a multitude of sins. In all, he talks warmly of communism, but in the world of this novel we cannot see it in action. That is the task, admirably carried out, of *Le Cheval de Troie*. As Emmanuel Berl points out: "*La Conspiration* is a pre-communist book. Its heroes are not sure about communism, but they are sure that life is not worth very much outside it."[27] But we see in Pluvinage, and within the same Party, the very antithesis of Carré: not a man of inner and supported strength, but a pathological misfit.

From the start, Pluvinage is the odd man out in the student group. He is fully aware that he is mistrusted for external reasons, for instance, his face ("une sale gueule de faux témoin et d'agent double," as Régnier prophetically notes).[28] After Carré has been arrested in the police swoop, and suspecting Pluvinage's part in it, Laforgue and Rosenthal subject him to a reciprocally embarrassing inquisition. All three show off irrelevantly. The suspicions of Rosenthal and Laforgue breed uncontrollably and they write to the Party to denounce Pluvinage as a police informer. Nizan remarks cuttingly on their pharisee attitude: "Rien au monde n'est plus lourd que la

[27] Emmanuel Berl, "Deux contemporains," p. 35.
[28] "He's got the ugly mug of the false witness and the double agent" (p. 130).

166

nécessité de juger; ils étaient enfin allégés de ce fardeau."[29]
Pluvinage has hardly got away from one trial than he has to
face another more indirect and wordless scrutiny at his cell
headquarters. Here, Nizan outdoes Sartre himself in the
realm of the *louche*: that uneasy state in which the suspect
feels himself being turned to a stone object by the judging
gazes of other people. Although Pluvinage's hands are not
limp or clammy, his shifty eyes betray him. But, going back
in time, Nizan spins the wheel: it was the judging gaze of
others that had in the first place created in the adolescent a
sense of guilt (as Sartre later diagnosed in the case of Genet).
Eventually, Pluvinage plunges head first into his guilty fate.
Via a diary, however, Nizan takes care to disclose the conditioning and motivation that led him there.

The first thing worth noticing is that the manuscripts of
this diary are written stylishly, as if Pluvinage were a failed
or foiled novelist. The reason might be, as has been said of
Conrad's fascination with the informer as a psychological type,
that "the informer who serves the established world by prying into the world beneath it" may be seen as "a projection
of the writer who pries, not without guilt, into the depths of
motive. The informer informs on his comrades, the writer on
himself."[30] This argument would more plausibly implicate
Nizan in Pluvinage's dilemma than in the later hysterical
outcry from Party hatchet men (after he had left the Party
in protest against the Hitler-Stalin Pact) that he was an arrant
traitor and that his understanding of Pluvinage proved it. It
is true that Nizan shows great patience in probing into this
young man's act of betrayal. What this proves is that Nizan
had learned the most precious lesson furnished by good novels: the duty to create a living opposition to the approved
characters, with its own codes of action. Like Lange in *Le*

[29] "The heaviest burden of all is the need to pass judgment on someone else, and they were finally lightened of it" (p. 180).

[30] Howe, *Politics and the Novel*, p. 83.

*Cheval de Troie*, Pluvinage is a nihilating presence, a hole in being, who himself responds to the call of the void.

Pluvinage's father directed the Paris "burial office." The boy was conditioned by death from early childhood; when other lads cut out bits from engineering catalogues, he collected pictures of coffins and tombstones. Nizan presents him to us with the overtones of the Dostoevskian morbid intellectual, a marginal man afraid of becoming altogether superfluous. He is obsessed by the number of "mondes clandestins qui gravitent autour du monde patent où on occupe sa vie."[31] This early intuition of the complexity of social organization, of underworlds and overworlds, prepares the ground both for his later adhesion to the Communist Party and for his switch from it to the French secret police. He lives in a district of Paris overweighted with those administrative centers "where the mysteries of a citizen's life are enacted": police, law courts, hospitals, prisons, his father's department, and the municipal waste disposal. An infrastructure, in short, of dregs, "J'ai grandi dans le monde qui se voue à l'élimination des déchets urbains et à l'enregistrement des catastrophes privées."[32] It is a world ruled, like that of Noah's sons in the face of their father's nakedness, by shame. Pluvinage believes that only a few doctors can live on both the ignoble and the everyday levels of life without becoming corrupted. It is a world of irrevocability, of final recording, which normal men visit rarely and only under compulsion. His upbringing was poisoned in addition by his tearfully solicitous mother. Like Gide's Armand, in *Les Faux-Monnayeurs*, the only outgoing compassion he can summon up is for a relative cruelly exploited by a hypochondriac mother. He almost loves the girl, but his hatred of his own flesh leads him to miss his chance. His con-

[31] "clandestine worlds gravitating around the wide-open world where people work for a living" (p. 210).

[32] "I grew up in a world given over to the disposal of urban waste and the registering of private catastrophes" (p. 219).

fession is honest. He does not try to enlist pity by making out that his whole young life has been one long misery. In his account we watch the interplay of his own ineradicable and rootless nature with the influence of others on him.

When he is lifted into the educational elite at the lycée Louis-le-Grand, he is struck by the "thunderbolts of envy." He envies the unexplained passwords, the easy triumphs of Laforgue and Rosenthal, and marvels at their apparent solid essence. It is a dizzy state: jealousy receding to infinity. Just as Rosenthal and company found a gap between dreams and facts, so Pluvinage finds an abyss between his own self-estimate and their valuation of him. Ashamed at being excluded, he needs to prove himself, as if he believes that a man's life were a geometrical theorem. He fears what the future holds (and the image noted at the outset recurs, with a twist) if he fails to hoist himself up to their level: "quelque destinée humide et noire d'insecte de la pourriture."[33] Most of all, like Anouilh's Bitos, he knows he lacks natural grace, lovability. In a bitter perversion of Montaigne's famous shorthand statement of friendship, he admits: "Je ne me pardonnais pas plus d'être moi que je ne vous pardonnais d'être vous."[34] He is jealous even of Rosenthal's suicide, which impresses him as stylish and inimitable. But, before that event, he realizes that the only way to assert himself is by choosing some course opposite to theirs. His choice is an inversion of values: informing on comrades instead of, as in Rosenthal's conspiracy, on enemies.

Before reaching his final impasse as a traitor, he goes through a stage of feeling almost justified and superior to the group. He joins the Party for largely neurotic and therapeutic reasons: "Je voyais en la révolution le lieu de toutes les chances

[33] "some dank, dark fate of an insect living off rotting matter" (p. 227).
[34] "I could no more forgive myself for being what I was than I could forgive you for being what you were" (p. 227).

possibles de réparation, de ressentiment assouvi, et comme le paradis des anciens vaincus."[35] This new society seems to him devoid of hierarchies (on Rosenthal's periodical he had been assigned only the hack jobs). In terms almost identical with those of Carré, he describes his cell comrades as having given him "la seule idée que j'aurai d'une communauté humaine; on ne guérit pas du communisme quand on l'a vécu."[36] Nizan could second such a declaration. Though an intellectual, Pluvinage is granted full active membership in the Party, and no mention is made of his bourgeois provenance, that "social original sin." This lonely youth meets a genuine warmth, "a physical complicity, an almost biological sense of belonging to the same species," for the first time in his wretched life. But the fragility of his commitment is severely tested when government and police begin a campaign of oppression against the Party. This born loser wants to be on the winning side. As a result, when his mother's lover Massart, a chief of the Secret Police, starts to serenade him, he is, though initially repelled, finally seduced. A few days after approaching Régnier for advice and glimpsing Carré, he dreams of denouncing the fugitive to the police. Nizan describes succinctly the underground process of temptation: "Quand une idée paraît, c'est qu'elle a fait un long chemin. Elle arrive parfaitement formée et adulte, il est trop tard pour la tuer."[37] The idea of betrayal haunts Pluvinage and then solidifies "like a gleaming jewel." When he finally drags himself to Massart's office, it is like a journey back to his dead father and death-ridden childhood. He is a marked man, inside and out, and

[35] "I saw in revolution the perfect opportunity for getting my own back, for satisfying my resentment; it offered a kind of paradise for people who had been failures" (p. 228).

[36] "the nearest thing to a community of men I'll ever know; you never get over communism when you've been through it" (p. 230).

[37] "When an idea comes to you, it's been on the way for a very long time. When it arrives, it's fully developed and grownup, and it's too late to kill it off" (p. 238).

so malleable that he is easily molded further by Massart's tempting theories.

Even when involved in the Party, Pluvinage had been attracted less by the glorious future promise and more by the present state of illegality and "underhand dealing," so suited to a man cursed with a giveaway face. In Massart there hangs over a good deal of Vautrin and the philosophizing detectives of Balzac's *Une Ténébreuse Affaire*. He rejects all prevailing myths about the police defending society against crime. His faith concerns his own *police pure*. Before his hypothesis is dismissed, we might remember the multitudinous activities of the C. I. A. and the French *police parallèle*. (Politzer was once arrested by a highly-educated police detective, who expounded to him a theory very similar to Massart's.)[38] Massart's line is that, contrary to Bossuet or to Marx, there is no discernible shape to history. Only Pascal, with his "policemen's world view," based on the random nature of events, nears the truth, which is that "big events are created by small chances and small men" (p. 211). Such a myth obviously appeals to the young failure who wants to take revenge for having been belittled by others. What Massart adds to Pascal is the belief that chance can be controlled. The hero of his system is the secret, anonymous, abstract network of backroom researchers who record in dossiers such information as will provide a means of *possessing* an individual citizen without his knowledge, in short, a highly organized system of blackmail, operating almost omnipotently: "that's how real power is exercised and historical events are fabricated" (p. 212). In fact, Massart is so self-assured that he can say frankly to Pluvinage that all policemen are drawn from the ranks of life's failures, that Pluvinage himself has always been "a humiliated little wretch," and that "joining the police is like committing suicide" (p. 212). Rosenthal takes his own life; Pluvinage turns

[38] See Henri Lefebvre, *L'Existentialisme*, pp. 51-52.

informer: two forms of self-destruction after two abortive lives.

Utterly alone, Pluvinage confesses himself to his woman, who deserts him after striking him in the face. When he tells himself that "the discipline demanded of work in the police information service is as severe as Loyola's Spiritual Exercises" (p. 214), it is clear that he needs a new religion to devote himself to. His anguish does not slacken. He faces lucidly if impotently the suicidal choice he is making and which is being made for him: "Une dénonciation, ce n'est rien, c'est une phrase qu'on dit, mais c'est une métamorphose dans les profondeurs, une rupture: on est *hors l'être*, comme dit Montaigne des morts."[39] He has achieved that irreversibility which escaped Rosenthal until his death. But even now, like Sartre's Daniel, Pluvinage does not coincide with his duplicity, for treachery opens a crack in being. There is no issue, only a permanent trap. As Nizan once said of Dostoevski: he who is at home in moral decay is alien to revolution. After Pluvinage has committed himself to collaboration with the police, he sees without self-delusion that "winner takes nothing," and he reverses Massart's theory: "L'homme qui veut jouer l'histoire est toujours joué, on ne change rien par de petits moyens. La révolution est le contraire de la police."[40] At the end, he admits: "A terrible fate drags me back to my father's world" (p. 243). Rosenthal goes out, Laforgue gropes forward, Pluvinage regresses. His diary ends in confusion, but the logic of his dilemma has been powerfully conveyed throughout. This confession of "unavowable" resentments generates some of that holy horror provoked by any renegade. His position recalls that of the tortured man in Baudelaire's fragment, also

[39] "Informing on people is nothing, it's just a word; but deep down it's a complete transformation, a break with your previous life. As Montaigne said about the dead, you are *outside being*" (p. 241).

[40] "The man who tries to outwit history is always outwitted himself. Nothing is altered by petty means. Revolution is the opposite of the police force" (p. 243).

called *La Conspiration*, who is haunted by the idea of suicide, rediscovers a taste for living when he learns of a plot against the authorities, and ends by tossing up to decide whether to denounce the conspirators to the police. He says: "There was bitterness in my enjoyment of life." Through Pluvinage, Nizan warns that communism may "save" only those who devote themselves to it generously, and that it cannot be a foster home for the abandoned children of the bourgeoisie who refuse to grow up.

*La Conspiration* finishes not with Pluvinage's end-stopped position, but with Laforgue's inchoate transformation. The book, however, has dimensions other than that of individual case histories, first, that of public events.

One of the most invigorating memories the student group cherish is of the day in 1924 when Jaurès' ashes were transferred to the Panthéon. In Nizan's work, funerals reveal nakedly how men normally mask their true selves. The young students feel intense hostility toward the government officials at the ceremony who attempt to annex Jaurès to their camp. Nizan maintains an animated contrast between the anonymous but liquid crowd outside the doors, who treat the funeral as an occasion for joyous solidarity (it was in fact the first mass demonstration organized by the Communist Party), and the congealed notables inside, unsuccessfully wearing their public faces. As the notables proceed through the ocean of faces, there is a sustained and ironic parallel with the Parting-of-the-Waters. The waters threaten to engulf, the funeral turns into a protest, described in terms of blood flow. The youths feel buoyed up by the surging collective passions. Later in the book, the funeral of Marshal Foch, presented self-satirically from the viewpoint of the complacent upper bourgeoisie, provides a counterpoint. Throughout the novel, parallels between history and fiction, public and private life, serve as reciprocal commentaries. Chiasmus figures abound: leading Communists are arrested on inflated charges of espionage, while

173

Rosenthal and company carry out without sanctions their spying. Whereas the bourgeois fathers spout anecdotes on current
affairs, grow hard skins to ward off the news of distant suffering, and always apologize for "talking shop," their sons live
on their nerve ends and verbalize their problems without
qualms. Nizan never underestimates the power of conservative forces in society. Though farcical in manner, the police
mopping-up is an efficient operation. Poincaré speechifying to
a heckling crowd is reduced to a disarticulated dummy. But
the young men know in their bones that Poincaré heads a
France that is in a period of bourgeois quiescence, one of the
troughs of history, so that in desperation they feel obliged to
celebrate the Wall Street crisis as a foretaste of a French
upheaval.

The second extra-individual dimension is nature. Just as
Nizan always balanced public and private affairs, so he situ-
ates man in nature, for Marx's vision of an unconstrained
total man haunted him. The weather, the countryside have
their vital and more than decorative place in any account of
man. In the Panthéon district, some rustic elements survive
into the 1920s: cock-crows, occasionally a cow in the street, as
if to remind the urbanites, as Laforgue and Bloyé often remind themselves, of past links with the land. In Nizan's work,
as in most people's daily experience, the weather intrudes,
excites or casts down. Even well-insulated bourgeois families
do not feel immune to seasonal changes. In Normandy, the
Rosenthal clan "éprouvaient comme tout le monde une vague
angoisse devant toute cette végétation chuchotante, et ils
n'étaient pas fâchés de se retrouver dans la lumière protectrice
des lampes."[41] When Rosenthal himself visits Naxos to see his
sister, after being initially blinkered by cultural memories he
gradually learns to appreciate this self-contained landscape, just

[41] "experienced like most people a vague anguish in the face of all
that murmuring vegetation, and they were relieved to get back to the
protective glow of a lighted room" (p. 136).

as Nizan valued Epicurus' philosophical autarky. (These pages of *La Conspiration* show a Nizan less ironical and genuinely dazzled.) For Rosenthal it is a stalled moment of perfection in his frenetic life. As he enjoys his sister's charming frivolity, we see for the only time the hedgehog Rosenthal off his guard, at peace with a member of his family; and the natural setting has actively helped the relationship.

The third dimension is that of family life. Though the young men's families are treated often with derision, their influence is undeniable and ubiquitous, for example, "des enfants qu'on attendrissait sur les bêtes pour les endurcir sur les hommes."[42] Rosenthal's clan relies smugly on its cohesion and capacity for survival. Nizan indulges in a mocking and yet functional picture of their summer retreat to their Norman bolt-hole: their pompous pronouncements on nature and social hierarchies, and their envy of their neighbors who, as "captains of industry," frankly regard their employees as subhuman. When they meet to judge Rosenthal, the family is compared to prescient spiders, spinning webs of fantasies. The son refuses to enact the role of the Prodigal Son as expected of him. It is largely to escape such a frozen essence that he chooses to kill himself. When he is dead, the family instinctively curls up in a ball. Just as in *Les Chiens de garde* Nizan described the bourgeois view of Marxism as an alien malady, so here the family blames the death on some exterior agency. But the family survives the rebel. Nizan's bourgeois are not predictable, nor dissolvable by mere scorn: "Il n'y a pas de bourgeois en soi, c'est une espèce sociale infiniment ramifiée et très subtile."[43]

A further dimension is that of love and sex. The young

---

[42] "The children were encouraged to be sentimental about animals so that they would be hardhearted towards their fellow men" (p. 162).

[43] "There's no such thing as a quintessential bourgeois, because it's a social species with infinite and subtle ramifications." Nizan, "Ambition du roman moderne," p. 19.

men ridicule yet mix with their fellow bourgeois. Laforgue
has a half-hearted, and half-bodied, affair with a young dilet-
tante of the emotions. The "habit of analysis," the fear of the
real thing, push this girl into an area of monadic titillations.
As her elders practice the art of mental restrictions, so she reserves her body, in a form of sexual hoarding. In the opening
pages, Laforgue had been on the brink of a more frank experience, and on several later occasions the idea that prosti-
tutes are "the working women of a relaxed eroticism,"
stripped of theatrical fuss, knocks for admission. The private
miseries of bought flesh are compassionately evoked: "ces
gestes angoissants de coquetterie, d'humilité qu'ont les femmes
évéillées pour cacher un défaut de leurs seins, ou l'âge, ou les
signes mous du malheur."[44] Unashamed, Nizan often intrudes
to speak directly of love: "cette complicité de rire, d'érotisme,
de secrets partagés, de passé et d'espoir, cette union pareille à
un inceste permis, ce lien fort comme un lien venu de l'enfance et du sang."[45] His total commitment to emotional and
physical demands stands out strongly from such conjugations.
Honest and generous love would be one of the bases of that
more authentic life his young men strive to reach. The older
Régnier, too, is as much concerned with the problems of
established love, the *career* of love, as with those of writing
and politics.

With all its irony, this book is deeply serious. On the one
hand, Nizan in his blurb exclaims: "An adolescence as blind
and as absurd as theirs is very unusual." On the other, in the
novel itself he says these words, which give a clue to his appeal
to young minds today: "Un jeune homme se croit si mal établi

[44] "those distressing gestures of coquetry or humility that women
make when they're awake so as to hide some flaw of their breasts, their
age, or the flabby signs of unhappiness" (p. 21).

[45] "this complictiy made up of laughter, eroticism, shared secrets,
feelings about the past or hopes for the future, this relationship reminiscent of an authorized incest, this bond strong as childhood or blood
ties" (p. 194).

dans sa vie qu'il veut enchaîner l'avenir, obtenir des gages; il est le seul être qui ait le coeur de tout exiger et de se croire volé s'il n'a pas tout. Plus tard, il n'y aura plus que des contrats."[46] Nizan, who did not renege on his own youth, speaks from bitter experience. The writing of this novel was one way of keeping alive into maturity the meaning of his youth. Perhaps the dominant feature of his outlook was, from the beginning, a refusal of *establishment*, a constant vigilance, as if he lived permanently on enemy territory. The key words of *La Conspiration*: alibi, complicity, plot, password, are all terms connected with counterauthority activity. This is a world of meshed forces: Rosenthal versus his family, Laforgue against himself, the government seeking to muzzle the Communists. Subterfuge and struggle for survival predominate. Ideas clash as strongly as do personalities. Yet these hyperconscious young men never analyze themselves out of existence. And in case this novel might be considered dated, it should be stressed that France and other countries have not seen the last of intellectually precocious and family-ridden young men fretting against society's suffocation of their energies.

It could be that young minds respond to Nizan's tone, as to Stendhal's: the constant amused irony, the mixture of connivance and raillery at youth's operatic imaginings. In his letters to his wife from the front in 1940, Nizan often expressed his admiration for *La Chartreuse de Parme*, perhaps the epitome of the achieved political novel, balancing political and private passions. *La Conspiration*, like Stendhal's novel, depicts the conflict of quixotic youth and prudent middle age, and is equally obsessed with the vacillating communications between the young individual and his society. Of the denizens

---

[46] "A young man feels so insecure that he wants to imprison the future and get some reliable assurances; he's the only one with guts enough to demand everything and to think he's been robbed if he doesn't get it. When he's older, he'll settle for contracts" (p. 156).

of Parma, Nizan would prefer Mosca to the limp Fabrice and the extravagant Gina. Nizan within the Communist Party somewhat resembled Mosca within power politics, refusing its cant but partly contaminated by long exposure to it, and committing himself to what he felt to be both a social and a personal necessity.

Nizan's literary tact led him to choose for his area of study a tense period of recent French history, when opposing groups were lining themselves up with increasing clarity. Another member of the *Philosophies* group, later a leading expert— in the Party and outside it—on the problems of labor, Georges Friedmann, opted for a woollier context in his novel *L'Adieu*,[47] which might usefully be compared to *La Conspiration*. Friedmann's novel is slackly structured, almost invertebrate; its largely autobiographical material is insufficiently distanced by the author. Like Nizan's far more caustic *Aden-Arabie*, it is the complaint of a wounded sensibility and mind ("I will never forgive *them*"). The hero Jacques, as a *lycéen*, joins a Rollandist peace movement, and later goes to Italy, where he falls under the influence of Paul, a young disciple of Barrès and Gide who has clearly been cropping too long on their insubstantial "fruits of this earth" and their cult of the ego. Unattached, a spectator of life, a connoisseur of perfect moments, Paul gradually alienates Jacques, who discovers the need to draw distinctions between the various worlds present in society. Jacques rejects the goal of living life as a work of art and of using other people and places as a means to his ends. At the end, nebulously, he goes off to work "alongside his fellow men" on the side of the unexquisite underdog. Friedmann's extensive use of the first person and the present tense increases the impression of ingenuousness: everything is just that moment happening, and Jacques lacks perspective. As a backwards look on the twenties and the attitudes of

[47] Georges Friedmann, *L'Adieu*, Gallimard, 1932.

young educated malcontents, *L'Adieu* lacks the discrimination and the power of *La Conspiration*.

Critics are fond of drawing analogies between Nizan's novel and Barrès' *Les Déracinés*. One of the most important differences is that in *La Conspiration* it is not teachers who are held responsible for the young men's disorientation. They are answerable finally to themselves: a significant advance in maturity and likeliness, for all teachers know how ultimately impregnable students are. It is true that in *Aden-Arabie* Nizan does accuse the teaching body of almost leading the young astray with pervasive propaganda. But, by the time of *La Conspiration* the ball is back in the individual's court. A further difference is that Barrès made strident and dishonest attempts to discredit intelligence, whereas Nizan was concerned with the proper use of the mind. (He was fond of drawing cartoons which showed Spinoza booting Leibniz's behind.)

Nizan's novels form a bridge between the Stendhal type of fiction with its fluctuating emphasis on politics and the Orwell/Koestler type, almost completely dominated by politics. One way in which he keeps up a tension between the rival claims of politics and private life is by his great respect for opposition. There is a fair allocation of conflicting points of view. Nizan responded to the dialectical rather than to the totalitarian impulses of communism. The enemy is motivated and never abstract or puppet-like. Nobody comes off uncontested. Laforgue pricks Rosenthal's swollen intellectual jargon. And, Rosenthal is as much a cheat as Pluvinage, on whom he appropriately comments: "Which of us is not two-faced?" The notebooks of both the liberal Régnier and the crypto-fascist Pluvinage revolve around the problems of adhesion and direction of energy. This novel is both open-minded and open-ended. It was meant to be continued by *La Soirée à Somosierra* (the manuscript was lost when Nizan was killed), which would have shown Laforgue finding his feet during the Spanish Civil War and coping in Geneva with a complete

love affair. In his reviews Nizan repeatedly stressed his aversion to the "dead-end literature" (typified especially by Mauriac). So that Caute misreads when he remarks that *La Conspiration* ends "on a note of suicide and despair,"[48] just as Laforgue's mother misinterprets his tears of rebirth. The ending is neither tragic nor optimistic, but problematic. Nizan often endorsed Shaw's defense of "displeasing" literature, and attacked the smoothly flowing discourse of traditional analytical writers like Lacretelle. He was convinced that "we must not pander to the reader's worst instincts," but that, instead, the novelist must "point his complicity in the most challenging direction."[49] Such a view, which entails an honest persuasion of the reader, counteracts Sartre's dogmatic query about communist novelists and their responsibilities. For Nizan combines complicity and judgment. The first is often apparent in the very syntax, where the author's standpoint melts at times into that of the characters (". . . infidèle à son père qui a tant fait pour lui et qui ne se prive pas *mon Dieu* de le lui reprocher").[50] The judgment is conveyed by the constant irony and the unabashed readiness to generalize, which spring from his confidence. The generalizations serve to offset the various individual viewpoints, and, together with the unified tone, they provide the cohesion that occasionally appears lacking by reason of the number of central characters. As one critic remarked, Nizan's dogmatism is "an essential part of him, like the very marrow of his being."[51] At times, it must be admitted, complicity veers into condescension, confidence into flippant and irritating allusiveness. But this is the dross, the residue of snobbery, from any variety of elegance.

One of Simon's military judges is called Sartre. Nizan's

---

[48] Caute, *Communism*, p. 95.
[49] Nizan, "Ambition du roman moderne," p. 20.
[50] ". . . betraying his father who had done so much for him and who *damned well* never let him forget it" (p. 14).
[51] Jean Catesson, "Un Roman et ses personnages," p. 229.

friendship with his politically uncommitted friend clearly had its acid moments. Yet there was no rupture between them. Aragon and Henri Lefebvre, however, two erstwhile friends, lived to clamor Nizan's treachery when he left the Party. In their readings of this novel can be seen some of the problems Nizan, as a Communist writer, was up against. Aragon is quite blind to anything other than antibourgeois satire. Lefebvre petulantly dismisses *La Conspiration* as "a cold and desiccated caricature" of the *Philosophies* group at the École Normale Supérieure (whom he calls "the first-run existentialists of the earlier postwar period").[52] Now, it is probable that Rosenthal has in him elements of Politzer and Pierre Morhange (the André Breton of the clique, the deliverer of paltriness after vast promises); and it is likely that Nizan borrowed the central conspiracy from amongst the group's projects. But Rosenthal's liaison with Catherine is based on an intrafamily scandal. All writers exploit without mercy friends and relations. What is more, writing ten years after the group's disintegration, Nizan necessarily had to take the long view and exhibit hindsight. It is a fact that the group's activities misfired in practical terms. And it is the general phenomenon of youth making mistakes that Nizan analyzes, with honesty and without that mistaken fidelity that omits to judge on performance.

With all his faults of distortion, Sartre, of those who were close to Nizan, comes nearest to an accurate account of *La Conspiration*. But when he maintains that "its young people are not really fictional characters; they're not very active and they're hard to distinguish from each other," that this technique of presentation is deliberate, and that "Nizan would later make men of them," Sartre is yielding to that one-eyed belief (that made his *La Nausée* so brilliantly unjust) that characters whose values differ from those of their creator must be presented as interchangeable dummies. On Nizan's language, however, he strikes home: "these rhetorical sallies . . . suddenly pull up short and make way for a concise and icy epigram." But then again his dogma interferes: "It's not a novelist's style, full of secret allusions; it's a propaganda style, a weapon."[53] On the contrary, Nizan's style is that of a *combative novelist*. His target is clear, yet all is not subordinated to one aim; there is room for those "irrelevant" details that are the mark of the true novel. Unlike Gide, who employed symbols for the sake of indirectness, Nizan's symbols are there to reinforce his argument. Simply, he says what he thinks (which does not abolish mystery). The man who as a student dressed like a dandy writes like a nudist. *La Conspiration* is a densely-packed novel, intelligent, taut, generous, and partial. Its complexities correct the dogmatism Nizan often slipped into in his polemical writings, as when he asserted: "Since 1914, life has become public, the age of private life is over."[54] This novel proves in action how public and private lives intermingle and influence each other, yet it does not pretend that there is any final solution to their dialectical struggle, which is the very stuff of life itself. As Sartre said, "This revolutionary was singularly lacking in blindness."[55]

[53] Sartre, *"La Conspiration,"* p. 29.
[54] Nizan, *"Été 1914,"* p. 96.
[55] Sartre, "Paul Nizan," p. 181.

# CHAPTER SIX

# BREAKS AND FIDELITIES

IN THE projected novel *La Soirée à Somosierra*, Laforgue was to be involved in the Spanish Civil War. As a journalist for *La Correspondance internationale*, Nizan had made several trips to Spain just prior to the outbreak and shortly afterwards. In his series of articles for this journal, Nizan displayed Stendhalian powers of swift, evocative notation of what he had observed on the spot. Similarly, the tone adopted is a mixture of generosity and acidity. As in all his journalism, he appears extremely well informed of events and of their background. For instance, he makes a real effort to give a balanced account of local traditions of anarchism and libertarian communism. He writes hopefully about peasant attempts to collectivize farming in some areas. When the war broke out, his articles, while imbued with a certain lyrical rhetoric, looked beyond the immediate and necessary violence for signs of a coming permanent change, and not merely of an ephemeral holocaust. In November 1936, with Vaillant-Couturier, Romain Rolland, Gide, Sadoul, Politzer, Langevin, and Joliot-Curie, he signed a "Declaration by Republican Intellectuals on the Events in Spain." This group deplored the policy of nonintervention, took up Yvon Delbos' phrase, "neutrality must not be an illusion," and demanded the immediate renewal of trade relations with the Spanish Republican Government. In July 1937, Nizan attended a writers' congress in Madrid, then under bombardment, and was moved by the spirited morale of the people in a crisis. At Valencia, he told a colleague that he felt at home in such a revolution, and that he did not feel cut off from comprehension of what was happening, as he often did in Russia. It might be wondered whether, here again, Nizan was in a way lucky to be in on the early days, before the Stalinist take-over bid acquired momentum and the shaky Republican solidarity began to disintegrate entirely.

Throughout 1938, Nizan was very busy writing on foreign affairs and reviewing books for *Ce Soir*, which he codirected with Aragon. Like his friend, the Communist deputy Gabriel Péri, he expended a great deal of energy warning of the threatening growth of Hitler's power and ambitions. His analysis of the international situation stressed the need for Britain and France to take positive action on Central European affairs, so as to avoid "another Spain." He followed in detail the crumbling of Austrian resistance. On the League of Nations, his commentary centered on the elaborate word games and the perpetual procrastination of the gathered diplomats. He was very alert to the problems of reading between the lines and of collating; and his little pen portraits of the chief speakers read like initial drafts for his planned novel *La Soirée à Somosierra*. As a member of the Party, he had obviously to follow the official line on matters connected with the U. S. S. R. Thus, when Anglo-Italian negotiations were started, he emphasized that France must stand by her earlier pact with Russia and have no truck with any anti-Soviet coalition the British might be hatching. As well as examining the details of each nation's dilemmas, he was convinced that Europe as a whole represented an interconnected war problem. With Yvon Delbos, he visited Poland, Czechoslovakia, Rumania, and Yugoslavia. He was scathing in his denunciation of the British tactic of "gentlemen's agreements" and her policy of "wait and see." He went to London in April 1938 to cover the talks between Daladier, Bonnet, and Lord Halifax. Alexander Werth, in his account of his meeting with Nizan, reports that Nizan remarked: "Daladier is made all of one piece—he is a bit of a rustic, and quite simple to understand. Bonnet is a much more intricate character, full of funny complexes. . . . He is a man who wants to be loved and who suffers at the thought that he is not lovable. . . . Instead of friends, he has 'contacts'; he is very intelligent, very ambitious—and thoroughly hard-boiled. . . . His wife is known as 'Soutien-Georges.' "[1] Werth considered this young Frenchman, blessed with a sense of humor and a novelist's eye for the motivation of character, a first-rate commentator on the events and personalities of foreign affairs.

As the Czech crisis bloated up, Nizan continued to harp on the evils of secret diplomacy, and to call on France and Britain to act more clearly and forcibly on the Sudeten problem. When the Munich agreement was signed, Nizan wrote in *Ce Soir*: "It is not merely a question of recording the loss of Czech friendship, but of grasping that the whole system of French security has just collapsed. A diplomatic disaster has occurred."[2] On the Munich question, the Communists found themselves in strange company. In addition to *Ce Soir* and *L'Humanité*, the only French papers to criticize the policy of appeasement were the right-wing *L'Ordre* and *L'Époque*, the mainstream *L'Oeuvre*, and (Beuve-Méry in) the conservative *Le Temps*. All of these disparate voices denounced both Hitler's elaborate psychological campaign aimed at emasculating French willpower, and the French collapse in the face of what these critics imagined to be Hitler's enormous bluff. In the French Chamber, after the signing of the agreement, only seventy-five deputies voted disapproval: the seventy-three Communists, a Socialist, and Kérillis, a right-wing columnist on *L'Epoque*. Meanwhile, the crowds outside were hysterical with relief over "peace in our time." The Communists were going out on a limb, and it seems in the main true to say that, in the late thirties, "the Communist Party was behind the times in national affairs and ahead of them in international affairs."[3]

Nizan too found himself in unusual company. He praised

---

[1] Alexander Werth, *France and Munich*, pp. 134-35.

[2] Nizan, *Ce Soir*, 4 October 1938, p. 6.

[3] Jacques Fauvet, *Histoire du parti communiste français*, vol. I, p. 218.

Montherlant's caustic attack on French cowardice in his *L'Équinoxe de septembre*. Nizan responded to Montherlant's insulting wit, his effort to displease, his honesty. Montherlant rejects the label of "warmonger," affixed by proappeasers on those like himself who cried out against the failure of France to assert herself at Munich: "It's not a matter of proclaiming that we prefer peace. It's a matter of being strong enough to impose peace on those who want war. And this strength has been sapped of its power in our country by claptrap like this."[4] An aggregate of inertias, he remarks, makes up a terrible force; and peoples get the governments they deserve. This writer, famous for his celebration of individual toughness both in opinions and in the body, had received from Nizan, earlier in 1938, a similarly sympathetic review of *Les Olympiques*. Nizan detected in Montherlant's corporal lyricism something healthy, something that could be compared to Greek physical sanity. In his writings on Epicurus, Nizan had stressed the need to develop the total resources, bodily and mental, of the human person. And, though no sportsman himself, in *Aden-Arabie* he had praised the English cult of leisure-time activities. In the midst of his foreign affairs reporting for *Ce Soir*, he took some time off in July 1938 to cover the "Tour de France." It was in many ways a revelation. "Il est admirable de se sentir absolument profane, de tomber de je ne sais quelle lune diplomatique, quand on connaît quelques secrets lunaires, dans un univers violent dont on ignore tout, les lois, les conventions, les moeurs, les langages: je tombe dans le Tour de France comme il y a dix ans en Arabie du Sud, comme il y a quatre ans dans le Pamir."[5] The tone is one of elegant ex-

---

[4] Henry de Montherlant, *L'Équinoxe de septembre*, p. 142.

[5] "It's splendid to feel yourself completely one of the crowd, to get out of the diplomatic ivory tower in possession of some of its secrets and to enter a violent world whose laws, mores, and language are all quite unknown to you. I'm stumbling into the Tour de France as I stumbled into South Arabia ten years ago and the Pamir range four years ago." Nizan, *Ce Soir*, 15 April 1937.

hilaration and yet fellow feeling, as he reports on the circus and funfair atmosphere of the event. Searching for the basic meaning of the exercise, he remarks: "the only thing in the world which seems to me to be really serious is the war waged by man on Nature," and he describes the squad of cyclists instinctively forming a triangle against a high wind, like migrating birds. Less honorably but no less genuinely, the spectators' observation of other people's suffering also plays a part in the general phenomenon of the race. Nizan is excited: he is discovering France and rediscovering, in particular, Brittany. All he saw, little or big dramas, alternating go-slow stages and violent surges, provided real nourishment to a man "usually caught up in more abstract permutations." The whole venture was a holiday and a lesson. Nizan never stopped learning, or relearning, from his experiences.

*Ce Soir* probably owed its existence to the energy of Willy Muenzenberg, the creator of the "front organization" corralling writers, scientists, and artists sympathetic to Russia, and of the "International Workers' Aid" fund, which helped to finance such schemes. *Ce Soir* had at its disposal a splendid body of contributors in addition to Nizan and Aragon: Jean Renoir on films, Robert Desnos reviewing records, Darius Milhaud on concerts, Andrée Viollis as roving reporter. It ran an open forum in which Attlee, Duff Cooper, Duclos, Radicals, and farmers' spokesmen took part. Aragon for some time wrote a column entitled "One Day in the World," a synoptic view of world news. Nizan, in addition to his foreign affairs coverage, reviewed books of all varieties in a fashion far more freewheeling than on *L'Humanité* in the early thirties. He could display his cultural perceptiveness with no apologies and with elegance. He could continue his indictment of "official" philosophy. Most of his journalism is factual, well informed, balanced, soberly but wittily expressed. In the preface to his *Chronique de septembre*—a post-mortem examination of the Munich crisis—he analyzes his own journalistic standards. His

187

main argument is that foreign correspondents must act like historians, though the tempo of research, clearly, is vastly accelerated. There is, he admits, always a strong element of risk, of gambling, as there is one of distortion. But even lies inform: the wishes of interested parties are also historical facts. Nizan is yet again blowing the gaff, voicing what most people know or suspect but prefer to hush up. The seeker after truth in foreign affairs must "take account of the personal variations of the correspondent and the collective variations of the news agency. This critique of sources and of reliability is well-nigh endless."[6] He is fully alive to the corporate nature of journalistic information: like novels or poems, newspapers feed off each other. They are linked externally to events but internally to products like themselves. He points out that the policies of newspapers are more overt than those of news agencies. In the end, he is forced to acknowledge that his prescriptions are ideals and that only approximation to them is feasible. A combination of psychology, detective work, and the magic powers of Lesage's prying demon would be the ideal, but at least the actual journalist must know when he is simplifying. At the end, he quotes Fustel de Coulanges (a fellow Breton, taciturn, honored by the Action Française, yet the author of *L'Histoire des institutions politiques de l'ancienne France*, which antagonized officialdom): "History does not solve problems; it teaches us how to study them." History, Nizan remarks, is often discontinuous. Only a flexible mind can hope to cope with it. In his journalism he managed in the main to keep his mind open.

The amount of free thought which he retained was put to its severest test in August 1939, when Stalin and Hitler signed their nonaggression pact, which created an almost impossible situation for the French Communist Party. It was a pact not only of nonaggression, but also of division of booty: Poland

---

[6] Nizan, *Chronique de septembre*, p. 10.

188

was due to go to the same fate as Czechoslovakia's a year earlier, except that she would be doubly raped, by West and East. After the announcement of the pact, there was no editorial in *L'Humanité* by Thorez, no articles by Duclos or Péri, as might have been expected in the case of an event of such magnitude. It was left to an assistant editor to comment on the pact, which he approved as serving the interests of peace and French security! This nonparticipation by the Party's leading spokesmen in *L'Humanité* and the inept and flabby *Ce Soir* editorial by Aragon, whose distorted syntax betrays his disarray, his persistent funambulism and mystifications ("Put a gag on the pack of anti-Soviet hounds. . . . The day has come when people will have to realize that something has changed in the world and that because of the U. S. S. R. countries cannot just make war how they like.")[7]—these speak for themselves. Not all French Communist reactions in favor of the pact, however, can be ascribed to such duplicity. Some were due to a weird simplemindedness, evident in this testimony from a Party official who eventually broke away, Auguste Lecoeur: "In 1939, matters were quite simple for a Communist. The capitalist countries had tried to lead the U. S. S. R. into an ambush, and just in time the U. S. S. R. had turned the tables on them."[8] A partial history of the French Communist Party, by Gérard Walter, quotes in justification of Stalin's maneuver Lenin's letter to American workers in 1918. In this letter, Lenin declares that he made contact with a French monarchist officer, when German troops were directed against Russia, with a view to expedient collaboration. Similarly, Lenin adds, he would not hesitate to side with the Germans if French or British troops were used against Russia: "Those who believe in the proletarian revolution only if it plays fair and square are not real revolutionaries."[9] But

[7] Louis Aragon, *Ce Soir*, 22 August 1939, p. 3.

[8] Auguste Lecoeur, *Le Partisan*, p. 117.

[9] Gérard Walter, *Histoire du parti communiste français*, p. 357.

French Communists could appreciate Stalin's motives from the point of view of Russian self-protection, though not from that of foreign Communist parties which were thereby left in the lurch. Before the end of August, Communist deputies were excluded from the Commission for Foreign Affairs in the Chamber, and shortly afterwards others resigned or were arrested. *L'Humanité*, *Ce Soir*, and *Regards* had already been seized. Events took another violent turn, when Hitler invaded Poland and France was dragged into war. In the Chamber, the Communists applauded Daladier's patriotic speeches and voted extra military budgets. Thorez and other leading Communists joined their regiments. None of this was in accord with Stalin's plans. The French Party was deluding itself but no one else. For Stalin, as the Party was later obliged to admit, the war *was* a war between two forms of imperialism, in which Russia had no part (at least as long as she was not threatened). It took the French Party several weeks to catch up with the official line dictated by Moscow: a refusal to participate in an imperialists' war. As Fauvet puts it, the Party was forced to move from "national defense" to "revolutionary defeatism."[10]

Where does Nizan stand on this whole complex issue? He had said to Werth in June 1939: "Our governments are mishandling these Moscow talks; but, honestly, these Moscow chaps seem a mighty queer bunch; and I wish I knew what they were really up to."[11] Nizan was away on holiday in Corsica when the news broke of the pact. He had met Sartre and Simone de Beauvoir in Marseilles a month earlier—the last time they were to see him alive. At that point, he was cheerful and convinced that a tripartite pact between France, Britain, and Russia would be signed to counter Hitler's threat. Three weeks later, when Merleau-Ponty met him in Corsica, Nizan was no longer confident that the enemy could be

---

[10] Fauvet, *Histoire*, vol. 2, p. 40.
[11] Werth, *New Statesman and Nation*, 2 December 1939, p. 12.

checked without a long struggle. He was appalled by Aragon's articles. After the pact, he published nothing himself. In fact, as he was in the first group for mobilization, he was soon called up in early September. On 25 September he sent a letter to *L'Oeuvre* (the one paper to protest against the seizure of *L'Humanité*), which published the following announcement: "Paul Nizan, ex-student at the École Normale Supérieure, *agrégé*, in charge of the foreign affairs section of the newspaper *Ce Soir*, has just sent to M. Jacques Duclos, vice-president of the National Assembly, the following letter: 'I am sending you my resignation from the French Communist Party. My present situation as a soldier of the French Army prevents me from adding anything further to these few lines.'" The tone is drily factual. Nizan published nothing by way of self-justification for his decision. What dictated his gesture? For Merleau-Ponty, it was the idea that years of work devoted to antifascism and to persuading his compatriots that the French Party was indeed French in outlook and behavior could be so easily turned to derision. "To get past the pact in the accepted way, Nizan would have to have been a mere dummy and be shattered in the process. And he did not become a Communist so as to enjoy being cynical."[12] For his part, Sartre brushes aside the political reasons for his act which Nizan offered privately later, and opts for his own "metaphysical" interpretation, his view of Nizan as a permanent adolescent who, after witnessing the sorry spectacle of a father robbed and mystified by superiors, was himself lied to by the Party hierarchy and thereupon regressed to his initial position of anarchic revolt. Such a view presupposes a Nizan flawed with some original sin of secession, some inability to really adhere to a group. It is hard to imagine how an intelligent man with allegedly itchy feet could stay put for eleven years. To approach the real reasons for Nizan's resig-

---

[12] Maurice Merleau-Ponty, *Signes*, p. 43.

nation, we must look at what he wrote in his letters from the front.

Nizan had an international outlook, and never exhibited that chauvinism that Party spokesmen often opportunistically displayed. He must have had doubts about the wholehearted-ness of the French will to resist Germany, but, given the logic of his position, after preaching for years the need to fight fas-cism with every means, he could only continue to play his own part in that combat. In the army, he soon met a good number of Communists in the ranks who shared his basic hostility to the mess created by Russia and ignobly endured by the French Party, and who felt like him that the only thing left was to join in the fight against Hitler. Nizan's first book, *Aden-Arabie*, is identical in intention with his last political act: a confession of a mistaken faith, a deflation of an illusion he had held himself. He had the courage of his convictions, and it might well be that it needs more courage to divorce an illusion than to espouse one. The pact was the last straw, the final alienation. Apart from the support of fellow Communists in the army, Nizan also received sympathetic letters from Gabriel Péri, who had been hit hard by the pact, and who would later, according to some accounts, keep up only very strained relations with the Party.

In his letters from the army, it is clear that Nizan's act of resignation was not a headstrong impulse, but a calculation. He was immediately concerned with the consequences of the pact, the future of Communism in France, and the need for the reconstruction of a ruined organization. He never ceased to think of himself as a communist after leaving the Party, and was caustic about orthodox Stalinists, who "confuse faith-fulness with dumb acquiescence to the hierarchy's views. They're a bit too apostolic and Roman" (20 December 1939). He was sure that the first essential was to understand the situ-ation without blinkers, but equally sure that all political crises are infinitely complicated: "It's a great mass of triple or quadruple permutations" (24 October 1939). As he pointed out, to decipher what was happening Marx's *Complete Works* were of less use than Voltaire's *Histoire de Charles XII*, than Clausewitz or Lenin. Repeatedly, he asserted that he did not leave the Party for ethical motives, but on the contrary because the *French* Communist Party had lacked the necessary political cynicism, "the political power to lie," to *put on a show* of disassociation from Stalin's strategy. This Russian strategy of self-protection was perfectly comprehensible to Nizan, though he was naturally repelled by the kind of logic that had to be paid for in French lives. And Polish ones. The Russian invasion of eastern Poland struck him as naked and unjustifiable *Realpolitik*. Faithful Party men like Moussinac who appeared to have "a good conscience *because* they're beaten" seemed to him particularly laughable. He appreciated easy consciences only in conquerors or in defeated people who have previously tried all means to win. In all, he protested, "scruple mongers make me sick" (22 October 1939). He told his wife, also a Party member, that she had no need to feel herself answerable to the Party. (His wife was in fact instructed by Moussinac to disassociate herself from her husband. She refused.) As Nizan reminded her, they were not alone. Péri, Luc Durtain, Malraux, Jacques Kayser, Louis Martin-Chauffier, Geneviève Tabouis, Sartre, Mandel were just some of the many and varied holders of political opinions who exchanged letters with Nizan during his last months. In January of 1940, Nizan could say: "Despite what people usually say, glory be to those who provoke scandals." His humor did not desert him in this testing period; he describes the snow as "unsure of itself and ambiguous, like everything that's happened these last few months" (14 December 1939).

If he had survived the collapse of the French Army, in what activity would Nizan have involved himself? Of his correspondents, Péri, Martin-Chauffier, and André Ullmann were all deported to Germany: Nizan seemed instinctively drawn to the resisters. Would he have joined in ideological resistance, like his old friend Georges Politzer, who was later to be executed by the Gestapo? Early in 1941, Politzer's virulently anti-Nazi pamphlet *Révolution et contre-révolution au XXe siècle* was circulating in France. It was a counterattack on the "spiritual colonization" represented by Rosenberg, a *Reichsleiter* in charge of ideological indoctrination, who in a speech in Paris declared his intention of settling accounts with "the philosophy of 1789." Rosenberg's twin themes were blood and gold. The first stood for the mystique of the German master race, and the second, for the plutocracy in the rest of the world that Germany would annihilate. Politzer denounced Nazism as a gigantic and lethal advertising campaign whose copy had to be unremittingly knocked by its competitors. Its racialism pointed to its regression towards obscurantism. Nizan, with his experience of "countereducation," could easily be visualized joining in such demystification drives as those of Politzer. But would he have been given the chance? In the Resistance, the Communists learned to cooperate with Socialists, Radicals, Catholics, and many others. But those they considered renegades were another matter altogether. We will see later their lasting hatred for those who left their ranks, for whatever motive.

In the army, Nizan was by no means solely occupied with going over the pact and his break with the Party. He was much concerned, as always, with the behavior of writers. The contributions of Maurois and Mauriac to *Paris-Soir* struck him as pure comedy: all these at-home scribblers writing while feigning to wear woolen socks so as to imaginatively share the common soldier's lot. As Nizan commented: "For my part, war would be more likely to make me want to write books while wearing silken hose" (7 October 1939). He thought of writing a *Chronique de septembre II*, "from the point of view of the historian and the mystified soldiers in the army" (15 October 1939); and he praised "Pertinax" in

194

*L'Europe nouvelle* for "the first nonabsurd views on the war I've come across." In contrast, Giraudoux in his broadcasts was trying hard, Nizan felt, to "invent the genre of novelettish propaganda" (30 September 1939). Nizan was fully alive to the whole deadly farce of the Phony War, and his observations on military life were clear-eyed.

His strabismus excused him from combat duty, and at first he was attached to a regiment of Pioneers near Strasburg, acting as a kind of annalist of the military operations. He recalled Racine's post as royal historiographer, but notes drily that he himself has little to chronicle, except the demise of a pack horse. The "mad military world" described in *La Conspiration* is reborn when he tells the anecdote of the head of army supplies who decreed that all the men were to be equipped with umbrellas: "And thus the tactic of the umbrella squad is reborn, reduced to individual proportions. We ought to acknowledge this homage paid to the individual by mass society" (21 October 1939). His tone is witty and light as he talks of the officers, the moderate discomforts and privations of soldiers at a front where nothing is happening. Yet he remarks that the average soldier seems ill-resigned to being "the raw material of secret diplomacy" and remaining inactive. In this war of nerves, they would almost welcome frank battles. In his frequent spare time, he enjoyed reading the limericks of Edward Lear and Lewis Carroll, from whom he quotes "curiouser and curiouser," adding: "This whole business is lit up by an absurd comedy reminiscent of *The Man who was Thursday*" (28 October 1939). But at the same time the meanings of words had changed, and this war was something radically new. Because of censorship but also by reason of temperamental preference, Nizan often slips in "a word to the wise," as he talks elliptically, allusively, uses initials, and so on. Stendhal's *La Vie de Henry Brulard* is his breviary, and he speaks warmly of *La Chartreuse de Parme*. He betrays some envy of this novel in which Fabrice, even when he was in prison, had Clélia at hand, messages from La Sanseverina, and a panorama of the Alps: "Prison is nothing. It's vacuum that's terrible—and repetitiveness" (9 January 1940). Unlike his friend Sartre, he had always loathed Kierkegaard and German phenomenology, but he now finds himself in the depersonalized world of Heidegger's system, and his loathing is reinforced. Now that he is confined to stasis, he refutes Pascal's injunction to sit still alone in a room, which he had quoted with approval in *Aden-Arabie*. He remarks that the army command shows concern for the morale of its men, but wonders whether this concern goes deep enough, since "even peasants have to come to terms with the void, the mystery of time, just like Kafka" (9 January 1940). A few weeks later, he wrote: "Perhaps I'm mistaken in envisaging an entirely Kafkaesque kind of world where I would have to be subjected to a process of 'purification' and 'expiation,' and all sorts of ordeals. But I'll always have a certain persecution complex" (29 February 1940). It is difficult to know how well informed Nizan was of the campaign of defamation then under way, organized against him by the Party. Perhaps, simply, he knew the orthodox reflexes well enough not to be under any illusions about his own reputation once he had definitively marked his distances. As well as mythological allusions to "expiation" and so on, he makes frequent reference to literature. The mysterious distillation of news by the authorities is likened to the enigmatic world of Villiers de l'Isle Adam. While making such comparisons, Nizan recognizes them as a kind of private luxury: "Perhaps I'm the only one, with my professional deformation, who can extract some kind of consolation from that sort of allusion" (4 November 1939). He expresses doubts, too, about the validity of the novel he is writing, but in general he sticks to his old and rooted belief that "the novel is an instrument of knowledge," a means of understanding more acutely both himself and the world of other men.

In a situation where there was one big danger, and not multiple nibbling responsibilities and distractions, he found at first a peace conducive to work. Yet later he confesses that hibernation is fine for cold-blooded animals, but not for soldiers or novelists. On the whole, he got on well with his writing of what he called alternately *La Soirée à Somosierra* and *Les Amours de septembre*. He was projecting a third volume (the first being *La Conspiration*), which would cover the first months of the war. The second volume was devoted to the attempts of Laforgue and a reformed Catherine to sustain a love affair while coping with the events of the Spanish Civil War and Geneva and elsewhere in Europe. In one letter, Nizan quotes a scene where Laforgue phones Catherine from Cracow, saying: "There are too many listening posts between us. In Europe even people in love are spied upon" (15 April 1940). He was obsessed particularly with technical problems, but admitted that it was difficult for him to talk of his novel, or to write like Gide a *Journal des Faux-Monnayeurs*: "No novelist splits himself in two less than I do" (15 April 1940). In other words, Gide's cat-and-mouse games were not for him: he needed to be totally present and involved in his fiction. He was very conscious of his own inability to invent. Everything he wrote is strongly marked by personal experience. The experience of writing clearly meant a great deal to him at this time, and no doubt, if he had survived the war, he would have been as devoted to novel-writing as to politics. He was also planning a book of short stories based on the region: the miners, their families, and the local bourgeoisie.

After much petitioning, he got himself transferred in March 1940 to a British regiment, the Fourteenth Army Field Workshop, as an interpreter and liaison agent. Though often tired of having to "live in English," in the main he enjoyed the civilized company, the comradely atmosphere. He translated for the officers when they went to buy expensive perfumes for their wives, and for the engineers repairing septic tanks. He was with this regiment in May 1940 when, while in an upstairs room, he was shot in the head by a stray bullet. In *Le Cheval de Troie* he had written: "While they are alive, people think of houses as protection against death; if the doors and windows are closed, it can't get in." Most of the officers were also killed and several hundred prisoners were taken in this battle at Audruicq (Pas-de-Calais). One of the prisoners, a sergeant, buried Nizan's manuscripts on his way to a POW camp in Germany; they have never been recovered.

Nizan's instinct that his name would be persecuted proved justified. Though his position at the outbreak of the war was certainly shared by other leading Communists (e.g., Péri, Cachin, and Jacques Sadoul (the Paris correspondent of *Izvestia*) also believed that France's safety and independence must come first), Nizan was denounced by Thorez. In an article in *Die Welt* (the successor to *La Correspondance internationale* and published in Stockholm), Thorez maintained that in August 1939, "under the cover of a plan for collaboration with bourgeois newspapers so as to get round the legal veto on the Communist press, Nizan was spreading the idea of a 'National Communism.' In other words, communism in word but nationalism in deed."[13] This sounds like a gross travesty of Nizan's idea that the French Communist Party should have behaved in a more Machiavellian fashion at the time of the pact. The same accusation that Nizan was a traitor, along with the dissident Communist deputies, was taken up in a clandestine Party pamphlet in early 1941. Some of these dissident deputies were murdered after the war by Communist *maquisards*. Would Nizan, if he had survived the war, have escaped their fate? Party memories and grudges were long-term. The rumor was spread that Nizan had informed on his ex-comrades to the Ministry of the Interior. As Rossi notes, this was a late invention, as the Party press never men-

---

[13] Maurice Thorez, "Les Traîtres au pilori," p. 12.

tioned it before the liberation.[14] The man who had in fact acted as a police spy was Marcel Gitton, a Party secretary, about whose double game the Party had been informed by Albert Bayet in 1935, but whom it had not decided to liquidate until late 1941. (Nizan himself had serious doubts about Gitton's genuineness.) Because Nizan had friends outside the Party, when he left it he was accused by means of the technique of "the amalgam" (you can tell a man by the company he keeps) and the linked theories of "objective guilt" and "consequentiality" much used at the Moscow Trials. These theories assumed that the accusers needed only the proof that the accused's ideas could lead logically to the acts they contain in embryo.

These various methods of calumny were used with some expertise by Nizan's former friend Henri Lefebvre in his book *L'Existentialisme*, which appeared in 1946. Lefebvre describes Nizan as "solitary, lucid, desperate, supremely detached,"[15] and the *Philosophies* group as wondering what his terrible secret was. (This was 15 years before Nizan's break with the Party.) His secret, according to Lefebvre, was treachery: Antoine Bloyé betrays the class he stemmed from; Pluvinage informs on his comrades; Lange joins the fascists. Further, *La Conspiration* itself is a long betrayal of Nizan's fellow students, and, like Drieu la Rochelle's *Gilles*, is a false testimony. Throughout *L'Existentialisme*, which is otherwise concerned with demolishing Sartre's pretensions of philosophical innovation by maintaining that existentialism had been begotten already by the *Philosophies* group in the 1920s, Lefebvre sustains a deliberate parallel (often implicit) between Nizan's shifty activity and the noble career of Georges Politzer, who died heroically under torture at the hands of the Gestapo. In 1946, a man of the Resistance (even if it took the Party a couple of years or more after the outbreak of war to realize the

---

[14] A. Rossi, *Physiologie du parti communiste français*, p. 442.
[15] Henri Lefebvre, *L'Existentialisme*, p. 17.

need for resistance) was obviously superior to a serving member of the defeated French Army who also happened to have been killed. Lefebvre protests later (in *La Somme et le reste*) against the official telescoping of Politzer's life to the moment of his death in prison, and rants against the "mystification, moral blackmail and ideological swindling," behind such a distortion.[16] Much the same could be said of *his* version of Nizan, which makes out that the man who worked to understand the mainsprings of treachery must have been a traitor himself. Nizan's understanding of the Party's enemies was held against him. In this later book, *La Somme et le reste*, written after his exclusion from the Party, Lefebvre admits that *L'Existentialisme* "is not a good book. Not because it's insincere but because I wrote it out of defiance."[17] Such word juggling reveals no desire for authentic self-criticism, and he makes no attempt to reopen "the Nizan affair." The jesuitry of his attitudes is revealed in the following description of an official self-criticism to which he once submitted: "I backed down without backing down while backing down." Perhaps the best rejoinder to Lefebvre's accusation of Nizan's treachery came from that splendid rogue elephant, René Étiemble: "My dear Lefebvre, prove to me that from the time you used to have dealings with him as an existentialist Nizan stank of treachery. If you can't, leave him in peace! For the sake of your beliefs I must hope that you can't find any proof, for, if you had sensed for years that Nizan was the police spy he's supposed to be, what were you doing in his company? And if the Party for years was proud of an informer, who are we to blame except the Party's blindness, or its complicity?"[18]

Aragon, who was probably the source of the calumnies against Nizan, joined in the act after the war. (Perhaps he had heard that Nizan wrote in a letter, 8 April 1940, about

[16] Lefebvre, *La Somme et le reste*, p. 421.
[17] *Ibid.*, p. 511.
[18] René Étiemble, *Hygiène des lettres*, p. 123.

Aragon's *Les Voyageurs de l'impériale*, which had been appearing in the *N. R. F.* until Drieu took over its direction: "Aragon's novel bores the pants off me.") After the Liberation, at an exhibition of writers' works of the previous six years, Aragon threw a fit when he saw Nizan's books on display; he hurled them to the floor, and no one had the guts to protest.[19] In 1949, he published a volume of his novel cycle, *Les Communistes*, in which Nizan figures as a journalist, Patrice Orfilat. The general tone is one of snide gossiping, allegations of marital infidelity and of blue funk at the approach of war. Orfilat is principally worried about not getting his wages from the newspaper that employs him if its management finds out his psychic disarray over the pact. He goes to the Ministry of Foreign Affairs and, amid tears, begs for "a little job" there. Later, a crippled old *Humanité* newsvendor, about to be beaten up by *Action Française* thugs, appeals to Orfilat for help, but Orfilat, like the Pharisee, passes quickly on the other side of the street. Lastly Orfilat visits Felzer (i.e., Politzer), a Party militant who is unmoved by events and is carrying on as usual with his work. Felzer quotes the example of Barbey d'Aurevilly's spying for the Versailles authorities on the Communards in 1871, and concludes: "Whatever he's written so far will be henceforth traitor's literature, spy's literature."[20] When Orfilat finally stammers out that Stalin has played a dirty trick on them all, Felzer orders him angrily to shut up and to leave at once. Rossi is quite right to speak of Aragon's "sadistic imagination" in the creation of such a monstrous parody, and of "his virtuosity in the 'dialectic' of lying for which he is by nature and to a high degree gifted."[21] Auguste Lecoeur produces further evidence of Aragon's total unscrupulousness, when he tells how Aragon asked him for

[19] Rossi, *Physiologie*, p. 442.
[20] Aragon, *Les Communistes*, p. 171.
[21] Rossi, *Les Communistes français pendant la drôle de guerre*, pp. 20, 42.

information on a militant's activities during 1940. Lecoeur told him the man had deserted his post. But, as Aragon had promised Jeanette Vermeersch that he would draw a flattering portrait of this militant, he willfully falsified the information provided by Lecoeur and used this untrue version in *Les Communistes*.[22]

In 1957, the posthumous trial was still going on. There is an equally grotesque portrait of Nizan in Simone Téry's *Beaux enfants qui n'hésitez pas* (the title is a line from an Aragon poem). This is a silly book, of embarrassing naïveté and romanticism, published by the Communist "Éditeurs français réunis." Nizan appears, virtually unrecognizable, as Pierre Dumont, a Party member who initiates the heroine, a bourgeois intellectual leading an empty life, into the meaning of communism. Dumont is drawn to her, almost succumbs, flinches back, and finally withholds his love. He dies at Madrid in the International Brigade, after fleeing from the passion he aroused. The term "literature of wish fulfilment" takes on its full meaning in this novel. It is impossible to picture Nizan euologizing Thorez, as Dumont does. But then Simone Téry herself, in *L'Humanité*, was wont to harp on the theme of Thorez as "our leader . . . this born leader." Nizan is extensively trivialized in this version, which presents him as emerging "straight out of a Cornelian world, a world where everyone made a simple sacrifice of his love life, his career, his happiness, his life, so as to lead an existence of grandiose humility."[23] This self-propelling, self-indulgent gush of words misrepresents Nizan as totally as does Aragon's small-minded viciousness. But, on the other hand, Nizan himself would not have quibbled over the conclusion, in which the heroine is rescued from suicide and given friendly therapy by the Party: "The Party is something quite different from Pierre Dumont."

It was Nizan's friend Sartre who took charge of his defense

[22] Lecoeur, *Le Partisan*, p. 150.
[23] Simone Téry, *Beaux enfants qui n'hésitez pas*, p. 157.

after the war. He informed Henriette Nizan of the rumors spread around Communist circles by Aragon that Nizan was a police spy. She wrote to Aragon, to Thorez, and received no reply. She went to see Laurent Casanova at the "Ministère des Anciens Combattants" who replied with sibylline threats: "I advise you not to take any steps whatsoever against the Party."[24] Sartre collected an impressive list of protesters, and they sent a collective demand to the French Communist Party, via the Comité national des Écrivains, requesting proof of its accusations. The letter was signed by Aron, Breton, Benda, Caillois, Camus, Merleau-Ponty, Mauriac, Brice Parain, and Jean Paulhan. The challenge went unanswered. In *Qu'est-ce que la littérature*, Sartre declared that the writer who joins the Communist Party and writes for it is not only presumed guilty but is also laden "with all its past sins, since his name is linked with all the Party's mistakes, and he is the scapegoat of every political purge."[25] Later, Sartre was to feel excessive guilt at not having resisted the calumny against Nizan with enough vigor. It may be that he tried to make up for this imagined failure by depicting in his *Les Chemins de la liberté*, in the character of Vicarios, and to some extent in that of Brunet, his own version of the "real" Nizan.

If, in the following section, I assume that Sartre's novels are *romans à clefs*, it is not out of naïveté but because there is ample proof that Sartre's memory and imagination are haunted by Nizan, and that he tends to plunder his immediate circles of close friends and close enemies for his fictional material. As Mathieu is in many ways a parody of Sartre himself, so perhaps Brunet, as well as standing for the type of dogmatic Party man from which Sartre felt alien, might represent the more categorical aspects of Nizan's outlook. Physically, with his beefy build and red hair, Brunet sounds much closer to Politzer. Mathieu is envious of his old friend, who

[24] Henriette Nizan, "Lettre ouverte," p. 79.
[25] Sartre, *Situations* II, Gallimard, 1948, p. 283.

seems to possess, when we first meet him in the summer of 1938, "the slow-moving, silent-but-murmuring life of a crowd."[26] The analogy is two-edged, for Mathieu is both weary of his own isolationist individuality and afraid of the disciplined anonymity he sees in committed men. In return, Brunet believes he has nothing to learn from Mathieu, "this squalid intellectual, this watchdog." Realizing the bankruptcy of Mathieu's indistinct option, Brunet advises him to join the Party: "You're up in the air, you're suspended, you're completely abstract. . . . You've given up everything so as to be free. Take one step further, give up your freedom itself and you'll be repaid a hundredfold."[27] As Mathieu says in reply, this sounds like the spiel of a priest; and indeed it is difficult to imagine someone like Nizan talking in such terms, though he undoubtedly criticized his friend's lack of political conviction during the thirties. Despite his disrelish of Brunet's choice of words, however, Mathieu feels exposed, and he answers Brunet's probes in words to be used later by Hugo to Hoederer in *Les Mains sales*: "Everything you touch seems real. Since you came into my room, it seems real to me, and I feel disgusted with it." But Mathieu refuses to join the Party, because he has no "reason" for accepting. When Brunet leaves in disgust, Mathieu confesses in soliloquy: "I enjoy getting indignant about capitalism and I don't want it to be abolished, because then I wouldn't have any excuses for getting indignant." We remeet Brunet in the autumn, at the time of the Munich crisis, when he is accosted in the street by a proletarian militant Maurice and his girl Zézette. Maurice and Zézette are disappointed in Brunet, a journalist on *L'Humanité* who cannot answer their question: will there be war? Brunet, well dressed, feels uncomfortable in the presence of these workers, and thinks of himself as "an intellectual, a bourgeois, cut off

[26] Sartre, "L'Âge de raison," *Les Chemins de la liberté*, p. 46.
[27] *Ibid.*, p. 125.

from them for all time."[28] He tells himself that not only the workers but the Party itself has a right to mistrust intellectuals.

This first crack in the monolithic structure of the stereotype is widened in *La Mort dans l'âme*, where the personality of Brunet is further nuanced. At the start, after the rout of the French Army, he has given himself up to the Germans. In the prison yard he meets a soldier called Schneider, who looks vaguely familiar, with his habit (like Nizan) of staring with ironic eyes at his fingernails. Schneider devotes himself to a grass-roots communism, convinced that all the prisoners are in the same boat together. Brunet institutes a kind of boy-scout communism: physical jerks, cold showers, a war on fleas. On the political front, largely because he is in the dark about events in France, he instructs his agents in the camp to play the waiting game and to busy themselves with finding potential converts before the padre wins them over to his ends. Brunet actively wants his fellow soldiers to despair, to give up futile dreams of release, and so to harden themselves for the coming difficulties. Meanwhile, in his frequent verbal and ocular combats with Schneider, Brunet begins to doubt whether he is really in a position to act as leader. Schneider troubles him with the question: are you up to date on the Party line? Yet the two men are almost inseparable, so much so that they provoke sniggers ("Those two are as thick as thieves, they're always together or chasing after each other"). Frequently defeated in argument, Brunet protests that he is not a controversialist but a militant. Yet he envies his friend's closeness to the men, and believes he can see in him an effort "to slow his mind down, as if he were trying to adopt a more patient and dogged way of thinking." He senses in Schneider a human revolt against abstract systems, not on grounds of individualism but of the collectivity. Schneider accuses him of treating his human material as objects and of driving iron into their

[28] Sartre, "Le Sursis," *Les Chemins de la liberté*, p. 19.

soul with his methods of organization. In the last section of this volume, when the prisoners are on a train, Brunet is torn between his wish that they be taken to Germany, where an enemy environment might stiffen their resolve, and a fear of what might become of a desperate, homesick typographer if they are transported there. The "typo's" urge to get back to domesticity is countered by Brunet's assertion that the Party alone counts, to which the young militant replies: "When I'm knocking off a woman, the Party is not at the bedside holding a lamp for us," a rejoinder which leaves the puritanical Brunet speechless. He thinks to himself: "I'm a Communist because I'm a Communist. No more to be said." This sounds like that obsession with essences which, for Sartre, distinguishes men of bad faith, like Daniel. When the "typo" jumps from the train and is shot down by the German guards while trying to grab Brunet's hand to climb back aboard, Brunet and Schneider grip each other's hands in the need for warmth. Brunet, in this volume, seems to take over some of Mathieu's pseudo-metaphysical petulance, his fixation on ethical conundrums, his squatting on the horns of dilemmas.

In *Drôle d'amitié*, Brunet and Schneider, in a stalag, watch the arrival of Maurice and of Chalais, a Communist deputy in 1939.[29] Chalais recognizes Schneider as Vicarios, a journalist excluded from the Party after the Hitler-Stalin Pact, who had been chief editor of a fellow-traveling paper in Oran. Chalais informs Brunet that Vicarios was in tow with the government of Algiers. From this point on Brunet fluctuates between seeing his friend now as Schneider, now as Vicarios. Brunet asks him why he had worked with Communists in the camp, if he had left the Party, and is told: "I was sick of being on my own." There is a heavy-breathing scene of wounded feelings, when Schneider begs him not to believe the slander of his supposed treachery. Chalais, in a bid for supremacy, gradually undermines Brunet's position as leader by revealing to him

[29] Sartre, "Drôle d'amitié."

how outdated are his ideas on the Party line. Brunet clings to
the popular line probably believed by most ordinary working
Communists in France: that the war was still on against the
Axis, and that Russia would eventually intervene and crush
Germany. Chalais puts over the new line: keep out of the
imperialists' war, and do not listen to Gaullism; the Party's
real enemy is bourgeois France. Jesuitically, Chalais demonstrates that the Party line has never wavered. Brunet is mes-
merized by this "loudspeaker voice . . . the voice of the historical process, the voice of truth," and begins to hear the first
sounds of an inner voice, doubting the Party's competence. He
forces himself to conduct a self-criticism before two militants
questioning him whether he or Chalais is the official spokesman to be trusted. Now, like Mathieu, Brunet is in a midway
state, caught in viscous interior monologues ("A thought inside a head is nothing, just an internal haemorrhage"). He
comes to see himself as a "reluctant schismatic," who polarizes
the resistance of the others to Chalais, even though he tries to
efface himself for the sake of not disturbing discipline. Brunet
sums up his dilemma in these terms: "If the Party is right,
I'm more isolated than a lunatic; if it's wrong, *all* men are
their own and the world is finished." For the first time, he
begins to think outside the framework of the Party's corporate
mind. His realization of the Party as a mortal and fallible
organization like any other is undoubtedly helped by Schneider's example, Schneider "the out-and-out Communist eventually sickened of the whole business by the Party."

When Schneider admits he wants to escape in order to defend himself against lies, Brunet realizes how akin they are to
each other. Every Party member is a "potential exile."[30] He
defends his friend by wittingly jumping into a trap set by
Chalais, and thereby losing all claims to command. Yet he is
glad to have erupted out of a state of suspension. Schneider's

[30] Fauvet, *Histoire*, vol. i, p. 32.

complaint about the Party is: "Since I left you I've only been half alive; but you weren't satisfied with that and you've tried to turn me into a rotting corpse." The Party had spread lies alleging his pro-fascist tendencies, whereas he had done his utmost to help the cause in his own way by drawing careful distinctions. After having been deformed by the Party machine, he was worked to sap Brunet, yet he feels no elation at having succeeded. His comment on Brunet's state of mind could apply also to himself: "Anyway, the worm is in the apple, now." Brunet opts to escape with him. During the attempt (which has been tipped off to the guards) their bodies are flung together and the "fingers of friendship" depend on each other. Brunet flounders in despair when Schneider is shot and dies murmuring: "The Party is the cause of my death." Brunet whispers: "I don't give a damn about the Party; you're my one and only friend." Part of him dies with his friend.

The novel was uncompleted. In *La Force des choses*, Simone de Beauvoir recounts Sartre's projected conclusion to *La Dernière Chance*, of which *Drôle d'amitié* forms a part. After Schneider's death, Brunet escapes again, reaches Paris, and finds that the Party's line is now anticollaboration, as Russia has entered the war. He manages to rehabilitate the name of Schneider and resumes militant work in the resistance. His "subjectivity" returns, through doubts, but, all in all, he has at last discovered freedom *within* commitment.

The relationship of Brunet and Schneider is the only real friendship in the whole of Sartre's considerable output, but even this is extremely awkward and peculiar: truly, "a rum friendship," partly explicable by reference to the queer, almost effeminate intimacy common amongst prisoners, and partly a distorted reflection of Sartre's very mixed-up feelings toward Nizan. As well as representing one of Sartre's own fears (the loss of identity consequent upon enrollment), Brunet could be seen as a (not unlikeable) parody of Nizan, which is gradually humanized under the influence of Schneider. Alternatively, Schneider represents Nizan, and Brunet, some archetypal Party man of an opposite and more mindless breed than Nizan himself. There is a touch of schizophrenia about the whole business. Sartre and Nizan were often mistaken for each other by third parties (they were sometimes called "Nitre et Sarzan," and Brunschvicg courteously congratulated Sartre for writing *Les Chiens de garde*!). Sartre often betrays green envy towards Nizan, as if he imagined him as an improved alter ego.

Amidst all the betrayals and fidelities discussed in this chapter, which position does Sartre occupy? A study of his preface to *Aden-Arabie* might reveal an answer. Simone de Beauvoir discloses that Sartre, in Havana at that time, was annoyed with himself for agreeing to write this text: "But he found it rewarding to contrast his own youth with that of Cubans today; his preface had a special effect on young men and women around twenty years of age."[31] Now, it is not often enough stressed that, in addition to his demolition work, Sartre has also sedulously pursued reasons for adulation, some person or people or place to believe in and to glorify. Cuba and Nizan were two such sources. In his preface to *Aden-Arabie*, we see both Sartre's caustic style at its most corrosive and his ability to enthuse over an admirable enterprise: Nizan's brief life. The burden of this text, as of *Les Mots*, is Mathieu's query: "What have I made of my life?" Sartre seems to be striving to live vicariously through this "vigorous corpse," whom he proposes as a living example to the shiftless youth of 1960. The account of Nizan is typical Sartrean melodramatized, cerebral pattern making. Sartre's method of "existential psychoanalysis" is a kind of reductionism: it reduces its objects of study to one knot of tensions. Thus, Sartre's Baudelaire is ruled by mother fixation; his Merleau-Ponty by a back-to-the-womb complex. His thesis on Nizan centers on the idea of intransi-

---

[31] Beauvoir, *La Force des choses*, pp. 522-23.

gence: "He became a revolutionary out of his rebelliousness, and when the revolution had to make way for war, he resurrected the violence of his youth and ended up as a rebel."[32] Sartre implies constantly that he was jealous of Nizan for dying before the age of compromise was really installed, after 1945, and that the survivors of that generation have been sunk in "deep-rooted impotence." He accuses himself for not seeing beyond the surface of Nizan. Merleau-Ponty, who like Nizan, though at a later date, helped to make Sartre politically conscious and to *activate* him, wonders whether the Nizan Sartre knew and misunderstood really existed in 1928, before his marriage, the publication of his books, his militant activities, and his break with the Party. In his view, Sartre makes the mistake of assuming that the whole man, formed over a lifetime, was present in every moment of it.[33] It is true that Sartre is short on a historical sense, though endowed with a strong dramatic flair. In *Les Mots*, Sartre does in fact recognize that we alter other people's lives by reconstructions after their death, but there he is talking of people who die old. He can be excessively humble in the face of real revolutionaries and real sufferers. In consequence, he romanticizes Nizan's vital dilemmas and actions just as he romanticizes "the workers." Nizan's protest against the multiple forms of alienation is translated by Sartre into a personal heartcry of the kind that sounds through *Les Mots*: "We're suffocated; from childhood on we're mutilated; we're all freaks."[34] What Sartre fails to see is that Nizan's father was not as "heavy" as Sartre's grandfather; that Nizan's neuroses were more socially orientated than Sartre's.

Sartre's self-disgust almost cripples him. He said in *Critique de la raison dialectique*, published the same year as his preface to *Aden-Arabie*: "The ideas we hold today are false because they've died before we have: some of them stink of

[32] Sartre, "Paul Nizan," p. 140.     [33] Merleau-Ponty, *Signes*, p. 36 .
[34] Sartre, "Paul Nizan," p. 130.

carrion and some look like little heaps of bleached bones. There's not much to choose between either of them."[35] The only remedy, therefore, is to keep thought on the move. Perhaps this is what Sartre fails to achieve in his study of Nizan, where his ideas stall into something not far removed from a Taine-type *idée fixe*. (As Camus warned in *La Chute*: "Watch out! The corpse is going to have some make-up put on it.") In intention, Sartre's approach is in his terms a "heuristic," in rhetorical terms, the art of finding out, of inventing. But the notion of invention is ambiguous: is invention a fiction or a development of some latent truth? Sartre describes this heuristic method as one of "to-and-fro shuttling," "progression-regression." It sounds like a Lobster Quadrille of the intellect. Yet, despite so apparently dynamic a method, Sartre declares: "The individual is always all of a piece," a view which substantiates exactly Merleau-Ponty's grievance that Sartre has a stalled concept of other people. Sartre does, however, make a plea for "comprehension," the act by which we try to live the existence of the other. (But he installs himself, like the cuckoo, in other people's nests. He lives vicariously through Genet, Fanon, Nizan.) One of his perennial complaints against Marxism is that it foregoes intuition and relies instead on frozen schemes of knowledge. In his preface to *Aden-Arabie*, as well as trying to comprehend Nizan, Sartre is also studying himself as a kind of poor relation, and describing his own flabby failure lit up by Nizan's splendid one. He is looking not only for Nizan's project, but also for his own, and thus his method of "to-and-fro shuttling," of reciprocity, is further compounded. The reader might be tempted to recall Robert Graves's lines: "Melancholy / And pale, as faces grow that look in mirrors."[36] Nizan spent his adult life, and Sartre has spent the last twenty-five years, trying to interiorize various external situations, to take them over consciously and

---

[35] Sartre, *Critique*, p. 74.
[36] "The Pier-Glass," *Robert Graves*, London: Penguin, 1957, p. 37.

make them their own. Not only Sartre but his readers may doubt whether he has succeeded in his attempt as fully as his friend did.

In all of Nizan's work there is strong evidence of a man working things out for himself, borrowing ideas when necessary, yet fundamentally independent. Sartre is mistaken when he depicts Nizan as deriving all from the Party. Rather, the Party provided a focus for his energy. Sartre's "portrait" is not false, but it is misleading. As it fluctuates between insight and error, it is difficult to know at what point Sartre is perceptive and at what point obtuse or perverse. Nizan was much surer of himself than Sartre makes him out to be. Perhaps Sartre should have remembered his own warning, in *La Nausée*, that "portraits," like would-be "realistic" fiction, are lies, that artists can make dwarfs look hefty and, conversely, Moscas appear Hamlets. Sartre acknowledges in his study of Flaubert: "I have 'schematized' this subject, quite outrageously, with the sole intent of demonstrating this permanence within his perpetual alteration."[37] Such word-chopping is what most distinguishes Sartre from Nizan. In addition, Sartre's politics are based more on hope and prophecy than on facts and personal experience. Perhaps Nizan *was* lucky to be politically active at a time when the choices were more clear-cut (but Sartre at that same time did not find them so), when courage and lucidity were a matter of following the obvious up to the hilt. The intellectual, for Sartre, remains in an anguished midway state, caught in the crossfire from right and left, a traitor to one class and refused integration into the other. Yet such a problematic man shoulders global responsibility. The result is that impotent Atlas complex from which Frantz von Gerlach suffers in *Les Séquestrés d'Altona*.

Nizan prefigures Sartre in many ways, some of which have been mentioned in earlier chapters. After Nizan named the

[37] Sartre, *Critique*, p. 72.

military judge in *La Conspiration* Sartre, Sartre returned the compliment by calling the uncle of the pederast-surrealist Bergère in *L'Enfance d'un chef* General Nizan. Lucien's vision of the viscous in this same story is foreshadowed in the young men of *La Conspiration* struggling to stand up in a gelatinous world. Nizan's motif of "alibis" leads on to the notorious Sartrean notion of "mauvaise foi." According to Henriette Nizan the cerebral Sartre never really understood Nizan's hypersensitivity, his physical response to every stimulus and obstacle. Sartre's account also neglects Nizan's humor, his domestic life (which Simone de Beauvoir treats despite her professed aversion to domesticity). But, then, Sartre's thesis of a neurotic rebel would have been diluted by including such reminders of Nizan's common humanity. Theirs was truly "a rum friendship." On the one hand, Nizan was a man who always labored to make his position clear, which does not mean that he sacrificed complexity or ambiguity. On the other hand, Sartre revels in the fishy situation, the unresolved mess. The result is that even works intended to be painfully honest, like his preface to *Aden-Arabie* or *Les Mots*, reek of some self-gratifying cruelty. Sartre shocks, he questions, and he provokes his readers to question. But he does not furnish any counterimage to what he demolishes. He, not Nizan, is "the negator *par excellence*," the gaping hole in the core of twentieth-century European literary and philosophical being, which, like a building excavation in the city, attracts crowds of gaping spectators. Nizan's preference for "displeasing literature" has already been noted. Sartre, speaking of a future sequel to *Les Mots*, says: "I will relate . . . how it was that I was led to think systematically against myself, to the extent that I began to measure the validity of an idea by the *distress* it caused me."[38] This is Sartre's fakir complex in a nutshell. His dialectics are self-contained. The only opening is through the win-

---

[38] Sartre, *Les Mots*, p. 210.

dow of the study, a kind of philosophical spying on the *activity* of others.[39] Sartre is a spectator and, in exceptional moments, a "witness" in the French sense of a man willing to stand up and be counted. In some ways, with his philosophy of the "gaze" he is the most many-sided voyeur of this century. Nizan sought *his* dialectics in a living exchange between the outer world and his private self; and he never made out that public self-laceration was an enjoyable occupation.

In this study of the relationship between Sartre and Nizan, before and after Nizan's death, Sartre has been judged harshly. He is a tough enough personality to stand any rough handling; he can take punishment as well as mete it out. Yet it would be unfair to end this study with the suggestion that Sartre was unworthy of his friend. Despite all the misunderstandings and conscious disagreements, there must have been some central area of affinity and sympathy which kept the two men friends over a period of twenty years or more. As Merleau-Ponty wrote of Sartre's preface to *Aden-Arabie*: "Sartre and Nizan have perhaps never been closer to each other than today, when their experiences illuminate each other."[40] It is fitting to end with the last words which the Pioneer Nizan wrote to the meteorologist Sartre, and which sum up their roles: "You and I are amongst the last six or seven naïve writers who are not working in the censorship department or with Giraudoux. We're looked upon with a certain amount of ironical amusement. Let's write our novels. Like you, I'm engaged in a self-interrogation, but weather-readings must take up less time than being a Pioneer does: I'm only up to my second notebook. And it can't be published for ages, anyway."[41] Sartre dispatching balloons into the blue, and Nizan keeping tabs on engineering and sanitary work. There

[39] See Sartre, *Critique*, pp. 197-98.
[40] Merleau-Ponty, *Signes*, p. 44.
[41] Nizan, letter to Sartre, quoted in Beauvoir, *La Force de l'âme*, pp. 491-92.

was a world of difference between them, but the heartening thing is that both of them made the effort to cross its frontiers and to meet on common ground in the truce of a friendship, however rum.

# CONCLUSION

Nizan did not care for confiding, except to his readers. The printed word acted as a means of distancing, of perspective. In this way the hated ghost of "inner life," that limp or rigid narcissism so common in French fiction, might be laid, or kept at bay. At the same time, Nizan was convinced that as well as craving honest relations with each other, all men have a "profound longing for dissimulation and secrets."[1] The same coexisting opposites of opening up and concealing are found in Stendhal. In Nizan's case, such a coexistence was made even more necessary by his belonging to a partly secret, partly public organization that demanded of its members outspoken ideological lying. It would be untrue to say, however, that Nizan wrote against the Party, but he was always insistent that the good writer writes also for himself and, like a craftsman, must care for the finished object. His novels, essays, and part of his journalism were in some ways a cathartic exercise. In them, he could get off his chest the ideas often repressed or unused by the Party. But his real subversive outcry was always directed against a society that needed urgently to be overhauled from top to bottom.

It is difficult to distinguish Nizan's style of life from his style of writing. Even his enemies recognized that he had a definite individual style of being and of acting. It was one of elegant self-containment and a troubling kind of detachment that secreted anger and scorn. He gave the impression of having reserves—of energy, and of doubt. He was concentrated, like a taut spring. He could work in the middle of a noisy room, no doubt inured to distractions by his experience as a journalist obliged to meet deadlines. He made very few notes, and his manuscripts exhibit hardly any deletions. Clara Malraux describes his working "in a sort of loggia overhanging the

[1] Nizan, review of Samuel Pepys, *Ce Soir*, 6 January 1938, p. 7.

216

front door. I was amazed that he could write in this exposed position, in a place where he could see everything that was going on."[2] He did not shut himself away to write or to live. His writing is not "confessional" in the pejorative sense given that word by Flaubert, but it is an act of decamouflaging and of owning up. We might apply to it what Orwell says of Henry Miller, who speaks directly to the reader because "he has chosen to drop the Geneva language of the ordinary novel and drag the *real-politik* of the inner mind into the open."[3] It is a style with a purpose: "Words are loaded pistols and therefore have targets."[4] Nizan's bark was his bite. He is not the ballerina type of French novelist (Giraudoux, Gide at times), flirting and pirouetting with words. But this does not mean that his writing is not witty. Many of the examples quoted in earlier chapters prove Lefebvre's point that "as regards language, dialectical thinking begins with ambiguities and wordplay."[5] Nizan does not neglect to play with words. Some of his images would be commonplace, were it not for the reader's awareness that Nizan is seeking to rejuvenate language as well as to reanimate slothful minds and life patterns. In *La Conspiration* he writes, describing how a crowd is suddenly infused with surging life at Jaurès' funeral procession: "the boulevard suddenly deserved its other name: an artery." Gide often asserted that the "gait" of a writer reveals more about him than any other stylistic feature. Nizan's gait adjusts itself to the subject matter in hand: plodding on or swirling around a central vacancy in *Antoine Bloyé*; nervous, often exalted and proud in *Le Cheval de Troie*; alternately lyrical and cutting in *La Conspiration*. He is, like Stendhal, an antipomp writer, a deflater of hot-air balloons, his own or those

[2] Clara Malraux, "Le Voyage à Moscou," p. 84.

[3] George Orwell, *Collected Essays*, p. 122.

[4] Brice Parain, quoted in Sartre, *Qu'est-ce que la littérature?*, Gallimard, 1948.

[5] Henri Lefebvre, *La Somme et le reste*, p. 130.

of others. Just as he had more than one song to sing, so he varied his gait to suit the terrain.

Is he what Roland Barthes called "un scripteur," halfway between the militant and the independent writer?[6] Barthes has in mind socialist realism, which, in his opinion, has taken over and exacerbated the faults of bourgeois fiction. One of his grievances against this modern form of "precious jargon" (particularly in the postwar novels of André Stil or Garaudy) is that it combines posh syntax and vulgar vocabulary. Aragon, he finds, is somewhat different, and has preferred to "tint his socialist realism with a slight eighteenth-century hue, mixing a bit of Laclos in with a bit of Zola." Though Aragon and Nizan were in the 1930s the only novelists of real weight in the Party, membership affected their writing in widely differing ways. Nizan, simply, was incapable of writing a hardly readable work like *Les Communistes*. Sartre's description of Nizan as "the negator par excellence" is true insofar as Nizan can be thought important not only for what he achieved, but for what he did not stoop to accomplish. In the last forty years, when, as regards literature, we have often had to be thankful for small mercies, what Nizan *spared* us is part of his success: facile self-absorption, eager toeing of Party lines. It is a negative definition, but part of the total picture. Lenin died before his young revolution hardened in the arteries. Nizan did not live to see the French Communist Party go totally Stalinist, nor the impotence of the French left-wing intellectuals after the Second World War.

Sartre wonders "how this Noble Savage" (a strange description of a very sophisticated mind) would have coped with adapting himself to the requirements of socialist production and interplanatory touring."[7] It is nearly impossible to forecast how Nizan "would have" developed. All that seems cer-

[6] Roland Barthes, *Le Degré zéro de l'écriture*, Seuil, 1953, pp. 101-103.
[7] Sartre, "Paul Nizan," p. 169.

tain is that he cannot be conceived as becoming a dedicated anticommunist of the Koestler type. When he had left the Party, Koestler adopted a tough man-of-the-world tone, as if he belonged to some exclusive political nightclub. He talks of "a lifelong hangover"; his favorite analogies are with booze and bedding women (cf., his bilious attack on Sartre and his followers: "Oh, you little masochists of the age of reason, how you itch with impatience to be raped!").[8] He compares himself to a fallen angel in comparison with the "semi-virgin pink intellectuals of St. Germain des Prés." Koestler belongs to the *God That Failed* company, who provide, except for the perceptive and humble Silone, pretty sorry reading on their great illusion. Perhaps those, like Nizan, who joined in the 1920s got off to a better start. The thirties were a different era, and there were no "good times" for the new recruits to look back on, except their prefabricated illusions before becoming Party members. As Deutscher says, the ex-Communist view of communism tends toward pure demonology, though even the indisputable demonic element of Stalinism "has to be translated into terms of human motives and interests." This is what Koestler failed to realize in his *Darkness at Noon*. For Deutscher, the ex-Communist is "haunted by a vague sense that he has betrayed either his former ideals or the ideals of bourgeois society. . . . He then tries to suppress his sense of guilt and uncertainty, or to camouflage it by a show of extraordinary certitude and frantic aggressiveness." The only remaining urge is to self-justification, "and this is the most dangerous motive for any political activity."[9] Nizan was a heretic, but not a renegade. He had set out willfully to betray his own class, and so he cannot have felt much guilt on that score. When he left the Party, he considered his break as a schism and not as an abandonment.

Nizan once wrote: "The revolutionary is the man who has

[8] Arthur Koestler, *The Trail of the Dinosaur*, p. 62.
[9] Isaac Deutscher, *Heretics and Renegades*, pp. 13-20.

triumphed over solitude."[10] Communism, and the Party in France, helped him out of his solo anguish. Why indeed maintain, as Orwell does, that "acceptance of *any* political discipline seems to be incompatible with literary integrity"?[11] Is a party necessarily, and uniquely, a constraint on a writer? Can it not be a source of warm comradeship, of direction of energy? As Malraux once said: "For Kassner, as for a good many other communist intellectuals, communism gives back a kind of fertility to the individual."[12] On the other hand, for Gide: "You think you're taking the side of the Party. But it's you who is taken in by the Party." The fact remains that Nizan marked off his distances with respect to any group he was associated with: *Philosophies,* the E. N. S., *La Revue marxiste, Bifur,* the A. E. A. R., the teaching profession, the Communist Party. He was both a lone wolf and a lonely man seeking solidarity. It was the conscious rupture of that international solidarity that most shook him at the time of the pact. Raymond Aron's complaint and definition cannot be applied to Nizan: "The talent of French intellectuals lies in ignoring or often aggravating the problems peculiar to their own country, out of an arrogant urge to be a conscience for the whole of mankind."[13] This sounds truer of de Gaulle than of left-wing intellectuals like Nizan, who proved their concern for their own country when it was threatened. Similarly Sidney Hook's gripe ("Outside their own immediate craft too many intellectuals are irresponsible, especially in politics. They don't know enough, don't think enough, and are the creatures of fashion.") reads like an accurate description not of intellectuals but of professional politicians.[14] Continuing this process of negative definition, we can see as the antithesis of Nizan, Orwell's metaphor

[10] Nizan, *Ce Soir,* 24 November 1938, p. 5.
[11] Orwell, *Collected Essays,* p. 432.
[12] André Malraux, *Le Temps du mépris,* Preface, Gallimard, 1935.
[13] Raymond Aron, *L'Opium des intellectuels,* p. 258.
[14] Sidney Hook, in *The Intellectuals,* George B. Huszar, ed., p. 531.

for Henry Miller and similar opters-out: "The whale's belly is simply a womb big enough for an adult. There you are in the dark, cushioned space ... with yards of blubber between yourself and reality, able to keep up an attitude of the completest indifference, no matter what happens. ... Short of being dead, it is the final, unsurpassable stage of irresponsibility."[15] Like his characters, Nizan wears no armor. He is vulnerable to other men, the weather, international and local events. In Merleau-Ponty's view, Nizan said what Sartre would later affirm: that we do not observe the world at a distance, but that we drink it and our fellow men in through our very pores.[16]

Nizan is the only French Communist novelist who expressed a genuine sensibility and intelligence. In his book reviews, he revealed himself to be an acute and sympathetic critic, not blindfolded by orthodoxy. In them, he goes straight to the core of the text under consideration and of the man who wrote it. He asks: what is behind all this? What is the basic premise, the working hypothesis of this book, this writer? He does not stab through the arras without first looking behind it. This concentration on the essential owed something to his Marxist training. Marx asked the crucial questions, even if his answers are often off center or plainly wrong. These crucial questions are ones of existential strategy, of the choice of sides, of the economy (in the widest sense), of a life choice. This kind of existentialism is more economic in manner than Sartre's profligate verbalizing. Together with men of the caliber of Péri, Vaillant-Couturier, and Politzer, Nizan helped to give the Party in the thirties some real fervor, some style, some hard intellectual bite. Just as he forms a bridge between the political novels of Stendhal and those of Koestler, so did he express hope in the future, expend energy in the present, and reveal a moving and controlled sympathy for the past (as exemplified in his care for period detail in *Antoine Bloyé* and

---

[15] Orwell, *Collected Essays*, p. 152.
[16] Maurice Merleau-Ponty, *Signes*, p. 38.

his tastes in literature and philosophy). A controversialist such as he would not expect unanimous approval for his choices. Henri Clouard dismisses him in these terms: "Just another revolutionary Barrès of the 1930s, Paul Nizan conformed to nonconformity, not without a certain university-trained pedantry of style."[17] Pierre Naville, commenting on the Party's denunciation of Nizan as a traitor, says: "Thus Nizan fell victim to the system which he had done his best to consolidate."[18] In contrast, Jean Guéhenno and André Chamson speak of him with great affection and respect. Merleau-Ponty, like several others, records his envy: "Just as when we look back to our childhood, it is in this lost comrade that I find fullness of being."[19] Nizan's friend Louis Martin-Chauffier concludes: "Nizan was a Breton, and Bretons are renowned for being nonconformists. Discipline, which he accepted in theory but could barely tolerate emotionally, made his silence all the more bitter, and this helps to explain his sudden explosion. It was like a deliverance from bondage."[20]

He was a man who wrote as powerfully of love as of hate, who did not choose between literature and politics. He would not have had the strength to break free from his Party if he had not had the strength to join. He responded to the central positive credo of Marxism: that a man is not doomed to one unchanging nature, that he can select himself, will himself to be other, not merely in mental attitude, but in praxis. Nizan changed his mode of life, yet remained true to what was best in himself.

[17] Henri Clouard, *Histoire de la littérature française du Symbolisme à nos jours*, Albin Michel, 1949, p. 316.
[18] Letter to the author, 6 May 1967.
[19] Merleau-Ponty, *Signes*, p. 37.
[20] Louis Martin-Chauffier, "Paul Nizan n'était pas un délateur," p. 5.

# BIBLIOGRAPHY

THE place of publication, throughout the footnotes and the bibliography, unless otherwise stated, is Paris.

### NIZAN: BOOKS

*Aden-Arabie*, Rieder, 1931; Maspero, 1960.
*Les Chiens de garde*, Rieder, 1932; Maspero, 1965.
*Antoine Bloyé*, Grasset, 1933.
*Le Cheval de Troie*, Gallimard, 1935.
*La Conspiration*, Gallimard, 1938; Éditions Rencontre, 1960; Club français du livre, 1965.
*Chronique de septembre*, Gallimard, 1939.
*Pour une nouvelle culture*, Grasset, 1971. Preface by Susan Suleiman.

### TRANSLATIONS

*Aden-Arabie*, translated by Joan Pinkham, New York and London: MR Press, 1968.
*Trojan Horse*, translated by Charles Ashleigh, London: Lawrence and Wishart, 1937.

### OTHER PUBLICATIONS

"Marx philosophe," in Karl Marx, *Morceaux choisis*, Gallimard, 1933.
Translation of Louis Fischer, *The Soviets in World Affairs*, as *Les Soviets dans les affaires mondiales*, Gallimard, 1933.
Translation of Theodore Dreiser, *An American Tragedy*, as *L'Amérique tragique*, Rieder, 1933.
Preface to *Les Matérialistes de l'antiquité*, Éditions sociales internationales, 1936; Maspero, 1965.
Adaptation of Aristophanes, *Les Acharniens*, Éditions sociales internationales, 1937.
Preface to Henri Lefebvre, *Le Nationalisme contre les nations*, Éditions sociales internationales, 1935.
Nizan and Sartre collaborated on a revision of the translation of Karl Jaspers, *Psychopathologie générale*, by Kastler and Mendrousse, Alcan, 1928.

### SELECTED ARTICLES

*La Revue marxiste*:
   "La Rationalisation," 1 February and 1 March, 1929.
*La Revue des vivants*:
   "La Littérature révolutionnaire en France," September-October 1932.
*Commune*:
   "L'Église dans la ville," July 1933.

"Les Enfants de la lumière," October 1933.
"Jeune Europe," November 1933.
"Renaissance de l'Espagne," September 1936.
"Histoire de Thésée," November 1937.
*Europe*:
  "Sur un certain Front Unique," January 1933.
  "Sindobod Toçikston," May 1935.
  "Sur l'humanisme," July 1935.
*Nouvelle Revue Française*:
  "Les Conséquences du refus," December 1932.
  "Les Funérailles anglaises," March 1936.
  "*Été 1914*," January 1937.
*La Littérature internationale*:
  "André Gide," vol. 3, 1934.
  "Présentation d'une ville," vol. 4, 1934.
*La Cahiers de la jeunesse*:
  "Dostoïewski," 15 December 1938.
  "Ambition du roman moderne," 15 April 1939.
*La Correspondance internationale*:
  "Secrets d'Espagne" (11 articles), June-July 1936.
*Vendredi*:
  "Une Littérature responsable," 8 November 1935.
  "Drieu la Rochelle," 13 December 1935.
  "Le Tombeau de Timour," 22 January 1937.
  "Un Esprit non prévenu," 29 January 1937.
*Regards*:
  "L'Ennemi public numéro 1," nos. 61-65, 1935.
  "Nuits de Valence," no. 135, 1936.
  "Quand l'Amérique s'éveille," nos. 202-205, 1937.
  "Trois semaines d'Europe centrale," no. 207, 1937.
*Valeurs*:
  "Deux poèmes inédits," July 1945.

In addition, a large number of articles and reviews in *L'Humanité*, *Monde*, and *Ce Soir*.

STUDIES OF NIZAN: BOOKS AND CHAPTERS

Braun, Micheline Tison. *La Crise de l'humanisme*, vol. 2. Nizet, 1967.
Brochier, Jean-Jacques. *Paul Nizan: intellectuel communiste*. Maspero, 1967.
Étiemble, René. *Hygiène des lettres*, vol. 1. Gallimard, 1952.
Ginsbourg, Ariel. *Nizan*. Éditions universitaires, 1966.
Leiner, Jacqueline. *Le Destin littéraire de Paul Nizan*. Klincksieck, 1970.
Merleau-Ponty, Maurice. *Signes*. Gallimard, 1960.
Sartre, Jean-Paul. "*La Conspiration*." In *Situations* I. Gallimard, 1947.
———. "Paul Nizan." In *Situations* IV. Gallimard, 1964.

STUDIES OF NIZAN: ARTICLES

"*Les Matérialistes de l'antiquité.*" *Times Literary Supplement,* 30 September 1965.

Aragon, Louis. "*Antoine Bloyé.*" *Commune,* May 1934.

———. "Le Roman terrible," *Europe,* December 1938.

Arland, Marcel. "*Antoine Bloyé.*" *Nouvelle Revue Française,* December 1933.

Berl, Emmanuel. "Deux contemporains." *L'Express,* 9 June 1960.

Cabanel, Jean. "Paul Nizan." *Triptyque,* 1938.

Catalogne, Gérard de. "Enquête auprès des étudiants d'aujourd'hui." *Les Nouvelles littéraires,* 7 December 1928.

Catesson, Jean. "Un Roman et ses personnages." *Cahiers du Sud,* March 1939.

Connolly, Cyril. "The Nizan Case." *Horizon,* June 1947.

Dupeyron, Georges. "*Les Chiens de garde.*" *Europe,* May 1933.

Faye, Jean-Pierre. "*Aden-Arabie.*" *Esprit* 3, 1961.

Fréville, Jean. "*Antoine Bloyé.*" *L'Humanité,* 18 December 1933.

Garmy, René. "*Les Chiens de garde.*" *L'Humanité,* 6 September 1932.

Juquin, Pierre. "Critiques sans base." *La Nouvelle Critique* 118, 1960.

Lanteri-Laura, G. "Nizan et Politzer quarante ans après." *Critique,* August-September 1968.

Leiner, Jacqueline. "La Part de l'actuel dans l'oeuvre de P.-Y. Nizan." *Revue des Sciences humaines,* January-March 1968.

Marion, Denis. "*Aden-Arabie.*" *Nouvelle Revue Française,* May 1931.

Martelli, Giampolo. "Nizan e Sartre." *Dialoghi* 9, 1961.

Martin-Chauffier, Louis. "Nizan." *Vendredi,* 18 June 1937.

———. "Paul Nizan n'était pas un délateur." *Caliban,* 15 May 1947.

Nadeau, Maurice. "Paul Nizan: deux fois mort et ressuscité." *L'Observateur littéraire,* 30 June 1960.

Nizan, Henriette. "Lettre." *L'Express,* 6 October 1960.

Sénart, Pierre. "Sartre et Nizan." *Combat,* 2 July 1964.

Sigaux, Gilbert. "Il paraît." *Preuves* 113, 1960.

Simon, Pierre-Henri. "*Antoine Bloyé.*" *Esprit* 16, 1934.

———. "*Aden-Arabie.*" *Le Monde,* 27 July 1960.

Thibaudet, Albert. "Un nouvel anticléricalisme." *Nouvelle Revue Française,* June 1932.

Thorez, Maurice. "Les Traîtres au pilori." *Die Welt,* 21 March 1940.

Todd, Olivier. "Paul Nizan: An Appraisal." *Time and Tide,* 30 March 1961.

Vaudal, Jacques. "*Le Cheval de Troie.*" *Nouvelle Revue Française,* February 1936.

A special number of the review *Atoll* 1, November 1967-January 1968, was devoted to Nizan:

Buin, Yves. "Nizan ou le malaise."

Besnier, Bernard. "Modus vivendi."

Leiner, Jacqueline. "Un Portrait pirandellien."

Brochier, Jean-Jacques. "Fonction du traître."

Ginsbourg, Ariel. "Une Promenade politique avec Paul Nizan."

Malraux, Clara. "Le Voyage à Moscou."

Barou, Jean-Pierre. "Mort et vie d'un romancier."

Nizan, Henriette. "Lettre ouverte."

SECONDARY MATERIAL

Adereth, Maxwell. *Commitment in Modern French Literature*. London: Gollancz, 1967.

Andreu, Pierre. "Les Idées politiques de la jeunesse intellectuelle de 1927 à la guerre." *Revue des Travaux de l'Académie des Sciences morales et politiques*, 2nd semester 1957.

Aragon, Louis. *Les Communistes (February-September 1939)*. La Bibliothèque française, 1949.

Aron, Raymond. *L'Opium des intellectuels*. Calmann-Lévy, 1955.

Beauvoir, Simone de. *Mémoires d'une jeune fille rangée*. Livre de poche, 1958.

——. *La Force de l'âge*. Livre de poche, 1960.

Benda, Julien. *La Trahison des clercs*. Jean-Jacques Pauvert, 1965.

Berl, Emmanuel. *Mort de la morale bourgeoise*. Jean-Jacques Pauvert, 1965.

Bernard, Jean-Pierre. "Communisme et littérature (1921-39)." Ph.D. dissertation, University of Paris, 1964.

——. "Le P. C. F. et les problèmes littéraires (1920-1939). *Revue française de Science politique*, June 1967.

Caute, David. *Communism and the French Intellectuals*. London: André Deutsch, 1964.

Crossman, Richard, ed. *The God that Failed*. London: Hamish Hamilton, 1950.

Debray, Régis. *Révolution dans la révolution?* Maspero, 1967.

Demetz, Peter. *Marx, Engels and the Poets*. Chicago: University of Chicago Press, 1967.

Deutscher, Isaac. *Heretics and Renegades*. London: Hamish Hamilton, 1955.

Domenach, Jean-Marie. "Le P. C. F. et les intellectuels." *Esprit*, May 1949.

Fauvet, Jacques. *Histoire du parti communiste français*. 2 vols. Fayard, 1964.

Fischer, Ernst. *Art and Ideology*. London: Allen Lane, The Penguin Press, 1969.

Freedman, Robert, ed. *Marx on Economics*. London: Penguin, 1963.

Friedmann, Georges. *L'Adieu*. Gallimard, 1932.

226

――――. *De la Sainte Russie à l'U. R. S. S.* Gallimard, 1938.

Gide, André. *Retour de l'U. R. S. S.* Gallimard, 1936.

――――. *La Littérature engagée.* Gallimard, 1950.

――――. *Journal (1889-1939).* Pléiade, 1951.

Guéhenno, Jean. *La Foi difficile.* Grasset, 1957.

Hayward, Max, and Labedz, Leopold, eds. *Literature and Revolution in Soviet Russia (1917-62).* London: Oxford University Press, 1963.

Howe, Irving. *Politics and the Novel.* New York: Horizon Press, 1955.

Huszar, George B. de, ed. *The Intellectuals.* Glencoe, Illinois: Free Press, 1960.

Koestler, Arthur. *The Yogi and the Commissar.* London: Jonathan Cape, 1945.

――――. *The Invisible Writing.* London: Collins and Hamish Hamilton, 1954.

――――. *The Trail of the Dinosaur.* London: Collins, 1955.

Kriegel, Annie. *Les Communistes français.* Seuil, 1968.

Lecoeur, Auguste. *Le Partisan.* Flammarion, 1963.

Lefebvre, Henri. *L'Existentialisme.* Sagittaire, 1946.

――――. *La Somme et le reste.* 2 vols. La Nef, 1959.

Lenin, V. I. *What is to be done?* Moscow: Progress Publishers, 1967.

Lichtheim, George. *Marxism in Modern France.* New York: Columbia University Press, 1966.

Loubet del Bayle, Jean-Louis. *Les Non-conformistes des années 30.* Seuil, 1969.

Mander, John. *The Writer and Commitment.* London: Secker and Warburg, 1961.

Maxence, Jean-Pierre. *Histoire de dix ans (1927-37).* Gallimard, 1939.

Micaud, Charles. "French Intellectuals and Communism." *Social Research,* Autumn 1954.

Montherlant, Henry de. *L'Équinoxe de septembre.* Grasset, 1938.

Mounier, Emmanuel. *Oeuvres,* vol. 4. Seuil, 1962.

Moussinac, Léon. *Manifestation interdite.* Éditions sociales internationales, 1935.

Orwell, George. *Collected Essays.* London: Mercury, 1961.

Pierce, Roy. *Contemporary French Political Thought.* London: Oxford University Press, 1966.

Plumyène, Jean, and Lasierra, Raymond. *Les Fascismes français.* Seuil, 1963.

Politzer, Georges. *Révolution et contre-révolution au xxe siècle.* Éditions sociales, 1947.

――――. *Critique des fondements de la psychologie.* Presses universitaires de France, 1967.

――――. *Fin d'une parade philosophique.* Jean-Jacques Pauvert, 1968.

Racine, Nicole. "Les Écrivains communistes en France (1920-36)." Ph.D. dissertation, University of Paris, 1963.

———. "L'Association des écrivains et artistes révolutionnaires." *Le Mouvement social*, January-March 1966.

Revel, Jean-François. *Pourquoi des philosophes?* Jean-Jacques Pauvert, 1965.

Rossi, A. *Physiologie du parti communiste français.* Self, 1948.

———. *Les Communistes français pendant la drôle de guerre.* Les Iles d'or, 1951.

Sartre, Jean-Paul. *Les Chemins de la liberté.* Gallimard, 1945-49.

———. "Drôle d'amitié." *Les Temps Modernes*, November-December 1949.

———. *Critique de la raison dialectique.* Gallimard, 1960.

———. *Les Mots*, Gallimard, 1964.

———. *Les Écrits de Sartre.* Edited by Michel Contat and Michel Rybalka, Gallimard, 1970.

Smith, Colin. *Contemporary French Philosophy.* London: Methuen, 1964.

Stil, André, ed. *Vaillant-Couturier écrivain.* Éditeurs français réunis de poche, 1967.

Strachey, John. *Literature and Dialectical Materialism.* New York, 1934.

Téry, Simone. *Beaux enfants qui n'hésitez pas.* Éditeurs français réunis, 1957.

Thibaudet, Albert. *La République des professeurs.* Grasset, 1927.

Touchard, Jean. "Le P. C. F. et les intellectuels (1920-39)." *Revue française de Science politique*, June 1967.

———. "L'Esprit des années 1930." In *Tendances politiques dans la vie française depuis 1789.* Hachette, 1960.

Vallette, Geneviève, and Bouillon, Jacques. *Munich 1938.* Armand Colin, 1964.

Walter, Gérard. *Histoire du parti communiste français.* Somogy, 1948.

Werth, Alexander. *France and Munich.* London: Hamish Hamilton, 1939.

Wilson, Edmund. *To the Finland Station.* London: Fontana, 1962.

# INDEX

Aden, 4, 11, 22-28, 31-32, 105
Alain, 40, 44, 48
Amiel, Henri-Frédéric, 10
Anouilh, Jean, 169
Arabia, 24, 186
Aragon, Louis, 21, 31, 47, 72, 86, 99-100, 122, 147, 165, 181, 184, 187, 189, 191, 200-03, 218
Aristophanes, 90-91
Aron, Raymond, 10, 11, 32, 203, 220
Aron, Robert, 83
Attlee, Clement, 187
Auden, W. H., 106, 140
Austria, 82

Babel, Isaac, 89-90
Balzac, Honoré de, 171
Barbey d'Aurevilly, Jules, 201
Barbusse, Henri, 99, 165
Bardèche, Maurice, 116
Barrès, Maurice, 13, 84, 178, 179, 222
Barthes, Roland, 218
Baudelaire, Charles, 24, 46, 73, 153, 172, 209
Bayet, Albert, 199
Beauvoir, Simone de, 10, 11, 18, 32-33, 61, 78, 87, 111, 146, 148, 190, 208-09, 213
Bédé, Jean-Albert, 114
Belinsky, V. G., 89
Benda, Julien, 21, 34, 37, 42, 44, 83-85, 203
Béranger, Pierre-Jean de, 46
Bergson, Henri, 13, 17, 36-37, 43-44, 84
Berl, Emmanuel, 20-21, 33, 45, 86, 117-18, 166
Bernanos, Georges, 100
Besse, Antonin, 22, 25-26
Beuve-Méry, Hubert, 185
Bismarck, Otto von, 37

Bloch, Jean-Richard, 86
Blondel, Maurice, 17
Bolivia, 4
Bonnet, Georges, 184-85
Bossuet, Jacques Bénigne, 171
Bourg, 78-80, 123, 124
Bourget, Paul, 72
Boutroux, Émile, 36, 37
Brasillach, Robert, 116
Brentano, Franz, 44
Brest, 123
Breton, André, 14, 18, 181, 203
Brueghel, Pieter, 140
Brunschvicg, Léon, 13, 17, 20, 23, 36-41, 43, 209

Cachin, Marcel, 123, 198
Caillois, Roger, 203
Calvin, Jean, 101
Camus, Albert, 203, 211
Canton, 141
Carroll, Lewis, 195
Castro, Fidel, 5
Catesson, Jean, 180n
Caute, David, 94, 106, 107n, 109n, 142, 143, 180
Céline, Louis-Ferdinand, 70, 115, 118
Cellini, Benvenuto, 12
Cendrars, Blaise, 24
Chamson, André, 48, 110, 222
Chiappe, Jean, 105
China, 57, 60
Chirico, Giorgio de, 32
Clausewitz, Karl von, 193
Clouard, Henri, 222
Cocteau, Jean, 13
Cogniot, Georges, 80
Conrad, Joseph, 167
Cortés, Hernán, 140
Crevel, René, 135
Croce, Benedetto, 10
Czechoslovakia, 184, 189